Integrated Assessment and Management of Public Resources

NEW HORIZONS IN ENVIRONMENTAL ECONOMICS

Series Editors: Wallace E. Oates, *Professor of Economics, University of Maryland, USA* and Henk Folmer, *Professor of General Economics, Wageningen University and Professor of Environmental Economics, Tilburg University, The Netherlands*

This important series is designed to make a significant contribution to the development of the principles and practices of environmental economics. It includes both theoretical and empirical work. International in scope, it addresses issues of current and future concern in both East and West and in developed and developing countries.

The main purpose of the series is to create a forum for the publication of high quality work and to show how economic analysis can make a contribution to understanding and resolving the environmental problems confronting the world in the twenty-first century.

Recent titles in the series include:

Integrated Assessment and Management of Public Resources

Edited by

Joseph C. Cooper

Economic Research Service, United States Department of Agriculture, Washington, DC, USA

Federico Perali

University of Verona, Italy

Marcella Veronesi

University of Maryland, USA and University of Verona, Italy

NEW HORIZONS IN ENVIRONMENTAL ECONOMICS

RegioneLombardia

Edward Elgar
Cheltenham, UK • Northampton, MA, USA

Published by
Edward Elgar Publishing Limited
Glensanda House
Montpellier Parade
Cheltenham
Glos GL50 1UA
UK

Edward Elgar Publishing, Inc.
136 West Street
Suite 202
Northampton
Massachusetts 01060
USA

A catalogue record for this book
is available from the British Library

Library of Congress Cataloguing in Publication Data

Integrated assessment and management of public resources/edited by
    Joseph C. Cooper, Federico Perali, Marcella Veronesi.
        p.   cm. — (New horizons in environmental economics)
    Includes bibliographical references and index.
    1. Natural resources, Communal—Management. 2. Public lands—
Management. 3. Environmental economics. I. Cooper, Joseph C.
II. Perali, Federico. III. Veronesi, Marcella, 1979– . IV. Title. V. Series.
    HD1286.C67   2005
    333.7—dc22
                                                                    2005050623

ISBN-13: 978 1 84542 472 5
ISBN-10: 1 84542 472 7

Printed and bound in Great Britain by MPG Books Ltd, Bodmin, Cornwall

Contents

Contributors

Michele Baggio, Department of Economics, University of Verona, Italy and Department of Agricultural and Resource Economics, University of Maryland, USA.

Massimo Bianchi, Istituto Sperimentale per l'Assestamento Forestale e l'Alpicoltura (ISAFA), Villazzano, Trento, Italy.

Michele Carta, Studio ForST, Foreste e Sistemi Territoriali, Toscolano Maderno (BS), Italy.

Veronica Cicogna, Department of Statistics, University of Verona, Italy.

Joseph C. Cooper, Economic Research Service, USDA.

Paola De Agostini, Department of Economics, University of Verona, Italy.

Nicola Gallinaro, Studio ForST, Foreste e Sistemi Territoriali, Toscolano Maderno (BS), Italy.

Stefania Lovo, Department of Economics, University of Verona, Italy.

Francesco Pecci, Department of Economics Society Institutions, University of Verona, Italy.

Federico Perali, Department of Economics, University of Verona, Italy.

Nicola Tommasi, Centro Interdipartimentale di Documentazione Economica (CIDE), University of Verona, Italy.

Marcella Veronesi, Department of Agricultural and Resource Economics, University of Maryland, USA and Department of Economics, University of Verona, Italy.

Acknowledgements

This research has been commissioned by the Forestry Agency of the Lombardy region (ERSAF). We gratefully acknowledge the 'Ente Regionale per i Servizi all'Agricoltura e alle Foreste' (ERSAF) and its president Mino Galli for the financial support and for the unique learning opportunity that has been provided to the students of the Doctorate in Economia Politica, major in Environmental Economics, of the University of Verona. The book is in fact a joint effort, mostly of students of the Doctorate. We are also thankful to the Department of Economics of the University of Verona for a publishing grant.

We would like to express deep gratitude to all who helped directly and indirectly in the different phases of the research. In particular, we owe special thanks to the project manager Nino Di Girolamo, to Ugo Maggioli for his fond friendship and enduring trust in the scope and validity of the research project and to Claudio Sammarati for his contribution to the research. We are very grateful to Nora O'Leary Arnold, Deborah O'Leary and Marcella Lorenzini for their generous support in editing and translating the manuscript with highly professional editorial care. A special recognition also goes to Raffaella Castagnini and Barbara Gelmetti for helping with the survey management and data interpretation. We would like to show our appreciation to the staff of the Junior Enterprise in Applied Economics and Statistics (JEAESI) and of the Club of Applied Economics (CEA) of the University of Verona for the enthusiastic collaboration in the interviews of the questionnaires during the many visits to the spectacular areas of the Garda Lake.

Not least, we thank the 'Comunità Montana del Parco dell'Alto Garda Bresciano', with special regard to the director Dr Beatrice Zambiasi and the visitors of the High Garda Natural Park who agreed to be interviewed, for giving us the wonderful opportunity to implement this study.

DISCLAIMER

We accept full responsibility for the remaining errors and omissions. The views presented here are those of the authors, and do not necessarily represent the views or policies of the Economic Research Service or the United States Department of Agriculture.

For our ladies
J.C.C. and F.P.

For my family
M.V.

Introduction*

Joseph C. Cooper, Federico Perali and Marcella Veronesi

MOTIVATION

The general objective of this book is to provide a reference work on making integrated environmental policy decisions in managing public goods and natural parks. A public resource such as a natural park has many different functions (for example, production of marketed goods, ecosystem protection, tourism), and its management requires a multidisciplinary approach covering various areas of expertise.

This book is the result of a multidisciplinary effort in which the economics discipline plays a central role. Nonetheless, the proper management of public resources requires the knowledge of the physical, biological and ecological characteristics of the functions supplied by the resource and the value of each function and of the public resource as a whole. The innovative approach proposed in the book consists in the integration of the assessment and management aspects of the policy decision process.

In order to define the most efficient managerial strategy to improve the environmental sustainability and quality of a public resource, information about the natural area and how it interacts with the economy is required. Further, a project representing a consensus over how the public resource is best managed is also sustainable if the project continues to be considered socially desirable by the future generations of tourists or residents.

Considering that conflicts of interests often arise among local actors that result in the perpetuation of the *status quo* rather than in the adoption of a Pareto improving management project, the manager of the natural area can reduce potential conflicts if he or she internalizes the users' preferences in the project proposal. In general, this modern attitude of institutional listening is effectively implemented if the 'voice' of the users is given the importance and attention it deserves within the decision process, thus putting into action the Latin motto 'vox populi, vox dei', i.e. a 'grass-roots' approach. After all, the best strategy for harmonizing the natural, productive, protective and tourist functions of a natural area will not be implemented if it is not accepted by the local community, which is both the most frequent user and the main recipient of the legacy of the project for future generations.

SPECIFIC OBJECTIVES

The empirical case study has been developed from survey information gathered by the Department of Economics of the University of Verona in Italy, on the west side of Garda Lake, in June–October 1997, within a research project financed by the Lombardy region. This survey was part of an integrated analysis on the multi-functionality of the West Garda Regional Forest in order to evaluate the best mix of forest functions and their hypothetical values, to assess the impact of possible policies on the local economy and to define cooperative policies between institutions, local operators and visitors. As this analysis was requested by the regional park authorities, it reflects a real-world application of research of interest to policymakers.

We adopt multi-criteria techniques, thereby permitting us to integrate bio-ecological, territorial and economic information in order to achieve the objective of best coordinating the natural, productive, protective and tourist functions of a public forest or park. Such an analysis can be used to define policies that allow for interactions among institutions, local economic agents and park users while accounting for implications of those policies on the local economy.

METHODOLOGY

Our methodology integrates physical and social sciences in order to consider the forest system as a pool of different elements that interact among themselves and with external systems. In order to define the best combination of functions offered by the area, we use multi-criteria analysis techniques, which consider qualitative indexes of functions, integrating territorial information coming from a geographical information system (GIS) analysis with those related to the preferences of the park's users, estimated using the contingent (CVM) and travel cost (TCM) valuation methods.

The contingent valuation method is a direct (stated preference) method to estimate the value of environmental goods by using 'willingness-to-pay' questions that simulate market mechanisms. The travel cost method is an indirect (revealed preference) method that estimates the value of the non-market good through the number of recreational trips and the travel cost for visiting the natural area. The number of trips to the area approximates the quantity consumed of the non-market good and the change in the welfare estimates the value of the good. Novel methodologies for CVM and TCM are developed and then used in the empirical case studies.

The results of the environmental valuation exercises and the GIS analysis are integrated into the multi-criteria analysis in order to help the public authority to make those management decisions that maximize a social and environmental goal specific to the natural area. In general, these management decisions have an impact on the local economy whose effects, when measured, may affect the social preference ordering suggested on the basis of the results obtained from the analysis, considering the natural park and its users as an isolated bio-economy.

We evaluate the effects of the decisions about the natural area as an isolated economy within the local economy as a whole as represented by a local social accounting matrix. Traditionally, the information about what is best for the natural area and the local economy is not sufficient for guaranteeing the implementation of the suggested plan because of conflicts of interests among either political parties or interest groups. We incorporate this important aspect of the local political economy by studying game theoretic techniques for conflict resolutions within the context of the natural area of the west side of the Garda Lake.

ORGANIZATION OF THE BOOK

The book is organized as follows. The first two chapters estimate the quantities of the forest's non-market functions using GIS techniques. These chapters define the forest's supply of functions. In the third and fourth chapters we estimate the hypothetical prices of the forest's functions using CVM and TCM techniques. These chapters represent the consumers' demand for the forest's functions. In the fifth chapter we define the best mix of the forest's functions by using multi-criteria analysis, while in the sixth chapter we simulate the impact of each functional alternative on the local economy using a local social accounting matrix. Finally, Chapter 7 specifies the alternative levels of the functions that best satisfy the preferences of institutions, local economic agents and visitors to the forest, using techniques of conflict resolution. The book concludes with environmental policy recommendations. The Appendix describes the survey conducted on the west side of the Garda Lake. The organization of the book is summarized in the five stages depicted in Figure 0.1. These stages are further grouped within the two assessment and management parts of the research.

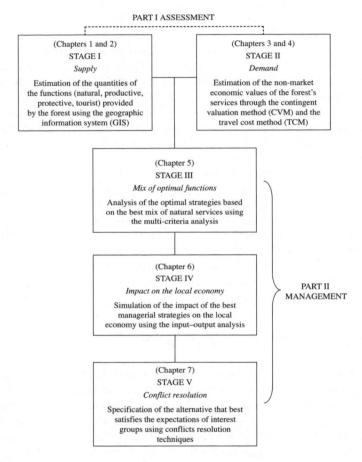

Figure 0.1   Book outline: analysis and chapter linkages

NOTE

*   The views presented here are those of the authors, and do not necessarily represent the views or policies of the Economic Research Service or the United States Department of Agriculture.

PART I

Assessment

1. Estimating the level of functions supplied by a natural area using GIS information

Michele Carta, Nicola Gallinaro and Massimo Bianchi

1.1 INTRODUCTION

The goal of this research is to define an operative instrument for mapping values of different functions supplied by forest areas. In contrast with a purely economic approach, we tried to map these values by developing for each function a set of indicators, and then aggregating them by a simple cartographic modelling procedure.

This instrument, which is based on the integration of geographic information system (GIS) and multi-criteria analysis (MCA) techniques, could be used in supporting decision making about forest planning strategies. It allows taking into account both monetary and non-monetary values. It can be viewed as a tool capable of considering both the socio-economic opportunities and the environment's carrying capacity in order to make the optimum planning choice.

The instrument has been developed and applied to the West Garda Regional Forest, a sizing about 110 square kilometres and located inside the High Garda Natural Park in eastern Lombardy region.

1.2 METHODOLOGY

It is well acknowledged that forests and other areas featuring a natural environment can be sources of products and services, among which public services play an important role. We may acknowledge that these areas provide some utilities and try to assign a value to them.

The scheme in Table 1.1 even if it is only applied to forest resources, can be easily adapted to the description of natural areas as well.

Functions having a global value, such as the environment function of

Table 1.1 *Classification of 'forest products' into homogeneous
            categories corresponding to different functions*

Function	Products	Services
Productive	Timber Food Pasture Resin, tannin Mushrooms Mosses, lichens	
Protective		Protection against: erosion wind avalanches floods
Naturalistic		Conservation of: species ecosystem diversity evolutive processes
Tourist		Landscape quality Tourism and sport Fishing and hunting

carbon dioxide retention of vegetal surfaces, have been excluded from this scheme because their estimation would be too complex. For the same reason we did not consider those functions that have a highly subjective component, such as spiritual and historical–cultural ones.

According to the value each function assumes, the territory can be divided into specific vocational categories:

- *areas with a prevalent function*: areas where one specific function prevails on others;
- *areas with multiple vocations*: areas where two or more functions prevail on others.

The multiple possibilities of combinations and the values functions can assume, determine many different cases.

In this process, we choose not to use predefined 'homogeneous' units, as for example the classic forest stand, but prefer to start from small land parcels according to a grid scheme. This choice is justified by the fact that zones which are 'homogeneous' from a mainly physiographical point of view, may appear strongly heterogeneous from other perspectives (such as tourism, hydrology, nature conservation, and so on). The identification and mapping of areas showing similar characteristics according to different viewpoints, is the main objective of this study.

The values assigned to each function have been mapped by means of a cartographic evaluation model based on MCA and GIS techniques. Given the practical, operative approach of this work, the parameters considered in the estimation are readily obtainable starting from the available data. Hence, a certain degree of simplification has been accepted.

In order to identify areas showing similar characteristics according to different functions, and represent homogeneous units from a functional point of view, a cluster analysis has finally been carried out.

1.2.1   The Evaluation Model

The evaluation model is intended as a support for operative, practical planning activities. Consequently, being conditioned by data availability and ease of use, its structure is rather simple. Besides a spatial database and a spatial analysis system, the model is based on a wide knowledge base: this gives it the characteristics of a knowledge-based system or 'expert system' (Zimmermann, 1987). The evaluation model is based on MCA concepts and methods. According to Eastman et al. (1993), criteria are elements or attributes of the environment or territory which, individually or in combination with others, can represent phenomena which are not directly measurable in physical units.

Criteria can be subdivided in constraints and factors: the former show just two values (0 = false, 1 = true) and are used to exclude some cells from the calculus (e.g. those above a specified slope threshold); the latter are continuously varying and are estimated through a scale of scores, defined and correlated to the function being evaluated. Thus, a standardization process is needed in order to express all the considered factors according to a common scale. The standardization has been made in a linear way through the following algorithm:

$$x_i = \frac{R_i - R_{\min}}{R_{\max} - R_{\min}} \cdot range,$$

where x_i indicates the score of a standardized scale, R_i the score of the original scale, $R_{\min}$ and $R_{\max}$ respectively the minimum and maximum value of the original scale and *range*, the interval of the standardized scale.

In this study, the value of functions has been evaluated according to a scale ranging from 1 (minimum value) to 10 (maximum value); however in intermediate steps different scales have been used as well.

Among several multi-criteria evaluation procedures (WLC, OWA, Boolean overlay) we decided to adopt a WLC (weighted linear combination), i.e. an additive model in which, besides a score based on a common scale, each factor has been assigned a weight that increases or reduces its importance of the final analysis.

This study extensively relies on the use of geographic information system (GIS) techniques, which represent the natural instrument while performing complex spatial analysis in wide areas. In general, this technology gives the possibility of handling interrelationships among different information layers, thus providing a powerful tool for turning data into information (Burrough and McDonnell, 1998; Aronoff, 1989).

More specifically, GIS allows the representation of spatial features in a raster (grid) format, made up by a set of square cells. The smaller the cell (or pixel) size, the more precise are the analysis and the mathematical elaboration.

The raster approach has been chosen due to its better performance in carrying out complex spatial analysis at a landscape level. The study area has been represented by a grid of 700 rows by 640 columns, with each cell sizing 50 × 50 m. Data were geo-referenced according to the Italian (Gauss–Boaga) reference system.

1.3 PROJECT STAGES

This project can be subdivided into the following phases:

- input of both cartographic and descriptive data into the GIS;
- database setup;
- analysis: GIS analysis functions together with external computer programs allowed the development of indicators and the definition of the evaluation model;
- output: the final results have been presented through graphics, tables, maps, reports.

The GIS software package used is GRASS, open source free software, formerly developed by the US Army Corps of Engineers Research Laboratory (USACERL, 1993), running in a Linux environment.

1.4   DATA INPUT AND DATABASE SET-UP

According to basic ecology concepts, the environment can be analysed by means of a set of ecological and anthropic factors, which in turn are represented by a set of lower level components. This way a sort of network of basic elements which make up the environmental system, and which correspond to information layers, may be defined. They can be summarized as follows in Table 1.2.

According to the following three phases, a complete database of both cartographic and attribute data named SINGARDO (Italian acronym for the environment information system of the West Garda Regional Forest) has been set up:

- phase 1: identification and collection of existing information;
- phase 2: integration of missing information by field work;
- phase 3: database set-up.

The database is made up by both spatial and tabular data. Attribute data have been organized into tables managed by a Relational Database Management System (RDBMS); spatial data have been structured in a vector component (useful mainly for data visualization) and a raster component used to perform spatial analysis.

The base map is the topographic map of Lombardy region at the scale of 1 to 10 000, referenced according to the Italian (Gauss–Boaga) system.

Table 1.2   Ecological factors and corresponding information layers

Ecological factors	Environmental components	Information layers
Abiotic factors	Climatic component Physiographical component Geological component	Climatic data Digital terrain model Geological maps
Merobiotic factors	Pedological component	Pedological maps
Biological factors	Vegetation component Faunistic component	Land use maps Vegetation/forest maps Faunistic maps and observations
Anthropic factors	Anthropic component	Human activities and infrastructures

1.5 THE ANALYSIS STAGE

1.5.1 The Tree of Knowledge

The first step in setting up the evaluation model is organizing the knowledge base in a hierarchically defined structure, known as the 'tree of knowledge' (Figure 1.1).

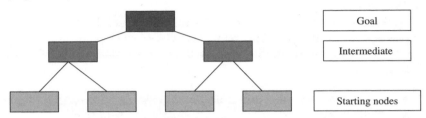

Figure 1.1 The tree of knowledge

At the lower level, each element can be represented by an information layer of SINGARDO. Higher levels of knowledge (*intermediate nodes*) are reached by combining these *starting nodes* one with another. The *goal* shows the highest level of knowledge reached by the expert system.

1.5.2 Value Assignment

1.5.2.1 Terminal nodes

The final nodes show values that are calculated for each pixel and for each estimated function, by mathematical functions that define the degree of membership of the estimated variables to the function being analysed (or to an element concurring to define it). Such a formulation is generally expressed as follows:

$$\mu(x) = f(x_i)$$

It comes from the fuzzy logic theory and gives back values ranging from 0 (no membership) to 1 (maximum membership).

The real analytic formulation depends on the element that has to be estimated; the two following cases can be distinguished:

- information varying in a continuous way can be represented by a continuous function, for example a logistic one which can be expressed as follows:

$$\mu(x) = 1/(1 + e^{-\alpha(x_i - \beta)}),$$

where α and β are coefficients of the logistic function. From a mathematical viewpoint α influences the steepness of the curve, while β is the point in which the function assumes the central value of 0.5 in the interval [0,1]; the two parameters are generally identified by an iterative method;

- information varying in a discrete way: in this case we keep on subdividing the variability field into classes and linking each one with a value of the membership function, always within the interval between 0 and 1.

1.5.2.2 Intermediate nodes

At this level the values attribution depends on the relations between terminal nodes, which can be of different type:

- additive relationships:

$$\mu(x) = a \cdot \mu(y) + b \cdot \mu(z),$$

where a and b are coefficients of a linear equation;
- multiplicative relationships:

$$\mu(x) = \mu(y) \cdot \mu(z);$$

- logical relationships:

$$\mu(x) = \mu(y) \text{ AND } \mu(z)$$

where AND operator implies that the membership function $\mu(x)$ is equal to the lowest value between $\mu(y)$ and $\mu(z)$; and:

$$\mu(x) = \mu(y) \text{ OR } \mu(z)$$

where OR operator implies that the membership function $\mu(x)$ is equal to the highest value between $\mu(y)$ and $\mu(z)$.

1.5.3 Weight Assignment

Weights have been assigned to each factor by using the pairwise comparison method (Saaty, 1987). According to this method, the weights are produced by means of the principal eigenvector of the pairwise comparison matrix.

1.5.4 Characteristics of the Evaluation Model

The model is characterized by a great versatility and adaptability towards the application context and the available data. It is also possible to add new indicators, and modify the combining criteria: the membership functions and the proposed weights.

Moreover, the model is able to express and compare different 'scenarios', allowing the simulation of the effect of different planning choices.

1.6   RESULTS

1.6.1   Ecological-vegetation Characterization

The preliminary phase of vegetation analysis consisted in the collection and interpretation of existing information. A vegetation map with a phyto-sociologic basis and a forest typology map, both at the scale of 1:10 000, have been chosen to represent the vegetation status. Field surveys and observations allowed the elimination of some inconsistencies between the two documents and the development of the final vegetation map used in the present study.

1.6.1.1   Forest vegetation

Mesophilous broadleaved woodland   The mesophilous broadleaved wood-land defined in the map corresponds to forest areas with a predominance of beech (*Fagus sylvatica*).

Species accompanying *Fagus sylvatica* may often be related to the phytosociological classes of *Fagetalia sylvaticae* and *Querco-Fagetea*.

The most represented species are *Ostrya carpinifolia*, *Laburnum alpinum*, *Acer pseudoplatanus*, *Corylus avellana*, *Betula pendula*, *Sorbus aria*, *Sorbus aucuparia* and *Fraxinus ornus*.

Inside this list there are some species that belong to the typical black hornbeam (*Ostrya*) woodland, by which the *Fagus* woodland often appears so permeated that it is rather difficult to define precisely the cartographic limits between the two groups.

In particular the manna ash (*Fraxinus ornus*), is a species characterized by a sort of ubiquity within the flora of the West Garda Regional Forest, since it can be found in most of the mapped vegetation types.

Species generally associated with these mesophilous forests are: *Pteridium aquilinum*, *Gymnocarpium robertianum*, *Erica carnea*, *Helleborus niger*, *Luzula nivea*, *Carex alba*, *Lonicera alpigena*, *Lonicera nigra*, *Lathyrus vernus*, *Veronica urticifolia*, *Prenanthes purpurea*, *Aposeris foetida*, *Cardamine sp. pl.*, *Hepatica nobilis*, *Laburnum alpinum*, *Viburnum lantana*, *Epipactis sp. pl.* and *Cephalanthera sp. pl.*

Semi-mesophilous to slightly thermophilous broadleaved woodland   These woods, largely managed as coppice, are referable to the *Orno–Ostryon*, with *Ostrya carpinifolia* as the predominant element.

The most frequent tree and shrub species are: *Fraxinus ornus, Sorbus aria, Berberis vulgaris, Corylus avellana* and *Viburnum lantana*. Beech is very rarely present in these woods; however, small beech areas included in the typical *Ostrya* wood can be found.

The shrub and the grass surface respectively highlight the presence of *Lonicra alpigena, Lonicera xylosteum, Daphne mezereum, Rhododendron hirsutum, Salvia glutinosa, Hepatica nobilis, Euphorbia dulcis, Cyclamen purpurascens, Cardamine sp. pl., Melampyrum italicum, Helleborus niger, Erica carnea, Sesleria varia, Brachypodium rupestre subsp. Caespitosum* and *Calamagrostis varia*.

This group also includes river-bed and hill impluvia vegetation, because of their limited extent – they are extremely difficult to map – and their similar naturalistic value.

In this last group the most common species are: *Salix eleagnos, Salix appendiculata, Peuceddanum verticillare, Eupatorium cannabinum, Cirsium eristhales, Adenostyles glabra, Salvia glutinosa, Tofieldia calyculata, Calamagrostis varia* and many other species common to the *Ostrya* woodland.

Scotch pine woodland   In the West Garda Regional Forest's vegetation, Scotch pine (*Pinus sylvestris*) is well represented. It usually (re)colonizes open spaces, especially located on south-facing slopes with very poor and thin soils. It often creates sparse woods where lawns of *Erica* and *Rhododendron sp. pl.* grow together with many species typical of mesophilous and semi-mesophilous woods.

However, in this vegetation unit only pinewood areas where this species prevails are included. Accompanying species are *Pinus nigra, Juniperus communis, Fraxinus ornus, Brachypodium rupestre subsp., Caespitosum, Sesleria varia, Teucrium montanum, Erica carnea, Cotoneaster integerrima, Amelanchier ovalis, Epipactis atropurpurea* and *Cephalanthera sp. pl.*

Mountain woods dominated by fir   In the West Garda Regional Forest, pure fir woods are rare, while a sparse presence of *Picea excelsa* can be observed inside mesophilous woods. *Pinus sylvestris, Laburnum alpinum, Crategus monogyna, Aposeris foetida, Neottia nidus-avis* and *Listera ovata* are also present.

Larch woods, which are rather scarce within the West Garda Regional Forest, are included in *Picea* dominated units, since they share similar naturalistic value.

Black pine reforestation   *Pinus nigra* has been extensively used in the past for reforestation, also thanks to its limited survival needs as it grows on arid and poor soils. It can easily be found in Scotch pine woods, since *Pinus nigra* shares similar ecological conditions. These woods are characterized by quite a good potential to evolve towards *Orno–Ostryon*.

Chestnut woods   Chestnut woods grow in small areas, mainly located in the western part of Garda Lake, especially near cultivated zones. Their presence is in fact strongly related to human activities. Their growth is fostered because of the wood and fruit they provide.

1.6.1.2   Shrub and herbaceous vegetation

Sparse mugho pinewoods   At the upper limits of the forest, sub-alpine shrub vegetation is mainly characterized by *Pinus mugo*, which can be included in the *Erica–Pinion* alliance. Besides *Pinus mugo*, there are also *Rhododendron sp. pl.*, *Amelanchier ovalis*, *Carex firma*, *Erica carnea*, *Globularia cordifolia*, *Genista radiata*, *Gallium verum* and *Phyteuma scheuchzeri*.

The herbaceous layer, generally identifiable as *Firmetum*, is locally developing towards the *Seslerieto–Semperviretum*.

Primary cacuminal grasslands   Among mountain pasturelands cacuminal heliophilous grasslands may be identified, often broken up by dwarf or creeping shrubs. From a taxonomic viewpoint, such species can be included in paraclimactic phases of *Seslerietea-variae* class, *Seslerietalia variae* order, *Caricion austroalpinae* alliance.

In these areas, trees grow with difficulty because of extreme pedologic and climatic conditions. The typical species of these grasslands are: *Carex baldensis*, *Carex sempervires*, *Carex humilis*, *Carex firma*, but also *Sesleria varia*, *Galium verum*, *Genista radiata*, *Helianthemum nummularium*, *Biscutella laevigata*, *Globularia cordifolia*, *Phyteuma scheuchzeri*, *Asperula cynanchia*, *Allium cirrhosum*, *Lilium martagon* and *Gymnadenia odoratissima* can be found.

Grasslands on basic soils and with Molinia coerulea   In the West Garda Regional Forest, grasslands growing on basic soil are often recolonized by trees and bushes, due to the regress of agricultural activities; even if slightly thermophilous species, expecially on southern slopes, can be found, they can be included in the *Seslerietum*.

In sub-mountain areas, on soil characterized alternatively by dryness and humidity, *Molinia coerulea* is extensively represented.

Secondary grasslands   In the West Garda Regional Forest secondary grasslands are mainly found near places with human presence: they are mostly nitrophil and sinanthropic species growing near mountain huts.

Cliff and rock vegetation   Vegetation of cliffs and rocks is often composed by 'permanent' associations, that belong to the *Asplenietea trichomanis class, Potentillion caulescentis* alliance. Among these, there are many endemic species, such as: *Physoplexis comosa, Silene elisabethae*, and *Saxifraga tombeanensis*. The presence of *Saxifraga arachnoidea* and *Daphne petraea*, other endemic species, gives further value to this type of vegetation.

1.6.2   Functions Value Estimation

1.6.2.1   Production value

By considering the factors generally used for determining the productive value of forests, for example cultural and ecological criteria, it is possible to assign a value related with the productive function of each forest unit.
  The productive function is estimated on the basis of two factors:

- *accessibility*, that is a measure of accessibility of forest units to mechanical vehicles;
- *cultural type* (e.g. coppice/high forest), defining wood products in terms of both quantity and quality.

Such an evaluation process allows for identifying the capacity of each forest unit to provide a competitive product, even if it does not consider whether a market exists linked to the products concerned.

Results   According to Table 1.3 and the corresponding map (Figure 1.2), within the West Garda Regional Forest, areas with a high production value (more than eight) are very few (0.9 per cent of the entire analysed area).

1.6.2.2   Protection value

The protective function provided by the vegetation has been considered in terms of protection against hydro-geologic degradation, and has been evaluated on the basis of two factors:

- *vegetation structural characteristics*, which define the protection potentiality, independently of the real characteristics of the territory;
- *geomorphologic characteristics of the territory*: slope steepness and presence or potentiality for hydro-geologic degradation phenomena.

Table 1.3   Functions value distribution

Function value		Covered surface (%)
0	Null	19.3
1–2	Low	1.1
3–4	Medium–low	13.7
5–6	Medium	45.8
7–8	Medium–high	19.2
9–10	High	0.9

Climatic data have not been considered since the study area can be considered quite homogeneous from this point of view.

Vegetation cover protects the territory against hydro–geological degradation in different ways. It is generally acknowledged that forest stands assume the highest protection value, towards both soil erosion and the control of floods, with respect to other vegetation cover types. This is due to action operating at different levels, such as:

- reduction of the kinetic energy of rain drops caused by boughs and leaves;
- slowing down water flow towards the soil;
- infiltration into the soil due to litter and to the high porosity of forest soils;
- action of mechanic holdback of soil parcels by roots;
- sub-surface water flow in the soil and delayed restitution to the hydrographical network.

The highest level of hydro-geologic efficiency is normally achieved by mixed highly dense forests, with high biological complexity.

In this study, structural characters of vegetation have been described through two *soil protection indices* which have been calculated for each vegetation unit of the land use map. This way it was possible to achieve a homogeneous classification of the territory, for each category of vegetation cover.

Table 1.4 is an index of protection against splash erosion. On a four-stage ordinary scale it shows the protection assured by tree and shrub strata, which is the anti-erosive function exerted by the vegetation on the impact of rain on the soil.

Table 1.5 describes the index of protection against diffuse erosion caused by surface water flow. In particular it considers the cover of herbaceous and

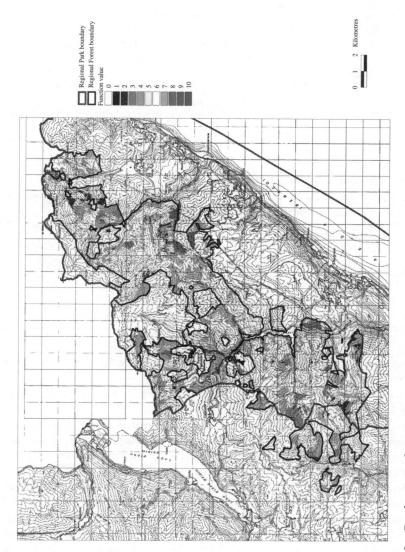

Figure 1.2   Production value map

19

Table 1.4   Index of protection against splash erosion

Class	Protection degree	Vegetation cover
0	Null–scarce	< 50%, sparse vegetation
1	Scarce	50–100%, open vegetation
2	Discrete	100–150% with vegetation made by a closed continuous arboreal stratum
3	Good	150–200% with a varied vegetation structure or covering >100% with a closed continuous tree stratum
4	Excellent	200% with a varied vegetation structure composed by trees and shrubs

Table 1.5   Index of protection against areal erosion

Class	Protection degree	Vegetation cover
0	Null–scarce	< 10% of herbaceous or mossy vegetation
1	Scarce	10–30%, discontinuous, impoverished, very sparse vegetation
2	Discrete	30–60%, discontinuous, rather sparse
3	Good	60–95%, continuous with elements of medium density
4	Excellent	100%, compact and continuous

mossy strata as an element which can help prevent degradation of the soil's surface.

The two indices have been synthesized into one *hydro-geological protection index*, by averaging them.

While the described function related to the hydro-geologic protection depends on the vegetation covering only, the real protective function is also related with the real territorial conditions, that is to slope steepness, soil erosion and geo-lithological characteristics.

In order to evaluate the soil loss caused by water erosion, it is also possible to use one of the widely adopted methodologies such as USLE (universal soil loss equation; Wischmeier and Smith, 1978). However, this method has not been applied since it needs a large data set. Therefore a simplified approach based on available data, such as slope steepness and presence of (or potential for) hydro-geologic degradation phenomena, has been chosen. Otherwise it is possible to use Gavrilovic's method, adopted in the Alpine mountains.

An approach based on models such as the soil conservation service (SCS) hydrological model or the USLE (Wischmeier and Smith's universal soil loss equation), has not been followed since it needs too large a data set. We chose a simplified approach based on available data, such as slope steepness and presence of (or potential for) hydro-geologic degradation phenomena. The physiographic element is particularly important in an alpine context since it strongly characterizes susceptibility to erosive phenomena and to land-slides. Thus a slope map has been created starting from the Digital Elevation Model and the corresponding membership function has been defined.

Based on available geologic maps, conditions of present or potential hydro-geologic degradation phenomena have been considered. Several categories are reported on the map but, in order to make the comparison with vegetation features easier, a reference table allowed the synthesis of these elements into two groups:

- group 0: no hydro-geologic degradation;
- group 1: presence of hydro-geologic degradation.

Results   The final estimate of the protective function (Figure 1.3) highlights the predominance of areas with medium–low values (66.9 per cent). Table 1.6 shows the distribution of the function value in the territory concerned.

1.6.2.3   Nature conservation
In estimating the nature conservation we assumed that naturalistic value derives from two main components, vegetation and fauna, which have been evaluated separately.

Vegetation component   On the basis of preliminary cartographic work, the natural degrees of the vegetation have been analysed. The process consists of the elaboration of an analytic estimation matrix, in which each vegetation unit is assigned a score for each of the following parameters:

1. *Rarity (Rt)*: indicates the facility of finding a particular vegetation type within the study area:
    - 8 = very rare (cover <1 per cent);
    - 4 = rare (cover 1–10 per cent);
    - 2 = common (cover 10–30 per cent);
    - 1 = very common (cover >30 per cent).
2. *Climax index (Cx)*: indicates the proximity to the climax:
    - 8 = flora and structure near the climax;
    - 4 = physiognomic predominance of climax elements;

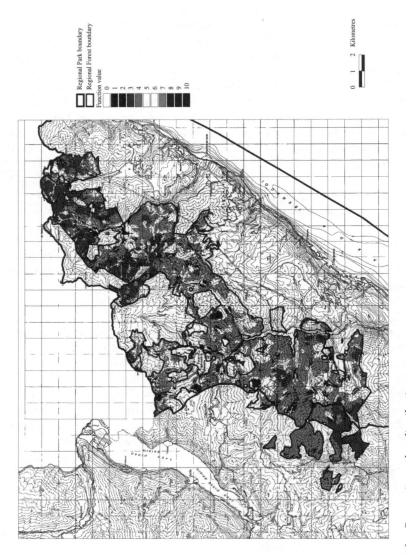

Regional Park boundary
Regional Forest boundary

Function value
0
1
2
3
4
5
6
7
8
9
10

0   1   2   Kilometres

Figure 1.3   Protection value distribution

Table 1.6   Distribution of the function value in the study area

Function value		Covered area (%)
1–2	Low	7.2
3–4	Medium–low	66.9
5–6	Medium	23.8
7–8	Medium–high	1.9
9–10	High	0.2

- 2 = structural and/or floristic climax elements;
- 1 = no climax elements.

3. *Structure (Sz)*: indicates the degree of complexity resulting from vertical spatial distribution of the species:
   - 8 = highly complex units, with at least three strata, one of them made up by trees;
   - 4 = shrub units;
   - 2 = compact herbaceous units;
   - 1 = sparse herbaceous units.

4. *Floristic set (If)*: indicates the disturbance degree caused by exotic species within the vegetation grouping:
   - 8 = scarce presence of adventitious species (<10 per cent);
   - 4 = adventitious species >10 per cent, but without a dominant role;
   - 2 = physiognomically dominant adventitious species;
   - 1 = adventitious and/or cultivar physiognomically or numerically dominant.

5. *Anthropic exploitation (Aa)*: estimates the degree and intensity of human activity on the several groupings:
   - 8 = no direct anthropic intervention;
   - 4 = interventions every 10 to 20 years;
   - 2 = cyclic non-destructive interventions;
   - 1 = yearly interventions and re-seeding.

6. *Evolutive potentiality (Pt)*: represents the auto-regenerative capacity of cenosis. It includes information related to the capacity of absorbing reversible impacts:
   - 8 = very high evolutive potential;
   - 4 = good evolutive potential;
   - 2 = medium evolutive potential;
   - 1 = null or very low evolutive potential.

7. *Floristic value (E)*: based on the presence of endemic or rare species growing at the margins of their ecological region, endangered species, species typical of peculiar vegetations, protected species:
   - 8 = excellent floristic value;
   - 4 = good floristic value;
   - 2 = medium floristic value;
   - 1 = null or very low floristic value.
8. *Biological diversity (Dv)*: estimated in order to compare the real situation and an optimal one for the concerned vegetation:
   - 8 = very high biological diversity;
   - 4 = good biological diversity;
   - 2 = medium biological diversity;
   - 1 = very low biological diversity.

Vegetation types have been evaluated on the basis of the above mentioned estimation indices. See Table 1.7.

The information provided by some parameters, such as the rarity index (Rt), must be considered in relative terms. The geographic extension of

Table 1.7 Score attribution to vegetation's types (Pn = Pinus nigra, L = Larix)

Vegetation type	Rt	Cx	Sz	If	Aa	Pt	E	Dv	Total
Woods with predominance of beech	1	8	8	8	4	8	1	8	46
Woods with predominance of black hornbeam	1	8	8	8	4	8	1	8	46
Woods with predominance of Scotch fir (Pn)	2	8	8	8	4	2	2	4	38
Woods with dominance of red fir (L)	4	8	8	8	4	1	2	4	39
Artifical black pine reforestation	8	4	8	4	4	1	2	4	35
Woods with dominance of chestnut	8	2	8	4	2	1	1	2	28
Mugho pine shrubs	4	8	4	8	8	4	4	8	48
Stable cacuminal grasslands	8	8	2	8	8	4	4	8	50
Grasslands on basic soils and with *Molinia coerulea*	2	4	4	8	4	4	2	4	32
Secondary grasslands	8	2	2	4	2	4	1	4	27
Cliff and rock vegetation	8	8	1	8	8	2	8	8	51

analysed units extends much outside the limits of the studied area and the suggested percentages apply only within the territory under analysis.

We should then consider the parameter used in absolute or relative terms, considering that a local value can often be much more significant than an absolute one.

RESULTS AND DISCUSSION   In the West Garda Regional Forest, areas with a medium–high naturalistic value prevail (55.2 per cent). Table 1.8 includes the distribution of the function value in the analysed territory.

Beech and black hornbeam woods are the most represented (within the first parameter of evaluation); they often create mixed woods with the two species co-existing in very different ways. Scotch pine woods follow – in percentage terms – even if with much lower values. Areas with a predominance of black pine, red fir and chestnut (adventitious species spread outside their areas by human activity) are rather few. The high naturality assigned to woody areas is due to the floristic set (If), which show a rare presence of adventitious species. The floristic set, expressing the degree of disturbance caused by exotic species, shows high values in groupings which have already been considered of high naturalistic value according to other parameters such as climax index, structure and biological diversity (the highest score is assigned to groups with a scarce presence of exotic species).

In contrast with the high naturality of woody areas, some vegetation types (black pine reforestation, chestnut woods, secondary grasslands) have lower quality characteristics, and this is also because of the presence of adventitious species. Secondary grasslands and chestnut woods are then simplified groups; they are characterized by a discontinuous flora quality which is damaged by frequent ingression of banal species.

As far as human activity is concerned (Aa), the less human activity there is over time, the worthier the vegetation types are considered to be. Also silvicultural techniques such as reforesting, thinning out and cutting,

Table 1.8   Distribution of the function values in the analysed territory

Function value		Covered area (%)
1–2	Low	2.1
3–4	Medium–low	13.1
5–6	Medium	21.2
7–8	Medium–high	55.2
9–10	High	8.4

even if they aim to increase the value of the forest ecosystem or keep it safe, determine a score (Aa = 4) that is less than other groups (stable cacuminal grasslands, mugho pinewoods) which belong to the higher score class (Aa = 8) because there is no human intervention.

The structure index (Sz) shows the complexity degree of vegetal cover: it is based on a vertical spatial distribution of the species and once again it highlights the typical woody features of the territory. Groupings of high complexity (score = 8) can be found in 60–70 per cent of the territory.

Considering the climax index (Cx), beech and black hornbeam woods show the highest values within the West Garda Regional Forest. *Ostrya* woods, typically referable to *Orno–Ostryon*, are relatively stable. They tend to grow in northern slopes, on soil with reduced evolution and showing a wide floristic variety (bounded to specific topographic conditions), according to their mesophilous or meso-thermophilous characteristics of cenosis.

Primary *Ostrya* woods are typically gorge areas with limited evolution capacity and are associated with a flora typical of humid zones, and of cliff areas on rocky soil.

Beech woods show a high climax index and grow on cooler slopes and on fertile soil. Considering tree species, the typical mountain beech wood presents a wide variety, in fact it can host many other species such as *Picea excelsa*, *Ostrya carpinofolia*, *Fraxinus ornus*, at a variable percentage.

Also cacuminal grasslands present cenosis with a high climax index. For instance *Seslerio–Seperviretum* can be considered as a very stable evolutional stage. Cliff and rock vegetation is somehow different, because of difficult ecological conditions, and it should be treated as a paraclimactic phase. Such vegetation component has been included in the high climactic group.

All typologies strongly influenced by human activity have generally very low climax values, which can be seen both in meadows surrounding huts, and in pasturelands. Natural evolution, which is mainly conditioned by edaphic elements, would take these units quite rapidly towards more stable cenosis – mostly referable to *Orno–Ostryon*.

The index related to the evolutive potentiality (Pt), indicates the auto-regenerative capacity of cenosis, thus expressing the possibility of absorbing impacts. In the analysed territory, the highest value has been reached by beech and black hornbeam woods.

Finally, the flora value (E), which has been calculated starting from an endemic or rare species set, reaches the highest values (score = 8) at vegetation typologies characterized by narrow ecological amplitude (cliff and rock vegetation, cacuminal meadows, mugho pine groups).

Among endemic entities it is possible to identify species both broadly

Table 1.9   Vegetation value

Class	Score	Value	Vegetation type
I	> 50	Excellent	Cliff vegetation and cacuminal grasslands
II	> 40	Good	Sub-alpine mugho pine shrubs, mesophilous and semi-mesophilous woods dominated by beech and black hornbeam
III	> 30	Medium	Mountain woods dominated by red fir, Scotch pine, black pine reforestation, grasslands on basic soil dominated by *Molinia coerulea*
IV	<= 30	Low	Chestnut tree woods, secondary grasslands with *Nardus stricta*

widespread in alpine zones (*Campanula carnica Schiede ex M. K.*, *Phyteuma scheuchzeri All.*), and others limited to the centre-alpine area (*Silene elisabethae Jan*, *Saxifraga tombeanensis Boiss*, *Physoplexis comosa (L) Schur*, *Centaurea rhaetica Moritzi*, *Carex austroalpina Becherer*).

The analysis of field-collected flora and vegetation data has been simplified by subdividing the total scores of vegetation typologies into four classes (Table 1.9).The first class includes units with high naturalistic value, which is cliff vegetation and primary cacuminal grasslands. They are stable associations, growing on very small surfaces and generally at high altitude.

The second class includes units of mesophilous, semi-mesophilous and slightly thermophilous broadleaved and sub-alpine shrubs with *Pinus mugho*. Broadleaved woods included here broadly characterize the West Garda Regional Forest.

All the coniferous woods belong to the third class (fir woods, Scotch pine woods and black pine reforestations), together with grasslands on basic soils dominated by *Molinia coerulea*. They have a naturalistic value which is intermediate between high-altitude grasslands and secondary ones.

The fourth and last class includes chestnut woods and secondary grasslands.

In general, the vegetation of the West Garda Regional Forest is generally characterized by a high naturalistic value. The class with the highest value is restricted to small areas; at the same time, vegetation units belonging to the fourth class are quite scarce. Medium–high quality classes are mainly represented by formations which are widespread within the West Garda Regional Forest.

Table 1.9 sums up the degrees of naturality.

Faunistic component   Without extensive, specialist fieldwork, one way to make a sufficiently good description of the macrovertebrate component in a specific territory is to carry out an environmental analysis procedure aiming to evaluate the land suitability to host the different zoocenosis components.

Given the practical objectives and time limits of the present research, the adoption of specific environmental evaluation models (EEM) could not be performed. Consequently a simplified evaluation process of fauna-potentiality has been adopted. The estimate of the faunistic value of the West Garda Regional Forest is based on zoogeographical and ecological criteria. In particular the final estimation is the result of cross-information relative to the presence and distribution of animal species and the degree of suitability that the territory shows towards them.

THE EVALUATION PROCESS   The base maps describing the fauna component are derived from the preliminary studies for setting up the environmental plan of the High Garda Natural Park, on a scale 1:50 000 and, in particular on the following cartography:

- environmental suitability for: deer, roe deer, chamois, mouflon, ibex, white hare, common hare, marmot;
- presence and density of: capercaillie, black grouse, hazel grouse, rock partridge;
- presence of Falconiformes;
- presence of other ornithic species.

The absence of maps describing other equally important taxonomic categories – such as entomofauna and ichthyofauna – did not allow us to include them in this research.

According to a multi-criteria evaluation approach, a value has been assigned to the faunistic component, operating in different steps.

First, a value has been assigned to each species based on existing documentation. Then a standardization procedure has been carried out, in order to express all values according to a common scale (from 1 as minimum value to 5 as maximum value). Finally, a weighted linear combination has been performed in order to achieve a synthesis map.

SPECIES EVALUATED ON THE BASIS OF LAND SUITABILITY   Land suitability for one or more species expresses land capacity to host those species. Land suitability evaluation has been carried out according to an ordinal scale ranging from 1 to 5, with scores increasing with suitability.

Table 1.10   Faunistic values: Falconiformes

Code	Species	Kind of observation	Biological value	Weight	Value
1	Black kite	Probable nidification	26	0.3	2
2	Buzzard	Nidification	26	0.4	2
3	Buzzard	Probable nidification	26	0.3	2
4	Short-toed eagle	Probable nidification	26	0.3	2
5	Short-toed eagle	Observation	26	0.15	1
6	Sparrow hawk	Sure nidification	26	0.4	2
7	Golden eagle	Regular observations	30	0.2	1
8	Golden eagle	Irregular observations	30	0.1	1
9	Golden eagle	Nidification	30	0.35	2
10	Kestrel	Sure nidification	26	0.4	2
11	Kestrel	Probable nidification	26	0.3	2

SPECIES EVALUATED ACCORDING TO THEIR PRESENCE   A map showing the naturalistic value related to the presence of rapacious species has been created. First of all, each species has been assigned a biological value according to specialized literature (Perco, 1990). Depending on the kind of observation, a weight factor has then been developed. The final values result from multiplying biological values per the corresponding weights, and finally rescaling the resulting values in the range 1 to 5. Values are shown in Table 1.10.

In areas where several categories overlap, the assigned score results from summing up the values of each analysed category.

A similar evaluation procedure has been applied for Galliformes as well (see Tables 1.11 and 1.12).

The presence of other birds has been evaluated in a similar way, but without the use of a weighting factor. Missing values have been subjectively introduced into Table 1.13.

FAUNISTIC VALUE: SYNTHESIS   After standardization, values of the different faunistic groups have been integrated by a weighted linear combination, thus yielding a synthetic map. The weighting function applied is based on the biological value of each species (Perco, 1990) (Table 1.14).

The calculated weights have been corrected in order to discriminate between evaluations made by suitability maps (mammals) and by presence maps (birds). Being a less direct evaluation, the former has been assigned a weight of 0.4, the latter a weight of 0.6.

Table 1.11   Faunistic value – capercaillie and black grouse

Code	Description	Score	Weight	Value
1	Presence of capercaillie in the last years	29	0.6	5
2	Presence of hybrid capercaillie – black grouse	26	0.4	2
3	Black grouse: slight or discontinuous presence	23	0.4	1
4	Black grouse: optimal density or regular presence	23	0.6	3

Table 1.12   Faunistic value – hazel grouse and rock partridge

Code	Description	Score	Weight	Value
1	Hazel grouse: minimum density or discontinuous presence	20	0.4	1
2	Hazel grouse: optimal density or regular presence	20	0.6	5
3	Rock partridge: minimum presence or discontinuous presence	19	0.4	1
4	Rock partridge: optimal presence or regular presence	19	0.6	4

Table 1.13   Faunistic value – other birds

Code	Description	Score	Value
1	Tengmalm's owl	25	5
2	Black woodpecker	21	3
3	Crag martin	18	1
4	Wall creeper – nutcracker	16	1
5	Raven	16	1

RESULTS   The results show a generally intermediate–low faunistic function (Table 1.15); however, the map shows some areas, mainly located in the higher part of the study area, characterized by high faunistic values.

Synthesis of naturalistic value   In order to express the naturalistic value through a unique index, fauna and vegetation components have been

Table 1.14   Biological value of each single species

Species	Average biological value	Weight
Deer	22	0.092
Roe deer	20	0.084
Chamois	23	0.096
Mouflon	18	0.075
Ibex	26	0.109
Common hare, white hare	18	0.075
Marmot	19	0.079
Golden eagle – other rapacious species	28	0.117
Capercaillie – black grouse	26	0.109
Hazel grouse – rock partridge	20	0.084
Other birds (different species)	19	0.079

Table 1.15   Distribution of the function value in the analysed territory

Function value		Covered area (%)
1–2	Low	41.6
3–4	Intermediate–low	35.4
5–6	Intermediate	18.5
7–8	Intermediate–high	4.1
9–10	High	0.5

synthesized. This has been done by a weighted linear combination, assigning the same weight to each component. The final map is reported in Figure 1.4.

1.6.2.4   Recreation value

In order to identify a complete and analytic model of evaluation of the recreation value of forest units, we referred to a work which has been developed by ISAFA in collaboration with the Provincia Autonoma of Bolzano, which integrates GIS methodologies and expert system. Such a procedure, named GARDEN (Carriero et al., 1998) allows estimating the recreation value of natural environments and represents the bibliography source of this research.

The attribution procedure is based on the analysis of both natural and anthropic factors, as shown in the corresponding tree of knowledge (Figure 1.5).

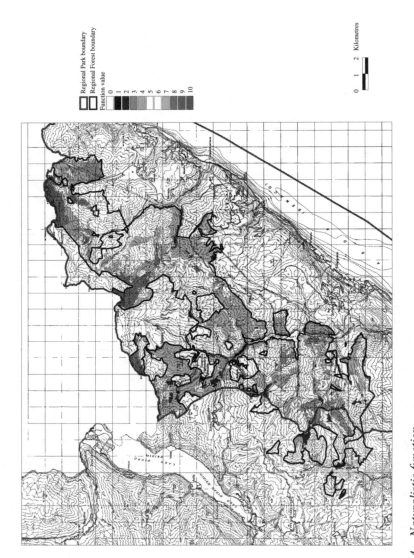

Figure 1.4   Naturalistic function

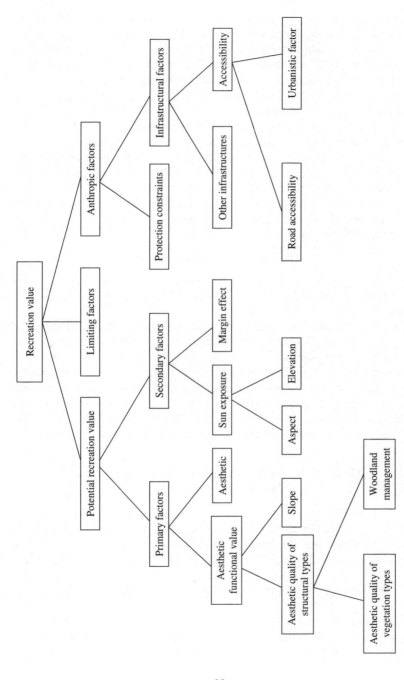

Figure 1.5   The tree of knowledge for recreation value

The evaluation process   The core of the analysis is the estimate of the aesthetic quality of woodlands. This property deals with the aesthetic appearance of woods, which can be considered in a passive way (just looking at the woods) or in an active one (using them for recreation). An aesthetic value has been attributed to every forest typology according to an estimation model developed by ISAFA (Scrinzi et al., 1995) considering Italian woods. This model assumes the existence of a relation between observable wood components (tree layer, underwood, etc.) and the functional–aesthetic quality perceived by the users.

The methodology refers to evaluations coming from observations made inside the wood. It does not consider then the landscape values obtainable by the observation from remote points.

The proposed relationship between the functional–aesthetic quality and the characters of the Italian woods has been formalized and interpreted through a multiple linear regression model:

$$Y_i = \beta_0 + \beta_1 x_{i1} + \beta_1 x_{i2} + \ldots \ldots \beta_k x_{ik} + u_i$$

with $i = 1,2,\ldots,n$, where the explicative variables refer to 25 elementary descriptors, synthesised then into six operative descriptors, according to Table 1.16.

The value-attribution of descriptors was made after a field survey based on forest typologies. At least three evaluations were made for each sample.

In each sample point a module was filled in and a photograph (10 × 15 cm) was taken. The evaluations obtained – based on the photographic atlas of visual inputs (attached to issue 95/2 of 'Comunicazioni di ricerca' ISAFA) – were mediated among them. It was thus possible to reach a value for the functional aesthetic quality for each forest typology. The evaluation model allows us to synthesize the information above through the following formula:

$$QEF = 3.811 + 0.676 \text{ tree layer} + 0.856 \text{ underwood} + 1.1178 \text{ uses} + 0.205 \text{ season.}$$

Results   The highest function values are present only near the road network: the analysis shows that the West Garda Regional Forest has a generally low recreation value. See Table 1.17 and the corresponding map (Figure 1.6).

1.6.3   Pre-arrangement of the Results for Further Analysis

In the present application, GIS provided the information in a directly accessible way to the cluster analysis procedure conducted by the Department of Economics at the University of Verona (see Chapter 2).

Table 1.16   Operative and elementary descriptors for the estimation
of the forest's aesthetic–functional quality.

Operative descriptors	Operative descriptors
Tree layer	Dimensions
	Inclination
	Branchiness
	Integrity
	Distribution regularity
	Dimension variability
	Density
	Epiphytic vegetation
	Chromatism
	Cover discontinuity
Underwood	Shrubs
	High plants/grass
	Grass mantle
	Chromatism
	Aridity/humidity
Management practices	Sparse residuals
	Concentrated residuals
	Sparse products
	Concentrated products
	Stumps
Soil	Slope
	Inaccessibility
Season	Seasonal suitability

Table 1.17   Distribution of the function value in the analysed territory

Function value		Covered area (%)
1–2	Low	5.8
3–4	Intermediate–low	57.2
5–6	Intermediate	32.0
7–8	Intermediate–high	4.7
9–10	High	0.3

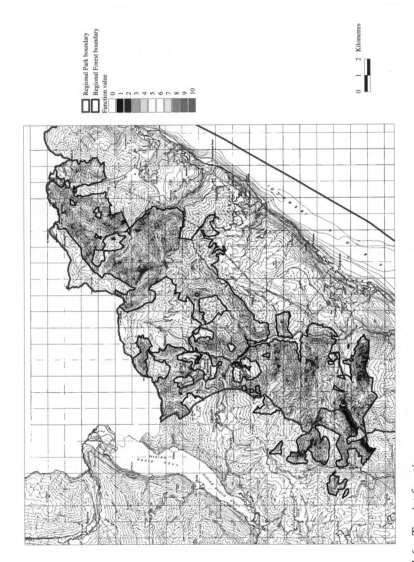

Regional Park boundary
Regional Forest boundary
Function value
0 1 2 3 4 5 6 7 8 9 10

0 1 2 Kilometres

Figure 1.6 Tourist function

36

The integration with the two analysis systems provided good results thanks to the perfect compatibility of the interchange data format. In particular, for each cell, a resulting value was provided for each of the estimated functions (productive, protective, naturalistic, tourist). This value, which synthesises the results of the analysis into just one number, represents the base reference on which the following subdivision into homogeneous units is based.

On this basis a cluster analysis procedure was carried out, which allowed the identification of homogeneous units according to a multifunctional space (Figure 1.7).

After a quick analysis of results, each group was preliminarily assigned the prevalent functions, as shown in Table 1.18.

However, in order to define precisely both the spatial extent and the associated functions of each homogeneous unit, further work is needed.

1.7   CONCLUSIONS

By using the described analysis system, an estimate of the current level of forest functions, based on both existing information and on field work, has been conducted. By visualizing the cartography, the user can immediately estimate each function and its spatial distribution. A set of information layers related to all the elements of the system, both elementary and intermediate nodes, may be derived at any time.

The subdivision of the West Garda Regional Forest on the basis of the prevalent functions shows that 28 per cent of the analysed territory is characterized mainly by the naturalistic function. The tourist function prevails on 10 per cent of the territory, depending strictly on its accessibility.

The methodology used also highlights the non-productive characteristic of the West Garda Regional Forest where only 9 per cent of the territory is characterized by important productive values (Table 1.19).

1.7.1   Further Research

A systematic and precise validation of this territory analysis model has not been carried out because of limited time and economic resources. This necessary phase of model calibration would make the model more reliable and also applicable to other contexts. A natural development of this work would involve the simulation of different land use changes by means of scenarios, by evaluating corresponding changes in the value of the different functions.

The flexibility of the model allows modifications aiming to satisfy particular knowledge needs at any point in time (allowing the introduction

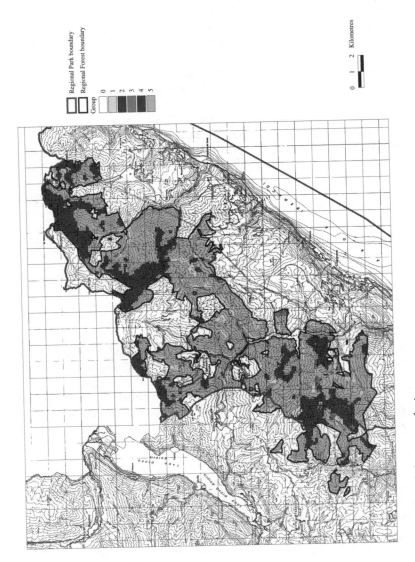

Regional Park boundary
Regional Forest boundary

Group
0
1
2
3
4
5

0 1 2 Kilometres

Figure 1.7 Results of cluster analysis

Table 1.18   West Garda Regional Forest subdivision by groups and prevalent functions

Group	Functions			
	1	2	3	4
1	Productive	Tourist	Naturalistic	–
2	Naturalistic	Tourist	Protective	–
3	Tourist	Naturalistic	–	–
4	Tourist	Naturalistic	Protective	–
5	Productive	Naturalistic	Protective	Tourist

Table 1.19   West Garda Regional Forest subdivision based on prevalent functions

Prevailing function	Covered area (ha)	Covered area (%)
Naturalistic	3102	28.1
Tourist	1160	10.5
Productive	1008	9.1
Protective	576	5.2
Multifunctional (two or more prevalent functions)	5209	47.1

of new parameters, modification of weights, and so on). Of course, only continuously updating the geographic database keeps the predictive capacity of the model up to date.

REFERENCES

Aronoff, S. (1989), *Geographic Information Systems, a Management Perspective*, WDL Publications, Ottawa, Canada.

Burrough, P.A. and R.A. McDonnell (1998), *Principles of Geographic Information Systems*, Oxford University Press, New York.

Carriero, A., G. Scrinzi, G. Tabacchi, V. Tosi and W. Weger (1998), *Integration between GIS and Expert System in the Evaluation of Territorial Tourist-recreation Suitability*, Proceedings of the AISF-EFI International Conference on Forest Management in Designated Conservation and Recreation Areas, 7–10 October 1998, Florence, pp. 491–500.

Eastman, J.R., P.A.K. Kyem, J. Toledano and W. Jin (1993), *GIS and Decision Making. UNITAR Explorations in GIS Technology*, 4, UNITAR, Geneva.

Perco, F. (1990), *Fauna Project*, Trento Autonome Province, Fishing and Hunting Service, Trento, Italy.

Saaty, R.W. (1987), '*The analytic hierarchy process – what it is and how it is used*', *Mathematical Modeling*, **9** (3), 161–76.

Scrinzi, G., A. Floris, T. Flamminj and P. Agatea (1995), *A Model to Estimate Forest Sites' Aesthetic-functional Quality*, ISAFA (Forest and Range Management Research Institute), Villazzano, Trento (Italy).

USACERL (1993), *GRASS User's Reference Manual*, US Army Corps of Engineers Research Laboratory, Champaign, IL, USA.

Wischmeier, W.H. and D. Smith (1978), 'Predicting rainfall erosion losses: a guide to conservation planning', *USDA-ARS Agriculture Handbook*, No. 537, Washington, DC.

Zimmerman, H.J. (1987), *Fuzzy Sets, Decision Making and Expert Systems*, Boston, MA: Kluwer Academic Publishing.

2. The supply of functions by homogeneous area using cluster analysis

Paola De Agostini, Veronica Cicogna and Federico Perali

2.1 INTRODUCTION

A forest system is composed of many different elements which interact among themselves and with the external system. In particular, forest productive processes are able to offer both private and collective goods. While production of private goods – such as wood and fruit – uses up space on the ground, production of collective goods – such as fauna protection and recreational activities – implies the conservation of the eco-system. Therefore, the management process of all these resources is complex. It is also important to consider that the forest productive system expands over a long-term period. For example, once part of the land has been devoted to the production of wood, it would be impossible to use it for other purposes for many years.

In order to advise the government on what policies should be formulated, it is necessary to take into account many aspects. It is important to gain insight into the decision-making process taking into account both bio-ecological, and social and economic characteristics, while resolving the conflicts of interest among institutions, local economic agents and park users. This can be done using mathematical and economic techniques (Nijkamp and Rietveldt, 1996; Rehaman and Romero, 1993).

The core purpose of this study is to define a management strategy for developing a natural area, such as the West Garda Regional Forest, through an integrated and participative analysis that will optimize the decision-making process. To achieve this goal, the first step is to evaluate the best mix of functions supplied by this natural area.

Data used in this analysis come from a detailed mapping system called a geographical information system (GIS). In particular, this data set provides indices recording the ability of each hectare of territory to offer naturalistic, productive, protective and tourist products and services. In order to help management decision-makers in defining the most efficient managerial strategy, it is necessary to identify a common policy for similar areas. Therefore similar macro-areas must be defined. In doing so, this chapter uses multivariate analysis to classify each hectare-cell into homogeneous macro-areas by bio-ecological characteristics and to identify their natural vocation.

This chapter is organized as follows. Section 2 discusses the cluster analysis methodology applied for organizing GIS data. Among cluster analysis methods, we choose the k-means technique, and after a general description of cluster analysis, we focus our attention on that method. Section 3 presents some preliminary tables that describe the main features of the West Garda Regional Forest and bio-ecological patterns. Section 4 adopts k-means cluster analysis techniques to identify five main macro-areas. Using factor analysis, we assign a name to each macro-area that emphasizes its natural vocation. Finally, Section 5 draws conclusions and assesses the extent to which the results can be generalized.

2.2   CLUSTER ANALYSIS METHODOLOGY

The cluster analysis combines a variety of statistical methods that assign elements to groups or clusters by their qualitative or quantitative common characteristics. There is no limit on the composition of the original set: it might contain individuals, objects, observations, variables, data or measures.

Thanks to the generality of cluster techniques, they have been extensively applied to many research topics (Friedman and Rubin (1967), Cormack (1971), Anderberg (1973), Everitt (1974) and Gordon (1981)).

The main aim of the multivariate statistical analysis is data analysis. In particular, cluster methods are useful for classifying elements belonging to a given data set into smaller subgroups based on measures of similarity or dissimilarity. The results obtained should emphasize that elements belonging to the same subset are as similar as possible, while elements belonging to two different subsets are as different as possible. In other words, this technique distributes observations into subsets considering internal and external similarity rates: within each group the natural rate of association is higher than between different groups. Therefore, clusters resulting from these applications show high homogeneity within the group and high heterogeneity between them.

Depending on the analysis method chosen, available data, scientific field and research interests, cluster analysis characteristics, such as flexibility and variety, make this method suitable for several tasks. In particular, this technique has been applied to model adaptation, prediction, hypothesis validation and testing, data exploration, hypothesis proposal and finally for reduction of the amount of data set observations.

Using *cluster* and *factor* analysis together allows identification of clusters and the determination of their relative positions. Moreover, more precise results can be derived using partitions and tree-structure studies in the preliminary data analysis.

In this study, we first apply cluster analysis in order to reduce the initial amount of information, identifying which micro-areas have similar bio-ecological functional characteristics and by using factor analysis we identify which environmental functions mainly characterize each cluster.

This chapter adopts a method of classification belonging to the family of non-hierarchical techniques known as *k-mean algorithm*. It is the best way of dealing with large amounts of data, counting hundreds or thousands of observations and its efficiency in producing meaningful empirical results is widely recognized.[1]

Applications of this methodology require fixing *a priori* the number k of groups that researchers expect to exist and some initial reference points. In this way, the first partition of the main set will be derived from these two assumptions. Once we have identified the first k clusters, for each group we calculate the centre point (see definition above). This method uses Euclidean distance as dissimilarity criteria. The second partition uses this definition and the minimum distance between all observations of the original set and new centres to create a new partition. This method is therefore iterated to find further partitions.

The advantage of using k-mean methodology is its ability to identify clusters that are stable. Past studies emphasize that the results of this evaluation can be reached relatively quickly, generally with less than ten iterations. Moreover, it is not necessary to store an initial distance matrix because it is sufficient to know the distance of clusters from each centre: thus this method can be used also to analysis large data sets.

K-mean analysis has been applied successfully for some environmental analysis, particularly for the identification of areas treated as homogeneous by social and economic services.

Assume we are looking for a partition of a set I containing n elements characterized by p variables. Let us define the Euclidean distance on R^p. We follow eight steps:

1. Predetermine a k number of clusters.
2. Identify the initial k reference points: $c_1^0, c_2^0, \ldots, c_k^0$. Define the initial partition P^0 as: $I_1^0, I_2^0, \ldots, I_k^0$.

3. Calculate the centre of each cluster and so define: $c_1^1, c_2^1, \ldots, c_k^1$ as the arithmetic mean of the elements assigned at each partition: $c = [c_1, c_2, \ldots, c_j \ldots, c_p]$. The centres are treated as elements and are used for the second partition.
4. Calculate Euclidean distances between each element and each centre obtained from the previous step.
5. Assign every element to the nearest centre group (minimum Euclidean distance). In this way we obtain k new groups.
6. Again calculate the average of each group and define new centres. From this we obtained a new partition P^2 using the same method we have already used for P^1.
7. Iterate this process from the third step until arriving at k new centres: $c_1^m, c_2^m, \ldots, c_k^m$ that do not change the partitions P^m found, for at least two successive iterations. Then we may say that the clusters or the partitions are stable.

2.3 GIS DATABASE AND DEFINITION OF THE FUNCTIONS OF THE NATURAL AREA

The High Garda Natural Park extends over an area of 38 000 hectares. Moving from south to north over the west part of Garda Lake this area covers nine town councils that are: Salò, Gardone Riviera, Toscolano Maderno, Gargnano, Tignale, Tremosine, Limone sul Garda, Valvestino and Magasa. The Regional Forestry Agency of Lombardy is responsible for the management of the park side belonging to the state, called West Garda Regional Forest. This area extends over 11 064 hectares and represents the object of this study.

The West Garda Regional Forest produces various environmental–ecological goods and services. We use data coming from the previous GIS analysis. This data set contains information about the ability of each hectare of land to supply products as criteria for classification of the micro-areas into the macro-areas, useful for determining the best managerial–environmental policy.

In particular, we consider four products or functions: naturalistic, protective, productive and tourist. We define these as:

1. naturalistic function: conservation of nature, wildlife and the eco-system;
2. protective function: regarding the structural feature of the canopy and territory: gradient, hydrologic characteristics and soil erosion;

Table 2.1   Descriptive statistics for West Garda Regional Forest (Obs. 11 064)

Variables	Mean	Std. Dev.	Min.	Max.
Naturalistic function	5.00	1.41	0	10.00
Productive function	4.16	2.43	0	10.00
Protective function	3.53	1.48	0	9.25
Tourist function	4.04	1.18	0	9.25

3. productive function: providing markets with competitive timber and non-timber products: mushrooms, fodders, resins, mosses, etc;
4. tourist function: it describes the capacity of offering recreational services: sports, and activities such as hunting and fishing, gathering flowers, mushrooms, fruits, and so on.

The data report indices summarize a quantitative evaluation of those four functions, and the functions are derived from an analysis of the ecological–territorial characteristics of each hectare of the area using GIS methodology (territorial, environmental, ecological and anthropological parameters) and from mapping data collection.[2] Those indices vary in a range [0–10] and they can be interpreted as follows: 0–2 low capacity, 3–4 medium–low capacity, 5–6 medium capacity, 7–8 medium–high capacity and 9–10 high capacity.

Summary statistics for this sample are reported in Table 2.1, while Figure 2.1 shows their distributions. This forest has a medium capacity to offer naturalistic services and a medium–low capacity to offer productive, protective and tourist services. In particular, Figure 2.1 shows that roughly 80 per cent of the area has low or medium–low capacity to offer protective services for the ecosystem (Figure 2.1c). However, much of it has a medium ability capacity to offer naturalistic and tourist products (87.15 per cent) (see Figure 2.1b and a). Looking at the productivity capacity (Figure 2.1d) it is obvious that there are two different types of territory: one with medium–high capacity of producing wood and other non-wood product covers roughly 53 per cent of the total area, while the remaining 47 per cent has a low capacity to produce marketable goods.

Given this functional diversity highlighted from a first exploratory data analysis, we continue to apply cluster analysis, in order to classify the total area into macro-areas by natural characteristics. This part of the study will be helpful in identifying differences existing among macro-areas.

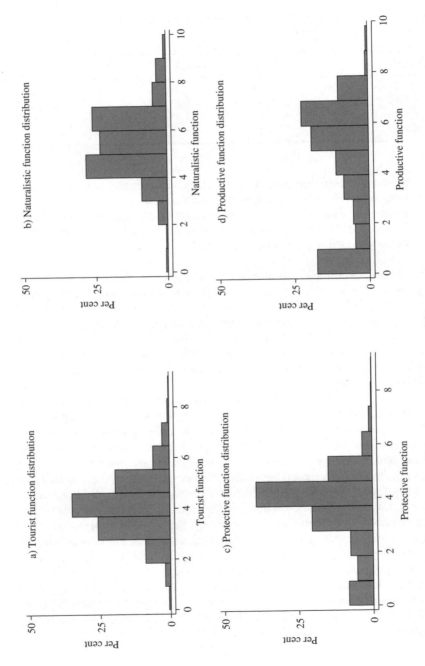

Figure 2.1 Function distribution in the West Garda Regional Forest

2.4 INTERPRETATION OF RESULTS

The results have been computed using SPSS (statistical packages for the social sciences, SPSS, 1997) applying k-means cluster methodology.

We divide the West Garda Regional Forest into areas of different sizes based on their natural characteristics. In this way, they could all be managed in a distinctive different and efficient way. In doing so, we use four variables recording naturalistic, protective, productive and tourist functions defined as described above.

The choice of the method depends on the aims of the study and data characteristics. Taking into account the dimensions of the data (a matrix of 11 064 rows and four columns), we decided to use the k-means method. This method is particularly useful for analysis of huge data sets because it does not need huge an enormous memory for the computations.

It involves knowing in advance the number of clusters the researcher wants to find. In order to choose the optimum number of clusters, we take into account the manager's needs and thus reduce the number of clusters to between a minimum of three and a maximum of eight. In fact the natural area can be more effectively managed in macro-areas, given its huge size. Identifying homogenous macro-areas based on functional characteristics allows defining a policy that will most effectively satisfy users' preferences and optimize the management of the natural resources.

Applying the analysis of variance to the k-means results for each $k = 3$, 5 and 8. The maximum dissimilarity between clusters results from $k = 5$. Therefore, we proceed the analysis dividing the park into five macro-areas.

2.4.1 Data Elaboration

Based on the data set described in Section 2.3, we have identified five macro-areas homogeneous by function. The method applied here started by choosing the initial centres randomly and ends after 22 iterations. The resulting clusters have means as shown in Table 2.2.

Table 2.2 Coordinates of final centres per group

	Cluster				
	1	2	3	4	5
Naturalistic function	4.92	7.41	2.52	4.15	5.19
Productive function	5.40	0.35	1.30	1.33	5.68
Protective function	1.15	3.02	1.26	3.78	4.26
Tourist function	5.29	3.68	2.08	4.03	3.95

Table 2.3   Matrix of Euclidean distance between centres

Cluster	1	2	3	4	5
1	–	6.14	5.36	5.06	3.41
2	6.14	–	5.35	3.50	5.91
3	5.36	5.35	–	3.24	6.05
4	5.06	3.50	3.24	–	4.50
5	3.41	5.91	6.05	4.50	–

Table 2.4   Size in hectares per area

Cluster	Hectares	Share of total area (%)
1	1335	12
2	943	9
3	621	6
4	2014	18
5	6151	55
Total	11 064	

Table 2.3 reports the Euclidean distance between centres. The most similar clusters are the third and the fourth.

Table 2.4 shows the area size in hectares per cluster and the percentage of surface belonging to each macro-area.

The table of resulting centres (Table 2.2) contains mean values of each variable per group, but it does not indicate anything about their variance. Therefore we use an ANOVA analysis applied to each variable and study the variance ratio both between and within clusters using test F.

The null hypothesis of this test presumes equality between variances. Table 2.5 shows the results of these tests: variance between and within groups, and their ratio (F-test value). High values of F and a low significance level mean that clusters are very different from each other. However, this test is meant to be only descriptive, because of the fact that clusters derived from this analysis aim to optimize differences between groups. Thus, the significance level is biased in this case and can be useful solely for testing equality between cluster means.

ANOVA results reject the null hypothesis of mean equality. Therefore, clusters are sufficiently internally homogeneous but different from each other:

Table 2.5   ANOVA analysis

Functions	Cluster		Error		F	Sig.
	Variance between clusters	df	Variance within clusters	df		
Naturalistic	2740.82	4	0.99	11 059	2764.55	0
Productive	12 775.74	4	1.28	11 059	9996.18	0
Protective	3608.10	4	0.88	11 059	4115.13	0
Tourist	805.21	4	1.09	11 059	735.88	0

Note: df = degree of freedom; sig. = significance.

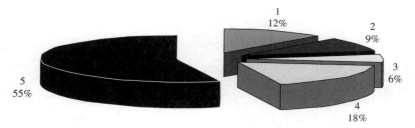

Figure 2.2   Distribution of macro-areas over total area

2.4.2   Results

Figure 2.3 shows the West Garda Regional Forest divided into five macro-areas resulting from cluster analysis.

Table 2.6 reports descriptive statistics for each independent variable. Their location has been affected by bio-ecological conditions: temperature, altitude, geomorphology, hydrographical network and soil use. These factors positively or negatively affect the existence of plant and animal populations and consequently they also limit the natural area's ability to supply natural products and services. The distribution of the variables among areas is shown in Figures 2.4 to 2.8.

In particular, the second group (Figure 2.5) shows that the natural area does not have a productive function since the wide variety of vegetation increases its naturalistic function. The fifth group (Figure 2.8), on the contrary is characterized by micro-areas with medium naturalistic and tourist function (95 per cent and 91 per cent respectively) and by some micro-areas with medium–high productive function.

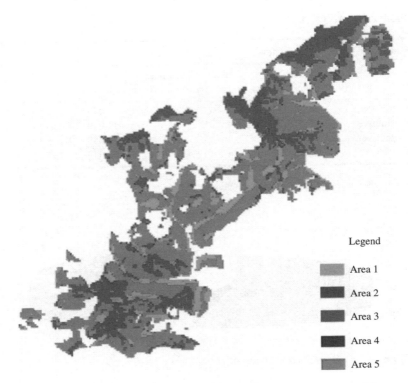

Figure 2.3   *West Garda Regional Forest by macro-area as derived from*
                cluster analysis results

Thus far, this study has identified five macro-areas within the park, but
in order to complete a more in-depth analysis, we continue with a factor
analysis. This methodology will be used to explore in detail the function of
each macro-area.

2.4.2.1   Identification of the functions characterizing the forest through factor analysis

After having divided the 11 064 hectares of park into five macro-areas
homogeneous according to ecological characteristics, it is necessary to
identify their principal functions in order to make it easier for the policy-
maker to determine the best environmental policy for each area. One
of the most used methods for doing so is called *factor analysis* (Cailliez
and Pagès, 1996). The basic thinking behind this statistical technique is
that values observable by the researcher might be affected by some other
variables not observable (latent variables). For example, a researcher can

Table 2.6   Descriptive statistics by macro-area

Variables	Cluster 1				
	N. Obs.	Mean	Std. Dev.	Min.	Max.
Naturalistic function	1335	4.91	0.98	2.00	8.00
Productive function	1335	5.40	1.22	1.75	9.50
Protective function	1335	1.15	0.99	0.00	4.25
Tourist function	1335	5.29	0.86	2.75	8.75

Variables	Cluster 2				
	N. Obs.	Mean	Std. Dev.	Min.	Max.
Naturalistic function	943	7.41	1.01	5.25	10.00
Productive function	943	0.35	0.84	0.00	3.75
Protective function	943	3.02	1.11	0.00	6.25
Tourist function	943	3.68	1.15	0.00	7.25

Variables	Cluster 3				
	N. Obs.	Mean	Std. Dev.	Min.	Max.
Naturalistic function	621	2.52	1.19	0.00	5.50
Productive function	621	1.30	1.31	0.00	5.00
Protective function	621	1.26	1.04	0.00	3.75
Tourist function	621	2.80	1.64	0.00	8.00

Variables	Cluster 4				
	N. Obs.	Mean	Std. Dev.	Min.	Max.
Naturalistic function	2014	4.15	1.00	0.50	6.50
Productive function	2014	1.33	1.28	0.00	3.75
Protective function	2014	3.78	0.92	0.00	9.25
Tourist function	2014	4.03	1.20	0.25	9.25

Variables	Cluster 5				
	N. Obs.	Mean	Std. Dev.	Min.	Max.
Naturalistic function	6151	5.18	0.97	1.50	8.00
Productive function	6151	5.68	1.08	3.00	10.00
Protective function	6151	4.26	0.89	2.00	9.25
Tourist function	6151	3.95	0.93	1.25	8.25

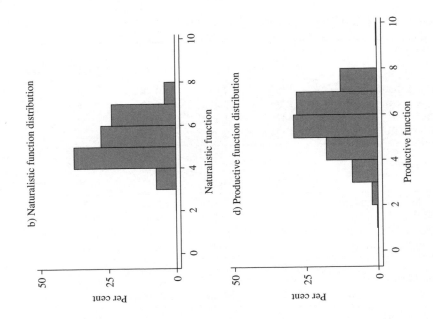

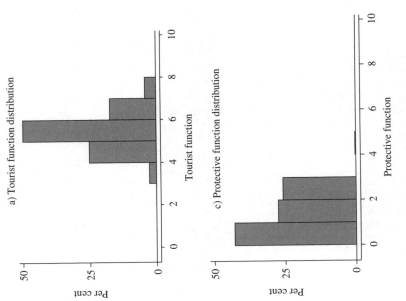

Figure 2.4 Function distribution in Macro-Area 1

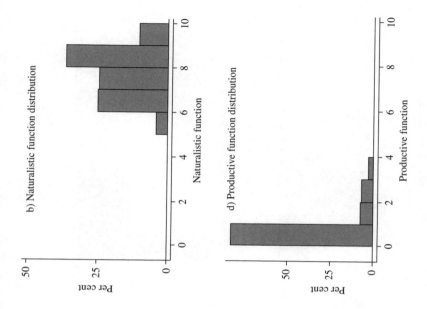

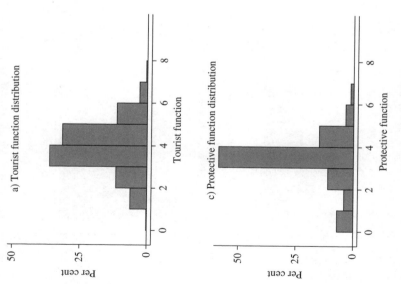

Figure 2.5   Function distribution in Macro-Area 2

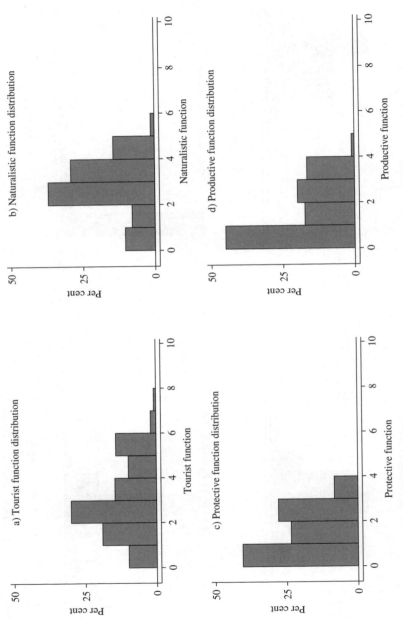

Figure 2.6   Function distribution in Macro-Area 3

54

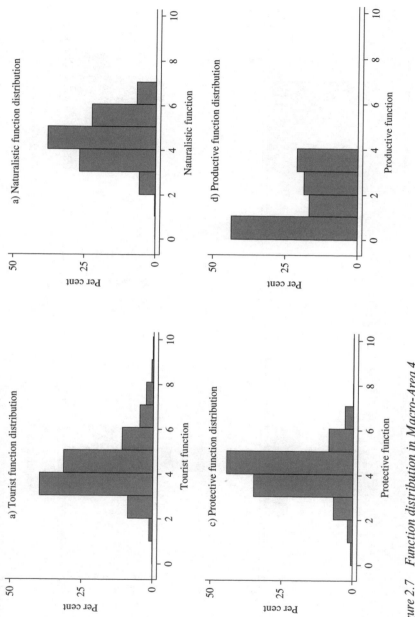

Figure 2.7 Function distribution in Macro-Area 4

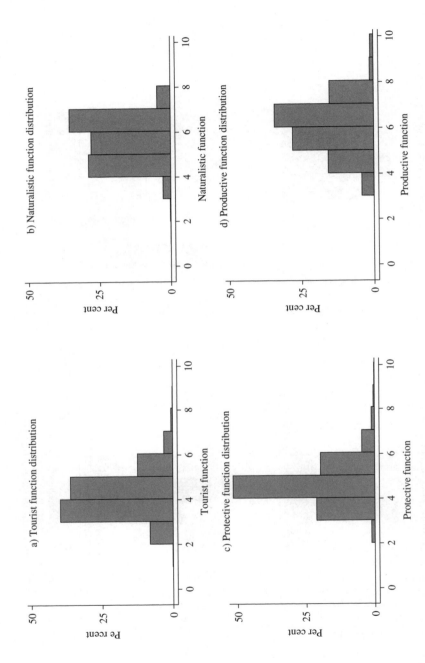

Figure 2.8   Function distribution in Macro-Area 5

observe the natural area's physical characteristics, such as its shape or types of plants growing over it, but he cannot observe directly the functional characteristic of a natural area. Using these observable characteristics it is possible to explain why an area might be more suitable in supplying some services rather than others, such as tourist services rather than wood products.

When a database has a large number of variables to describe an event, it might be useful to define a smaller number of variables. In this case researchers usually define some new variables derived from the original observed variables. How do we choose this new set of variables? Reducing the amount of descriptive variables means that part of the available information is lost. In order to minimize this loss, factor analysis defines new variables as a linear combination of the observed variables, in such a way that the variables are not correlated with each other and that each of them has maximum variance.[3]

The aim of the new variables is to explain the dependence between the original observable variables. For example, an area with several woods and wide grass prairies is shown to be more accessible for tourist purposes.

The main aim of this part of our study is to transform the original four observed variables – naturalistic, protective, productive and tourist functions – that are highly correlated with each other, into four new uncorrelated variables, called 'principal components'.

Given that this method identifies new variables based on their capacity to explain total variance, most of the variance can be explained only by some components. The research of the principal components suggests a reduction of the original space R^k into a space smaller than k. In this way the interpretation of the results is easier.

2.4.2.1.1 Factor analysis results The application of factor analysis is based on the four original variables representing the supply of services that are the object of this study. The number of principal components affects the interpretation and graphical representation of the results. Therefore it is useful to choose a small number of components in order to keep the representation simple. In doing so, the minimum number of common factors capable of explaining the observed variables with the least loss of information is chosen.

Information derived from the common factors is summarized by the eigen values. They are computed through diagonalization of the correlation matrix.[4] Each eigen value (Tables 2.7, 2.9, 2.11, 2.13 and 2.15) represents the variance of observed cases on each principal axis. In order to decide how many principal components we need to consider to continue with the analysis, it is convenient to interpret eigen values in relation with total variance. The total variance is derived from the sum of eigen values and it is equal to the number of variables because they have been standardized.[5] The ratio between each eigen value and the total variance represents the percentage of variance explained by the corresponding principal axis. For example, looking at the third group in our analysis (Table 2.11), the first factor explains 38.4 per cent of the total variance. Two axes explain more than 70 per cent of the total available information.[6] Three axes explain more than 90 per cent. Interpreting eigen values in this manner, we analyse the results per group identified by the cluster analysis. Representing our findings on R^2 seems the easiest way of looking at them. Therefore we have identified two principal axes per macro-area.

Tables 2.8, 2.10, 2.12, 2.14 and 2.16 report correlations between each observed variable and the first two principal axes obtained from the factor analysis (first and second columns), the square values of these correlations (columns three and four) and total by row of third and fourth columns. This last value represents the information explained by the axes for each of the four environmental functions. For example, for the first macro-area (see last column of Table 2.8), passing from R^4 to R^2 we are still able to represent 81 per cent of the total information about tourist function.

In order to give a clearer interpretation of the results, correlations between variables and principal axes are reproduced graphically using the so called 'correlation circle'. The correlation circle for each macro-area is reported in Figures 2.9, 2.10, 2.11, 2.12 and 2.13. The correlation circle's representations are obtained drawing a circle with a ray equal to one. On it, four 'function points' are represented: their coordinates are the correlation coefficients between variables and principal axes. To interpret these graphs let us go back to the last example about the first cluster (Table 2.8). For instance, 81 per cent of tourist information is explained by the two principal components, but only 39 per cent of productive function is explained. The same results can be obtained interpreting the graph, where the representation of a variable is more accurate the closer it ends up to the border of the circle. Therefore, it is evident that in Figure 2.9 the tourist function is the closest to the circle border, while the spot representing productive function is the closest to the centre.

In this way factor analysis shows the specific function of each macro-area. In particular, interpreting the results based on each area's physical and ecological characteristics (as variables represented through indices), factor analysis highlights that the first cluster is characterized by a prevalence of tourist services, owing to the type of vegetation and to the network of roads facilitating access to the natural area. The second and fourth areas are both characterized by protective and naturalistic functions, but in different manners: in fact the different territory composition shows different functional levels. The second area holds high mountains (Monte Caplano, Passo Tremalzo, Passo Nota) and it is characterized mainly by rocks and discontinuous pastures of grass and shrubs. This kind of land-scape explains the low productive function of the area and its high natur-alistic value: it is an optimal place for chamoises, marmots, buzzards and golden eagles. On the other hand, the fourth cluster is located on the pre-Alps area of the park (Monte Pizzoccolo and Passo Spino, area of S. Michele extending from Tremosine to Tremalzo). The easy access to the area and the presence of prairies, hard woods and pine trees make this natural area suitable for commercial and non-commercial wood produc-tion. The third area, characterized by woods and meadows, has an evident high tourist–naturalistic function: 83.78 per cent and 83.08 per cent respec-tively, and protective and productive functions at about 60 per cent. The fifth group is a wide area able to supply all types of services and goods we are controlling for, but it is mainly useful for naturalistic and tourist func-tions.

Finally this analysis allows us to label each area with a name highlight-ing its main character (Figure 2.14). Specifically we define:

1. a tourist area;
2. a protective–naturalistic area;
3. a tourist–naturalistic area;
4. a protective–naturalistic area;
5. a naturalistic–tourist area.

Therefore from this analysis, we can conclude that the West Garda Regional Forest is mainly characterized by a naturalistic function, and a low productivity function that does not appear to apply in all the five macro-areas.

AREA 1

Table 2.7　Total explained variance

Components	Initial eigen values		
	Total	% explained variance	Cumulative
1	1.26	31.41	31.41
2	0.96	23.97	55.38
3	0.90	22.41	77.79
4	0.89	22.21	100.00

Table 2.8   *Correlation matrix between variables and the first two principal axes*

	Correlations		Correlation squared		Sum of square correlations
	1	2	1^2	2^2	
Naturalistic function	0.57	−0.47	0.32	0.22	0.55
Productive function	0.59	0.18	0.35	0.03	0.39
Protective function	0.59	−0.35	0.35	0.12	0.47
Tourist function	0.48	0.76	0.23	0.58	0.81

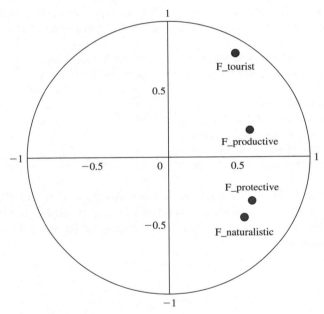

Figure 2.9   *Correlation circle*

AREA 2

Table 2.9   Total explained variance

Components	Initial eigen values		
	Total	% explained variance	Cumulative
1	1.51	37.75	37.75
2	1.10	27.64	65.39
3	0.94	23.62	89.01
4	0.44	10.99	100.00

Table 2.10   Correlation matrix between variables and the first two principal axes

	Correlations		Correlation squared		Sum of square correlations
	1	2	1^2	2^2	
Naturalistic function	0.69	0.58	0.48	0.34	0.82
Productive function	−0.41	−0.13	0.17	0.02	0.19
Protective function	−0.41	0.85	0.17	0.73	0.90
Tourist function	0.83	−0.13	0.70	0.02	0.71

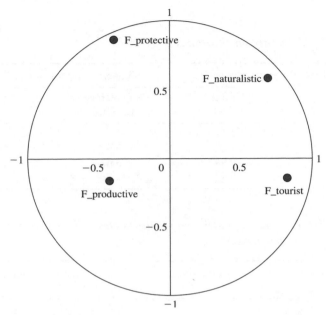

Figure 2.10   Correlation circle

AREA 3

Table 2.11   Total explained variance

Components	Initial eigen values		
	Total	% explained variance	Cumulative
1	1.54	38.43	38.43
2	1.34	33.59	72.01
3	0.76	18.99	91.00
4	0.36	8.99	100.00

Table 2.12   Correlation matrix between variables and the first two principal axes

	Correlations		Correlation squared		Sum of square correlations
	1	2	1^2	2^2	
Naturalistic function	8.42	0.35	0.71	0.12	0.83
Productive function	0.0006	0.75	0.00	0.57	0.57
Protective function	−0.16	0.78	0.03	0.62	0.64
Tourist function	0.90	−0.19	0.80	0.03	0.84

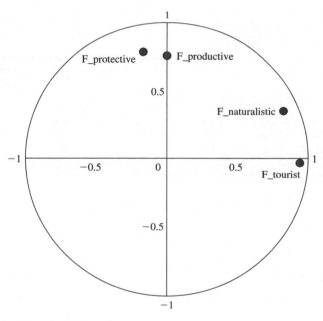

Figure 2.11   Correlation circle

AREA 4

Table 2.13   Total explained variance

Components	Initial eigen values		
	Total	% explained variance	Cumulative
1	1.47	36.84	36.84
2	1.09	27.31	64.15
3	0.93	23.23	87.38
4	0.50	12.62	100.00

Table 2.14   Correlation matrix between variables and the first two principal axes

	Correlations		Correlation squared		Sum of square correlations
	1	2	1^2	2^2	
Naturalistic function	0.84	−0.23	0.71	0.05	0.76
Productive function	0.79	0.13	0.63	0.02	0.64
Protective function	−0.09	0.89	0.01	0.80	0.81
Tourist function	−0.36	−0.47	0.13	0.22	0.35

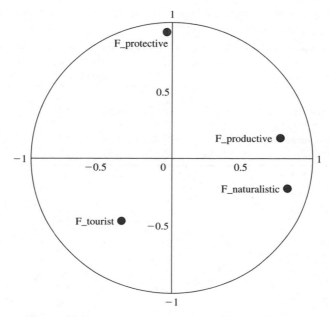

Figure 2.12   Correlation circle

AREA 5

Table 2.15   Total explained variance

Components	Initial eigen values		
	Total	% explained variance	Cumulative
1	1.40	35.10	35.10
2	1.05	26.18	61.28
3	0.80	19.95	81.23
4	0.75	18.77	100.00

*Table 2.16   Correlation matrix between variables and the first two
                principal axes*

	Correlations		Correlation squared		Sum of square correlations
	1	2	1^2	2^2	
Naturalistic function	−0.48	0.67	0.23	0.45	0.67
Productive function	0.66	0.39	0.43	0.15	0.58
Protective function	0.61	−0.42	0.38	0.17	0.55
Tourist function	0.60	0.53	0.37	0.28	0.64

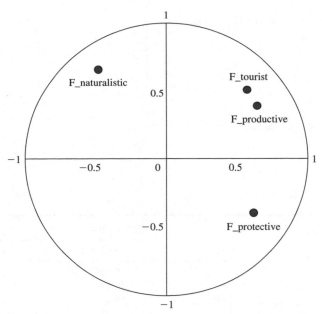

Figure 2.13   Correlation circle

2.5   CONCLUSIONS

This chapter shows the link between the GIS analysis results and the determination of the best environmental policy by the optimal combination of
West Garda Regional Forest functions. Because of the detailed information
derived from the GIS analysis over each hectare of land, GIS results cannot

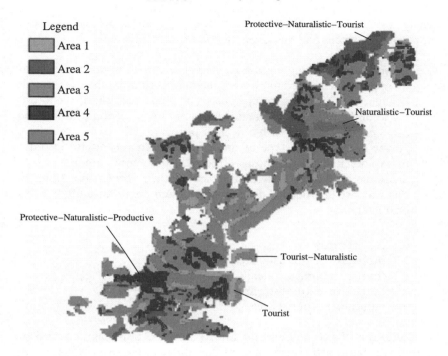

Figure 2.14   Function per macro-area

be immediately applied to the decision making process. Thus it has been necessary to aggregate the information into macro-areas homogeneous by physical and environmental characteristics based on their functions.

Considering the characteristics of GIS data set we used the *mean-k cluster method* due to Forgy (1965) like a method of aggregation. The advantage of this method compared with others is that it uses an iterated technique that identifies stable groups.

Each step of this research has been instrumental in highlighting the main elements that characterize the ability of the West Garda Regional Forest in supplying environmental products and services. From a preliminary analysis, it is evident that this area presents low productive and protective functions, while it is mainly characterized by naturalistic and tourist functions, although the latter depends very much on the level of accessibility to the natural area.

Multivariate analysis has analysed and confirmed these hypotheses. In particular, we studied the relations existing in the environmental system using relevant variables that we obtained from classification criteria and analysis objectives. In particular, multivariate analysis process has been applied in two steps and has given the following results:

1. *Cluster analysis using mean-k method*: The classification method that we applied determined five homogeneous macro-areas that were statistically robust. The first group consists of the 12 per cent of the forest, the second area of 9 per cent, the third one of 6 per cent, the fourth one of 18 per cent and the fifth one of 55 per cent.
2. *Factor analysis*: This type of analysis has been very useful in order to explore data, highlighting objectively differences among macro-areas and classifying them on the basis of their peculiar functions. In this way, we identified a description of each area that underlines its characteristics:

   a. tourist area;
   b. protective–naturalistic area;
   c. tourist–naturalistic area;
   d. protective–naturalistic area;
   e. naturalistic–tourist area.

Notice that the second and the fourth areas are both characterized by protective–naturalistic functions, but they differ in their functional levels. This difference is defined by the environmental characteristics of the territory where the tourist function predominates in some areas and the productive function predominates in others.

The results obtained from this study can be directly used by the policy-maker in the natural area in a way that directly affects the allocation of the natural resources. The macro-areas were not defined *a priori* in a random manner, but they were derived directly from the analysis of the environmental characteristics of the forest. Therefore, they can be used as reference points in the definition of efficient economic, managerial and environmental policies.

NOTES

1. Although several researchers have worked on the development of this method (Thorndike, 1953; Ball and Hall, 1967; MacQueen, 1967; Diday, 1971; Diday et al., 1979), the basic logical process underlying it is mainly recognized to be due to Forgy (1965).
2. For each micro-area, an index representing the function level capacity is estimated using fuzzy logic methodology (Zimmermann, 1987).
3. In order to create an artificial variable measuring an unobservable event, this variable should give a relevant 'informative contribution'. In other words its variability must be at

a maximum. In this way it is guaranteed that the new variable generates the maximum difference between the elements that are the object of study. Given that the most common measure of variability is the variance, we need to identify new variables with maximum variance.

4. If, the variables had not have been standardized, it would have been necessary to diagonalize the variance–covariance matrix.
5. When variables are standardized, their variances are equal to 1. Therefore each eigen value will be compared with the number of variables that are the object of study, which corresponds to the total variance.
6. Since the principal components are not correlated to each other, it is possible to add them together.

REFERENCES

Anderberg, M.R. (1973), *Cluster Analysis for Applications*, New York: Academic Press.
Ball, G.H. and D.J. Hall (1967), 'A clustering technique for summarizing multivariate data', *Behavioral Science*, **12**, 153–5.
Cailliez, F. and J.P. Pagès (1976), *Introduction à l'analyse des données*, Paris: SMASH.
Cormack, R.M. (1971), 'A review of classification', *Journal of Royal Statistics A*, **3**, 134.
Diday, E. (1971), 'La méthode des Nuées Dynamiques', *Revue de Statistique Appliqué*, **19** (2), 19–34.
Diday, E., S. Bochi, G. Brossier and G. Celeux (1979), *Optimisation en Classification Automatique (Tome 1 et 2)*, Rocquemcourt: INRA.
Everitt, B. (1974), *Cluster Analysis*, London: Heinemann.
Forgy, E.W. (1965), 'Cluster analysis of multivariate data. Efficiency versus interpretability of classifications', Biometric Society Meetings, Riverside, California.
Friedman, H.P. and J. Rubin (1967), 'On some invariant criteria for grouping data', *Journal of American Statistical Association*, **62**, 1159–78.
Gordon, A.D. (1981), *Classification*, London: Chapman and Hall.
MacQueen, J.B. (1967), 'Some methods for classification and analysis of multivariate observations', in L.M. Le Cam and J. Neyman (eds), *Proceedings of the Fifth Berkeley Symposium on Mathematical Statistics and Probability*, vol. 1, Berkeley, CA: University of California Press, pp. 281–97.
Nijkamp, P. and P. Rietveldt (1996), 'Multiple objective decision analysis in regional economics', in *Handbook of Regional and Urban Economics*, Amsterdam: North Holland.
Rehman, T. and C. Romero (1993), 'The application of the MCDM paradigm to the management of agricultural systems: some basic considerations', *Agricultural Systems*, **41**, 239–55.
SPSS Base 7.5 per Windows (1997), *User's guidelines Rel. 7.5*, Chicago: SPSS.
Thorndike, R.L. (1953), 'Who belongs in the family', *Psychometrika*, **18**, 267–76.
Zimmermann, H.J. (1987), *Fuzzy Sets, Decision Making and Expert Systems*, Boston, MA: Kluwer Academic Publishers.

3. A contingent valuation method incorporating fairness and citizen participation[*]

Joseph C. Cooper, Federico Perali,
Nicola Tommasi and Marcella Veronesi

3.1 INTRODUCTION

Concepts associated with envy, equity and 'superfairness' have received considerable attention in the last decade, being considered by both political scientists and economists (for example, Baumol, 1987; Renn et al., 1995; Zajac, 1995), although the theory has received little application (Zajac, 1995). An extensive discussion of fairness is to be addressed later, but an example of 'strict fairness' is giving two people a cake, letting one cut it in two, and the other choose which slice he wants. Concepts of economic justice, for example the 'just price', have a long history: for instance the discussions by St. Thomas Aquinas in the thirteenth century (St. Aquinatis, 1897) and earlier (for example Valerius Maximus), although these were later displaced through the efforts of Adam Smith and others (Zajac, 1995).

Generally discussed in the context of the concepts above is citizen participation. Adding fairness to interactions between policymakers and the household level is a way of encouraging citizen participation in policy decisions, as called for by the guidelines for sustainable agriculture and rural development (SARD), for example. People's participation is an essential element of any successful SARD policy. Unfortunately, however, much of what is written about participation, while long on rhetoric, is short on practical guidelines for implementation. In essence, in making a benefit valuation consistent with the guidelines of SARD, we are looking for instruments aimed at establishing a democratic and participatory process designed to involve all interested groups in decision making and implementing SARD. Given that concepts of fairness are relevant to the contingent valuation method (CVM), that CVM can be used to estimate the benefits associated with SARD, and that fairness can be linked with SARD, then it follows that CVM, fairness and SARD may be usefully linked.

While closed ended CVM (CE) is the CVM elicitation format recommended by the NOAA Blue Ribbon Panel (Arrow et al., 1993), forcing such a high level of control over the bid offers does not appear to be in keeping with the spirit of fairness. At first glance, the open-ended CVM (OE) elicitation approach may appear fair. Open-ended questions (as well as iterative bidding formats) have a strong participatory element because while the interviewer fixes the scenario, the respondent is free to choose the bid. However, it is unfair to the interviewer as it allows the respondent to engage in strategic response biases. Furthermore, in cases where the respondent does not intend to engage in strategic responses, just as it may be unfair to give the respondent no say over the bids, it may be unfair to give the respondent complete freedom over the bid; he may be placed in a difficult situation in stating an open-ended value to a good he has much less experience evaluating than does the interviewer. The multiple bounded discrete choice (MBDC) approach is arguably fairer than the open-ended and the closed-ended approaches. MBDC allows ample opportunities for strategic bias in the responses, but otherwise the level of flexibility is a compromise between OE and CE. However many researchers prefer CE approaches for the reasons stated earlier. Our goal is to modify the CE approach to incorporate a greater degree of fairness in Baumol's envy-free sense, while maintaining many of the desirable characteristics of CE. Bateman et al. (2004) observe that 'within stepwise formats the degree of scope sensitivity varies dramatically and significantly depending upon the direction order in which values are elicited' (p. 88).

Specifically, we revise the elicitation approach to let the respondents choose the bid, within bounds, that they want to respond to. What are the benefits in doing so? The answer is that we want to make the willingness to pay (WTP) elicitation process as participatory as possible while minimizing the response biases discussed above. To do this, we modify the one-and-one-half-bound (OOHB) approach (Cooper et al., 2002) to a fair one-and-one-half-bound (FOOHB) approach, instead of modifying the double bound (DB) approach, given that OOHB may have less potential for bias in response to the follow-up bid than DB (ibid). We increase fairness by allowing the respondent to choose whether they want to start the questioning process with the low bid or the high bid. In other words, the respondent is allowed to choose only the starting bid and not the value itself, as this would result in an open-ended question format.

Regarding the relationship between discrete choice (DC) and citizen participation, we note Renn et al.'s (1995) assertion that while referenda (a common payment vehicle for DC CVM) meet their criteria for fairness, by themselves they are not participatory. They suggest that referenda are an excellent way of legitimizing a final decision after it has been subject to review by citizens. The FOOHB approach, by allowing the respondent more participation in the bid offer process, can be considered a simple initial review process.

Pretty (1995) presents a discussion of moving from an 'old professionalism' to a 'new professionalism' in the strategy and context of inquiry, which is relevant to the association between discrete choice and citizen participation. Characteristics of 'old professionalism' include: investigators know what they want; there is a pre-specified research plan or design; information is extracted from controlled experiments; and context is independent and controlled. Characteristics of 'new professionalism' include: investigators do not know where research will lead; it is an open-ended learning process; understanding and focus emerge through interaction; and the context of inquiry is fundamental. To differing degrees, the various CVM elicitation formats fall into 'old professionalism', although to a large extent, the focus group and pre-testing stages that are part of a quality CVM survey embody 'new professionalism'. Of course, we do not move so far as to make the final CVM question completely characteristic of 'new professionalism', but placing the choice of starting bid in the hands of the respondent moves the discrete choice CVM question format more in that direction.

On the statistical side, OOHB is already designed to address response bias to the follow-up bid that sometimes is evident in multiple bound discrete choice surveys. So the difference between OOHB and FOOHB is the fairness concept embedded in the FOOHB. In fact, the two methods have two data generating process that are nested. To estimate the coefficients for the FOOHB model, we use the Welsh–Poe (1998) maximum likelihood specification for multiple bounded discrete choice. Welsh–Poe's specification is the most general (compared with Hanemann, 1994) in that it incorporates the Hanemann model, while at the same time allowing for endogeneity between the response and the bid amount. The FOOHB model lies between the Hanemann and Welsh–Poe model in flexibility.

While we can establish whether or not respondents prefer a more participatory process through survey questions, whether or not the FOOHB model produces more accurate results than the OOHB model requires knowing the true willingness to pay, which is expensive to elicit. However transferring the concepts of fairness to economic applications has proved difficult in practice. We are attempting a first stab at this, and concern ourselves at this point with how fairness can be applied, and not on its accuracy. Pre-testing our surveys in which we ask the respondents whether they prefer to respond to FOOHB or OOHB question formats indicates that they prefer FOOHB. While this choice could be influenced by some perception that FOOHB allows more possibilities for strategic bias than OOHB, the pre-tested group was unlikely to have these motivations. Their comments suggested that they preferred the more participatory aspect of FOOHB over OOHB.

The remainder of the chapter is organized as follows. Section 2 compares survey formats and formally describes the likelihood functions associated with OOHB and FOOHB formats. Section 3 presents an empirical comparison with the West Garda Regional Forest in Italy based on a split sample contingent valuation survey using the FOOHB and OOHB formats and presents the values of the functions supplied by the natural area. Our conclusions are summarized in Section 4.

3.2 COMPARISON OF THE SURVEY FORMATS

In this section we analyse different survey formats, the single bound (SB) format, the double bound (DB) format and the one-and-one-half-bound (OOHB) by Cooper et al. (2002), and we compare them with a new model: the fair-one-and-one-half-bound model (FOOHB). The log-likelihood functions for the survey formats are estimated using maximum likelihood techniques programmed in Gauss.

3.2.1 The Single Bound (SB) Format

In the single bound format, the i-th respondent is asked if she would be willing to pay some given amount b_i^* (the 'bid') to obtain a given improvement in environmental quality. The answer is 'no' if her own WTP is inferior to b_i^*, it is 'yes' in the opposite case (Figures 3.1 and 3.2).

We refer to 'full visibility' of the choice set when 'the respondent

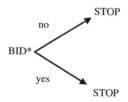

Figure 3.1   Single bound – full visibility – sequential representation

Figure 3.2   Single bound – full visibility – linear representation

perceives [the set of goods] the full extent of purchase options which will be made available in the course of that exercise' (Bateman et al., 2004, p. 75).

The probability of a negative answer is equal to the probability that WTP is inferior to the bid, while the probability of a positive answer probability is that WTP is greater than the bid:

$$\Pr(no) = \Pr(WTP_i < b_i^*) = F(b_i^*; \theta)$$
$$\Pr(yes) = \Pr(WTP_i \geq b_i^*) = 1 - F(b_i^*; \theta)$$

where F is the cumulative distribution function of WTP; and θ represents the parameters of the distribution.

The resulting log-likelihood function for the SB format is:

$$\ln L^{SB}(\theta) = \sum_{i=1}^{n} \{d_i^Y \ln[1 - F(b_i^*; \theta)] + d_i^N \ln F(b_i^*; \theta)\}.$$

where $d_i^j = 1$ if the i-th response is j ('yes' or 'no'), and 0 otherwise.

An individual should be willing to pay some given amount C, if her utility will be greater or equal to the utility before the payment. Thus:

$$U_0(Y; x) \leq U_1(Y - C; x),$$

where U_0 is the utility at time 0 and U_1 at time 1 following the payment of the amount C, Y is the individual income and x is a vector of demographic and attitudinal variables, such as the respondent's age or sex, or whether or not the respondent is an environmentalist; and possibly other variables relating to the willingness to pay. The utility function U is a random variable because it is not observable. We denote the mean of U by V. Then we consider a stochastic error ε_i identically distributed with a mean zero. The previous equation can be written as:

$$V_0(Y; x) + \varepsilon_0 \leq V_1(Y - C; x) + \varepsilon_1.$$

If $V_0(Y; x) = \alpha_0 - \beta Y$, where $\beta < 0$ and $V_1(Y - C; x) = \alpha_1 - \beta(Y - C)$, this expression can be written as:

$$\alpha_0 - \beta Y + \varepsilon_0 \leq \alpha_1 - \beta(Y - C) + \varepsilon_1$$

and in probabilistic notation:

$$\Pr(WTP \geq C) = \Pr(V_0 + \varepsilon_0 \leq V_1 + \varepsilon_1) = \Pr(\varepsilon_1 - \varepsilon_0 \geq V_0 - V_1)$$
$$= \Pr(\varepsilon_1 - \varepsilon_0 \geq -\alpha - \beta C)$$

where $\alpha = \alpha_1 - \alpha_0$.

Applying a logistic probability function to the utility model we obtain:

$$\Pr(WTP \geq C) = F_\varepsilon(\Delta V) = 1 - [1 + \exp(-(\alpha + \beta C))]^{-1}$$

where $F_\varepsilon(.)$ is the cumulative distribution funtion of $\varepsilon = \varepsilon_1 - \varepsilon_0$ and ΔV is the difference between the two utility functions V_0 and V_1. If we disarrange α in the sum of its components, in the case of a multiple regression with q explicative variables we obtain:

$$E(WTP|x_i) = \frac{\alpha_1 x_{i,1} + \alpha_2 x_{i,2} + \ldots + \alpha_q x_{i,q}}{-\beta}.$$

3.2.2 The Double Bound (DB) Format

The objective of the econometric model is to infer the maximum willingness to pay (WTP) starting from a given price and a series of dichotomous answers that we define as 'yes' and 'no'. We choose the starting values that minimize the average quadratic standard error of the willingness to pay using Cooper's procedure (1993).

The DB format starts with an initial bid b^*. If the respondent answers 'yes', she receives a follow-up bid $b_i^U > b_i^*$; if she answers 'no', she receives a follow-up bid $b_i^L < b_i^*$ (Figure 3.3). The possible outcomes are four: (yes, yes), (yes, no), (no, yes) and (no, no) (Figure 3.4).

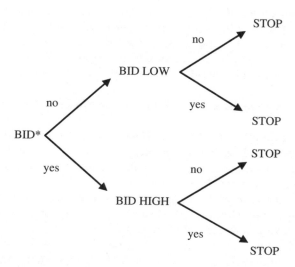

Figure 3.3   Double bound – sequential representation

Figure 3.4   Double bound – linear representation

The corresponding response probabilities are:

$$\Pr(yes, yes) = \Pr(WTP_i \geq b_i^U) = 1 - F(b_i^U; \theta);$$

$$\Pr(yes, no) = \Pr(b_i^* \leq WTP_i \leq b_i^U) = F(b_i^U; \theta) - F(b_i^*; \theta);$$

$$\Pr(no, yes) = \Pr(b_i^L \leq WTP_i \leq b_i^*) = F(b_i^*; \theta) - F(b_i^L; \theta);$$

$$\Pr(no, no) = \Pr(WTP_i \leq b_i^L) = F(b_i^L; \theta).$$

The double bound log likelihood (Hanemann et al., 1991) is:

$$\ln L^{DB}(\theta) = \sum_{i=1}^{n} \{ d_i^{YY} \ln[1 - F(b_i^U; \theta)] + d_i^{YN} \ln[F(b_i^U; \theta) - F(b_i^0; \theta)]$$
$$+ d_i^{NY} \ln[F(b_i^0; \theta) - F(b_i^L; \theta)] + d_i^{NN} \ln F(b_i^L; \theta) \},$$

where F is the cumulative distribution function of respondent WTP; b_i^* is the initial bid; b_i^U is the upper bid; b_i^L is the lower bid; θ represents the parameters of the distribution, which are to be estimated on the basis of the responses to the contingent valuation survey; $d_i^{YY} = 1$ if the i-th response is (yes, yes) and 0 otherwise; $d_i^{YN} = 1$ if the i-th response is (yes, no) and 0 otherwise; $d_i^{NY} = 1$ if the i-th response is (no, yes) and 0 otherwise; $d_i^{NN} = 1$ if the i-th response is (no, no) and 0 otherwise. Let $\hat{\theta}^{DB}$ the resulting maximum likelihood estimator (MLE), the associated information matrix, $I^{DB}(\hat{\theta}^{DB})$, is equal to minus the expectation of the Hessian of the maximized log-likelihood function.

3.2.3   The Multiple Bounded Discrete Choice Model (MBDC)

The multiple bounded model is the generalization of the double bounded model (Welsh and Poe, 1998). The respondent is asked to vote on a range of referendum thresholds and to indicate how she would vote if passage of the referendum cost her that amount.

Consider the case where the individual can respond 'yes' or 'no' to a wide variety of bids (Figure 3.5). We define b_i^U as the maximum bid amount that the individual would vote for, and b_i^L as the minimum bid amount that the individual would vote for. Her willingness to pay lies in the interval $[b_i^U, b_i^L]$. When the respondent says 'no' to every bid amount then $b_i^L = -\infty$ and when she says 'yes' to every bid amount then $b_i^U = \infty$.

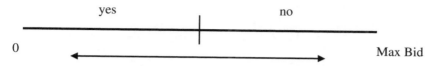

*Figure 3.5   MBDC – full visibility but sensitive to scope– linear
representation*

The corresponding log-likelihood function is:

$$\ln L^{MBDC}(\theta) = \sum_{i=1}^{n} \{\ln[F(b_i^U; \theta) - F(b_i^L; \theta)]\}$$

where F is the cumulative distribution function of respondent WTP with
parameter vector θ. $F(b_i, \theta)$ and $[1 - F(b_i, \theta)]$ respectively denote the probability that an individual votes 'no' and 'yes' to a specific bid amount b_i. The
probability WTP for individual i-th lies between any two bid thresholds and
it is equal to $[F(b_i^U; \theta) - F(b_i^L; \theta)]$.

As pointed out by Welsh and Bishop (1993), this most likely representation of the data generating process nests discrete choice models in general.
This is also true for the following survey formats: the one-and-one-half-
bound and the fair-one-and-one-half-bound models.

3.2.4   The One-and-One-Half-Bound Model (OOHB)

In the OOHB format the i-th respondent is given two prices up front and
told that, while the exact cost of the item is uncertain, it is known to lie
within the range bounded by these two prices, a lower bound and an upper
bound. A random process determines if the respondent has to start from
the upper bound or the lower one. In this case the choice set is 'partially
visible' because the respondent does not know the starting bid but only the
possible price range.

Another distinguishing feature is that the follow-up question is only
asked when the 'yes' response is given to the lower bound or when the 'no'
response is given to the upper bound. No follow-up question is asked when
in response to the initial question an upper amount is accepted or a lower
amount rejected (Figure 3.6).

Since the respondent is told about the possible range of costs at the
beginning of the survey, she is less likely to form false cost expectations,
enter into bargaining mindset, or experience loss-aversion when respond-
ing to the follow-up bid. The analytic analysis suggests that the loss of statistical efficiency from using OOHB instead of double bound model may
be small or negligible (Cooper et al., 2002).

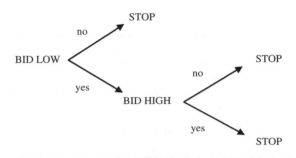

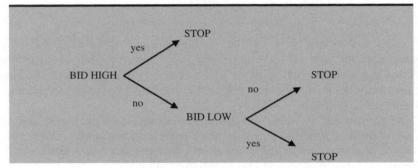

*Figure 3.6   OOHB – conditional sequential disclosure – partial visibility –
sequential representation*

Define a range of bid values as $[b_i^L, b_i^U]$ where $b_i^L < b_i^U$. If the lower price, b_i^L, is randomly drawn as the starting bid, the three possible response outcomes are (no), (yes, no) and (yes, yes) (Figure 3.7); if the higher price, b_i^U, is randomly drawn as the starting bid, the possible response outcomes are (yes), (no, yes) and (no, no) (Figure 3.7).

The corresponding response probabilities are:

$$\Pr(no) = \Pr(no,no) = \Pr(WTP_i \leq b_i^L) = F(b_i^L; \theta);$$

$$\Pr(yes,no) = \Pr(no,yes) = \Pr(b_i^L \leq WTP_i \leq b_i^U) = F(b_i^U; \theta) - F(b_i^L; \theta);$$

$$\Pr(yes,yes) = \Pr(yes) = \Pr(WTP_i \geq b_i^U) = 1 - F(b_i^U; \theta).$$

The corresponding log-likelihood function is

$$\ln L^{OOHB}(\theta) = \sum_{i=1}^{n} \{d_i^Y \ln[1 - F(b_i^U; \theta)] + d_i^{YN} \ln[F(b_i^U; \theta) - F(b_i^L; \theta)] + d_i^N \ln[F(b_i^L; \theta)]\},$$

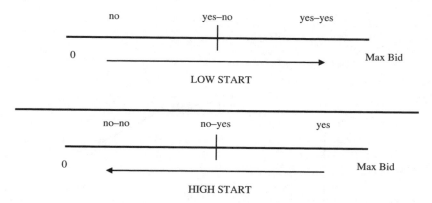

Figure 3.7   OOHB – conditional sequential disclosure – partial visibility – linear representation

where F^v is the cumulative distribution function of respondent's answer $v = \{$no, yes–no, yes–yes, yes, no–yes, no–no$\}$; d^v is a dummy variable equal to 1 for v and 0 otherwise; θ represents the parameters of the distribution, which are to be estimated on the basis of the responses to the CV survey; $d_i^N = 1$ if either the starting bid is b_i^L and the response is (no) or the starting bid is b_i^U and the response is (no, no) and 0 otherwise; $d_i^{YN} = 1$ if either the starting bid is b_i^L and the response is (yes, no) or the starting bid is b_i^U and the response is (no, yes) and 0 otherwise; and $d_i^{YY} = 1$ if either the starting bid is b_i^L and the response is (yes, yes) or the starting bid is b_i^U and the response is (yes) and 0 otherwise.

3.2.5   A Contingent Valuation Method incorporating Fairness: The Fair One-and-One-Half-Bound Model (FOOHB)

Open-ended questions (as well as iterative bidding formats) have a strong participatory element because while the interviewer fixes the scenario, the respondent is free to choose the bid. Discrete formats reduce the respondents' flexibility. To some extent, this reduction is positive from the interviewer's standpoint – respondents may have a difficult time giving an open-ended value for an unusual good, they may engage in strategic bias and generally, are used to buying products with take-it-or-leave-it pricing. By allowing the respondent to choose the starting point for the bidding process, FOOHB introduces fairness into discrete choice CVM question format. However since the interviewer still controls the bounds on the starting bids, the interaction between the two parties is not completely flexible.

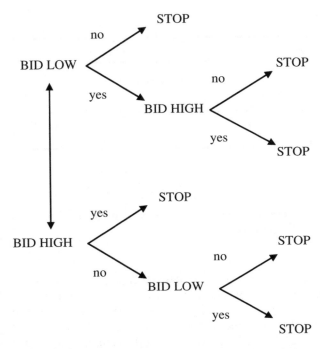

*Figure 3.8   FOOHB – unconditional (fair) sequential disclosure – full
visibility of a small choice set – sequential representation*

The relationship between answers and WTP is the same in the two
models as Figures 3.7 and 3.9 show. The difference consists in the fact
that the interviewer does not select at random one of the two prices and
then she asks the respondent if she would be willing to pay the price
selected. In the FOOHB model the respondent chooses the starting price.
The process consists of two phases: in the first phase, the respondent
chooses whether to start from the upper price or the lower one; in the
second phase, she chooses the value that she should be willing to pay
(Figure 3.8).

To estimate the coefficients for the FOOHB model, we use the Welsh–Poe
(1998) maximum likelihood specification for the multiple bounded discrete
choice model (MBDC). This specification is the most general (compared
with Hanemann, 1994) in that it incorporate the Hanemann model, while
at the same time allowing for endogeneity between the response and the bid
amount. The FOOHB model lies between the Hanemann (1994) and
Welsh–Poe (1998) model in flexibility (Figures 3.8–3.9).

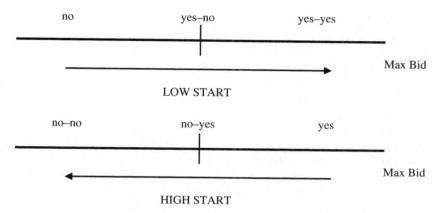

Figure 3.9   *FOOHB unconditional (fair) sequential disclosure – full visibility of a small choice set – linear representation*

The log-likelihood function using the FOOHB format is:

$$\ln L^{FOOHB}(\theta) =$$

$$\sum_{i=1}^{n} \left\{ \begin{array}{l} g_i^L \ln G^L \{ d_i^{YY} \ln[1 - F(b_i^U;\theta)] + d_i^{YN} \ln[F(b_i^U;\theta) - F(b_i^L;\theta)] + d_i^N \ln[F(b_i^L;\theta)] \} + \\ g_i^U \ln G^U \{ d_i^Y \ln[1 - F(b_i^U;\theta)] + d_i^{NY} \ln[F(b_i^U;\theta) - F(b_i^L;\theta)] + d_i^{NN} \ln[F(b_i^L;\theta)] \} \end{array} \right\}$$

where F, d_i and θ are defined as in the OOHB model; g_i^L is a dummy variable equal to 1 if the respondent starts from the lower bound (b_i^L), equal to 0 otherwise; and g_i^U is a dummy variable equal to 1 if the respondent starts from the upper bound (b_i^U) and equal to 0 otherwise; G^L and G^U respectively denote the probability that the respondent starts from the upper and lower bound.

Any bounded model, independently of the number of bounds, can be converted in a discrete choice model with no loss of relevant information given a suitable adjustment of the data (Welsh and Bishop, 1993). In the case of the FOOHB format the log-likelihood function becomes:

$$\ln L^{FOOHB}(\theta) = \sum_{i=1}^{n} \{ \ln[F(b_i^U;\theta) - F(b_i^L;\theta)] \}.$$

3.3   A FIELD TEST OF THE FOOHB AND OOHB FORMATS

We present the results of the contingent valuation survey conducted in Italy to value the West Garda Regional Forest. The survey was conducted by the

University of Verona in June–October 1997 and it took the form of on-site[1] interviews of adult visitors (mean age of 39 years). Access to the forest is currently free; in the contingent valuation survey, respondents were asked whether they would be willing to pay for an entrance ticket in order to improve the quality of the management and preservation of the area, and an annual subscription fee, which finances projects to improve the quality and quantity of recreational activities. The survey was prepared following the guidelines by the NOAA[2] Blue Ribbon Panel. In order not to incur bias, in the introduction of the survey it was emphasized that the objective was to improve the area and that the prices were hypothetical. To guarantee the consistency of the contingent valuation, before asking about the willingness to pay for a ticket the visitor was asked to give an opinion about the area as to whether it is crowded and if the number of visitors should be regulated.

In order to compare the results of the two models the sample was split between the OOHB (25 per cent of the sample) and FOOHB (75 per cent of the sample) elicitation formats, with random assignment between formats. In the OOHB version, respondents were first told that the price of admission to the forest will be somewhere in the range of b^L to b^U euros: they did not know the precise amount asked. One of the prices was selected at random by the interviewer and the respondent was asked 'If the price of this admission were [selected price], would you willing to pay for it?', with a follow-up question using the other price where this was logical. Fifty per cent of the OOHB sample started from the lower bound of the range and 50 per cent started from the upper bound. Examples of OOHB questions are the following (Box 3.1 and Box 3.2):

'Suppose the bureau of land management asks you to pay for a ticket to visit the area to improve the quality of the management and preservation of the area. Given these conditions, are you willing to pay for a ticket that may vary within a range of 2.07 euros and 4.13 euros keeping in mind that the *exact price is uncertain?*'

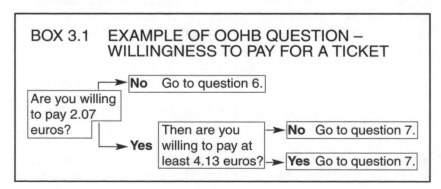

BOX 3.1   EXAMPLE OF OOHB QUESTION –
WILLINGNESS TO PAY FOR A TICKET

Are you willing to pay 2.07 euros?
→ No   Go to question 6.
→ Yes Then are you willing to pay at least 4.13 euros?
→ No   Go to question 7.
→ Yes Go to question 7.

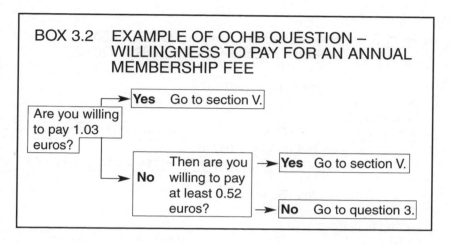

BOX 3.2   EXAMPLE OF OOHB QUESTION –
WILLINGNESS TO PAY FOR AN ANNUAL
MEMBERSHIP FEE

Are you willing to pay 1.03 euros?
→ Yes   Go to section V.
→ No   Then are you willing to pay at least 0.52 euros?
→ Yes   Go to section V.
→ No   Go to question 3.

'Suppose now that to gain access to the natural area you are asked to be part of an association called "Friends of the Mountains", which finances projects to improve recreational activities according to the preferences that you revealed in question no. 1. Let us hypothesize that the annual membership fee for each recreational activity may vary within a range of 0.52 euros to 1.03 euros. Are you willing to pay it?'

The FOOHB version was submitted to the remaining 75 per cent of the sample to improve respondent's participation to the survey and to inhabit strategic behaviour in the answers about their willingness to pay. Respondents were asked to choose if they would like to start from the lower bound or from the upper bound of the range of b^L to b^U euros. Respondents chose the starting price, not the interviewer, in order to make the survey fairer. For example it was asked (Box 3.3 and Box 3.4):

'Suppose the bureau of land management asks you to pay for a ticket to visit the area to improve the quality of the management and preservation of the area. Given these conditions, are you willing to pay for a ticket that may vary within a range of 2.07 euros (*point A*) and 4.13 euros (*point B*) keeping in mind that the exact price is uncertain?

'*Please, choose to start from point A or B as you prefer*, and answer questions following the directions. Note that your choice of the starting point does not affect the final results of the survey.'

'Suppose now that to gain access to the natural area you are asked to be part of an association called "Friends of the Mountains" which finances projects aiming at improving recreational activities according to the preferences that you revealed in question no. 1. Let us hypothesize that the annual membership fee for each recreational activity may vary within a

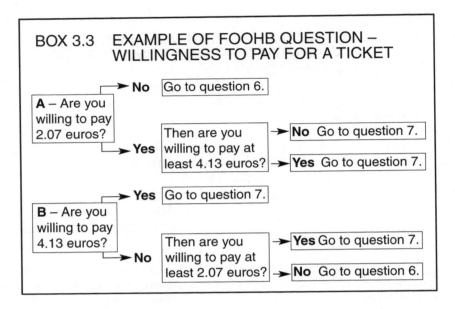

BOX 3.3   EXAMPLE OF FOOHB QUESTION –
           WILLINGNESS TO PAY FOR A TICKET

range of 0.52 euros (*point A*) and 1.03 euros (*point B*). Would you be willing to pay it?'

'*Please, choose to start from point A or B as you prefer*, and answer questions following the directions. Note that your choice of the starting point does not affect the final results of the survey.'

Different prices were randomly assigned across subjects in both models. These prices were derived on the basis of a pretest made in the area, using the bid design approach in Cooper (1993). Different ranges were divided equally in the sample (Table 3.1). Ticket prices ranged from a minimum of 1.55 to a maximum of 8.26 euros, while membership fees ranged from 0.77 to 3.62 euros. Table 3.2 shows the answers for both models. Table 3.2 shows that in the most cases of FOOHB format the respondents chose to start from the lower bid for both ticket and fee. This happens when the ticket cost more than the fee. So the OOHB format does not fairly represent the respondents' behaviour because it starts 50 per cent of the sample from the lower bound and 50 per cent from the upper bound, but most of the respondents would like to start from the lower one.

The survey also includes some questions about the reason for a negative answer to the willingness-to-pay question, in order to verify whether the FOOHB format increases the respondent's participation and, if so, whether it reduces the probability of strategic behaviour in the answers. When the reason for refusal was, 'It is a service that the state should offer to citizens

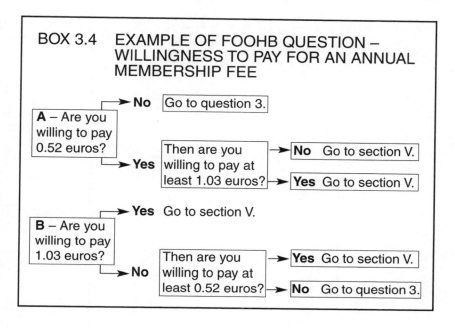

BOX 3.4 EXAMPLE OF FOOHB QUESTION –
WILLINGNESS TO PAY FOR AN ANNUAL
MEMBERSHIP FEE

A – Are you willing to pay 0.52 euros?
→ **No** Go to question 3.
→ **Yes** Then are you willing to pay at least 1.03 euros? → **No** Go to section V.
→ **Yes** Go to section V.

B – Are you willing to pay 1.03 euros?
→ **Yes** Go to section V.
→ **No** Then are you willing to pay at least 0.52 euros? → **Yes** Go to section V.
→ **No** Go to question 3.

Table 3.1 Price ranges (euros)

	Ticket			Fee	
Min.	Max.	%	Min.	Max.	%
1.55	3.10	20.22	0.77	1.55	20.22
2.07	4.13	23.27	1.03	2.07	23.27
3.10	6.20	18.84	1.29	2.58	18.84
3.62	7.23	18.28	1.55	3.10	18.28
4.13	8.26	19.39	1.81	3.62	19.39

and the cost must be paid by the state,' or 'It is my right to enjoy the area, you cannot ask me to pay,' then we did not consider the surveys to estimate WTP. The percentage of negative answers is greater when the question is about the WTP for a ticket than a fee because the lower bound for the ticket is higher than the one for the fee.

Note in particular that the percentage of rejections is lower in the FOOHB model than in the OOHB one. Table 3.2 shows that considering the WTP for the ticket, 26 per cent of FOOHB surveys were rejected versus 29 per cent of OOHB surveys. When we consider the WTP applied to the

Table 3.2   Frequency of willingness to pay using FOOHB and OOHB

Answers	Ticket				Fee			
	FOOHB		OOHB		FOOHB		OOHB	
	Frequency	%	Frequency	%	Frequency	%	Frequency	%
no	88	31.65	11	13.25	91	32.73	9	10.84
yes–no	99	35.61	16	19.28	62	22.30	16	19.28
yes–yes	42	15.11	12	14.46	55	19.78	14	16.87
Subtotal 1	229	82.37	39	46.99	208	74.82	39	46.99
yes	44	15.83	12	14.46	69	24.82	21	25.30
no–yes	3	1.08	15	18.07	1	0.36	5	6.02
no–no	2	0.72	17	20.48	0	0.00	18	21.69
Subtotal 2	49	17.63	44	53.01	70	25.18	44	53.01
Total	278	100.00	83	100.00	278	100.00	83	100.00
Rejected surveys	73	26.26	24	28.92	13	4.68	3	3.61

Table 3.3   Willingness to pay for a ticket using FOOHB and OOHB models (in euros)

	FOOHB	OOHB
Krinsky and Robb's confidence interval		
99% C.I.	$3.18 < WTP < 4.92$	$4.95 < WTP < 6.19$
95% C.I.	$3.86 < WTP < 4.77$	$4.22 < WTP < 5.95$
90% C.I.	$3.92 < WTP < 4.68$	$4.32 < WTP < 5.69$
Krinsky and Robb's mean	4.30	4.96
Krinsky and Robb's median	4.30	4.91

Source: Krinsky and Robb (1986).

Table 3.4   Willingness to pay a fee from FOOHB and OOHB models (in euros)

	FOOHB	OOHB
Krinsky and Robb's confidence interval		
99% C.I.	$2.14 < WTP < 3.15$	$2.15 < WTP < 3.85$
95% C.I.	$2.28 < WTP < 3.01$	$2.25 < WTP < 3.47$
90% C.I.	$2.35 < WTP < 2.94$	$2.30 < WTP < 3.27$
Krinsky and Robb's mean	2.62	2.73
Krinsky and Robb's median	2.61	2.68

Source: Krinsky and Robb (1986).

fee, we have the same rate of rejection in both models but in this case the fees are lower than the ticket prices.

In Tables 3.3 and 3.4 we compare the estimated WTP for both a ticket and a fee, applying the OOHB and FOOHB formats. These tables present the Krinsky and Robb confidence interval, mean and median (Krinsky and Robb, 1986). The variables used in the OOHB–FOOHB model are described in Tables 3.5 and 3.6 and the estimated coefficients in Tables 3.7 and 3.8. Note that the willingness to pay for a ticket is greater when applying the OOHB model (4.90 euros) than the FOOHB one (4.30 euros). But we have to consider that the subsets for the two models are different. If we consider the wiliness to pay a fee, the results are almost the same: OOHB–WTP is 2.69 euros, FOOHB–WTP is 2.61 euros.

Finally, before asking about the willingness to pay the fee to improve the recreational activities of the area, the visitor is asked how she allocates

Table 3.5   Descriptive statistics of variables using FOOHB and OOHB
models for ticket (in euros)

Variables	Mean	St. Dev.	Min.	Max.
*risp*1	1.142	1.128	0.516	3.099
*min*1	2.809	1.862	1.549	4.132
*max*1	5.618	3.724	3.099	8.263
*aff*1	4.608	1.728	1	10
ln_*clsr*	9.890	0.516	9.068	11.034
ln_*sp*2	7.482	0.640	5.225	9.127
istrz	12.651	4.062	5	21
eta	39.355	14.321	14	85
sex	1.442	0.498	1	2
ln_*valtxi*	1.036	1.897	0	6.142

Notes:
*risp*1	Answer to the question about WTP for an entrance ticket.
*min*1	Lower bound.
*max*1	Upper bound.
*aff*1	Crowding level of the area.
ln_*clsr*	Log annual income interval.
ln_*sp*2	Log annual leisure expenditure.
istrz	Education.
eta	Age.
sex	Sex.
ln_*valtxi*	Log WTP a fee to preserve the natural area.

her time during the visit between the functions offered by the forest. As Table 3.9 shows, from this question we derive that about 77 per cent of the visitors prefer spending their time on tourist activities (mountain biking, horse riding, hiking, picnicking, visiting historic places), about 20 per cent into naturalistic activities, such as harvesting flowers, mushrooms and going sightseeing, and the remaining percentage on hunting and fishing. We find the WTP for each function by summing the WTP for the ticket and the daily association fee, and multiplying this total WTP by the percentage of visitor's preference in time allocation. We found that the price for the tourist function is 3.37 euros and for the naturalistic function is 0.85 euros. We found the price for the protective function considering the answer to the specific question: 'How much are you willing to pay in order to preserve the area for the future generations if you have to pay a tax?'. The average visitor is willing to pay 21.10 euros per year in order to preserve the West Garda Regional Forest.

Table 3.6   Descriptive statistics of variables using FOOHB and OOHB models for fee (in euros)

Variables	Mean	St. Dev.	Min.	Max.
risp2	1.228	1.189	0.5165	2.582
min2	1.263	0.708	0.7747	1.808
max2	2.527	1.415	1.5494	3.615
qtai	7.300	1.258	4	10
ln_clsr	9.890	0.517	9.0684	11.034
ln_sp2	7.482	0.640	5.2253	9.127
istrz	12.651	4.062	5	21
eta	39.355	14.321	14	85
sex	1.442	0.497	1	2
ln_valtxi	1.036	1.897	0	6.142

Notes:
risp2   Answer to the question about WTP a fee.
min2   Lower bound.
max2   Upper bound.
qtai   Quality of the area.
ln_clsr   Log annual income interval.
ln_sp2   Log annual leisure expenditure.
istrz   Education.
eta   Age.
sex   Sex.
ln_valtxi Log WTP a fee to preserve the natural area.

3.4   CONCLUSIONS

This chapter introduces the fair one-and-one-half-bound model (FOOHB) as an alternative to the one-and-one-half-bound model (OOHB). By allowing the respondent to choose the starting point for the bidding process, FOOHB introduces fairness into the discrete choice CVM question format and it should decrease the potential for the respondent to consider the interview to be largely a top-down process that minimizes the input of the respondent to making simply a 'yes' or 'no' response. Adding fairness to interactions between policymakers and the household level is a way of encouraging citizen participation in policy decisions. We increase fairness by allowing the respondent to choose whether they want to start the questioning process with the low bid or the high bid. In other words, the respondent is allowed to choose only the starting bid and not the value itself.

Our real world data set suggested that respondents preferred the more participatory aspect of FOOHB over OOHB. The percentage of negative

Table 3.7   Coefficients of willingness to pay for a ticket using FOOHB and OOHB models

Variables	FOOHB		OOHB	
	Coeff.	St. Dev.	Coeff.	St. Dev.
constant	0.589	1.423	0.452	0.796
*risp*1	−0.048	0.018	−0.074	0.035
*aff*1	0.105	0.374	0.205	0.110
ln_*clsr*	0.057	0.055	0.153	0.124
ln_*sp*2	0.468	0.544	0.219	0.125
istrz	−0.150	0.191	0.133	0.134
eta	−0.011	0.066	−0.073	0.112
sex	0.066	0.182	−0.124	0.137
ln_*valtxi*	−1.523	0.172	0.149	0.115
mills	1.104	2.079	–	–
rho	−0.878	0.098	−0.861	0.153

Note: 361 observations; mills = inverse Mills ratio; rho = correlation coefficient; all other variables are described in Tables 3.5 and 3.6.

Table 3.8   Coefficients of willingness to pay a fee using FOOHB and OOHB models

Variables	FOOHB		OOHB	
	Coeff.	St. Dev.	Coeff.	St. Dev.
constant	−0.034	0.559	1.621	0.804
*risp*2	0.095	0.037	−0.259	0.081
qtai	0.021	0.051	0.184	0.159
ln_*clsr*	−0.094	0.145	0.664	0.258
ln_*sp*2	−0.068	0.301	0.189	0.172
istrz	−0.035	0.149	−0.667	0.173
eta	−0.053	0.054	−0.030	0.149
sex	0.108	0.247	0.024	0.015
ln_*valtxi*	−0.234	0.700	0.240	0.159
mills	2.102	2.254	–	–
rho	−0.850	0.155	0.632	0.318

Note: 361 observations; mills = inverse Mills ratio; rho = correlation coefficient; all other variables are described in Tables 3.5 and 3.6.

Table 3.9 *Willingness to pay and preferences (%) for West Garda Regional Forest's functions*

WTP for a visit of one day in euros (a)	4.366
% Preference for tourist function (b)	77.310
% Preference for naturalistic function (c)	19.240
% Preference for hunting/fishing (d)	3.450
WTP for tourist function in euros (e = a·b)	3.370
WTP for naturalistic function in euros (f = a·c)	0.850
WTP for hunting/fishing in euros (g = a·d)	0.151
WTP for protective function in euros	21.100

answers to the WTP is lower from the FOOHB model than the OOHB one. In most of the cases with the FOOHB format, respondents chose to start from the lower bid for both the ticket and the fee. While the OOHB model starts 50 per cent of the sample from the lower bound and 50 per cent from the upper bound, the respondent would like, in most cases, to start from the lower one. So the difference between OOHB and FOOHB is the fairness concept embedded in the FOOHB format.

NOTES

* The views presented here are those of the authors and do not necessarily represent the views or policies of the Economic Research Service or the United States Department of Agriculture.
1. Visitors were interviewed in the following places: Passo Spino (27.98 per cent of the respondents), Valvestino (17.17 per cent), Tignale (30 per cent), Tremosine (12.47 per cent), Tremalzo (4.16 per cent) and others ones (8 per cent). There were 400 respondents but after skimming the actual sample consists of 361 observations.
2. Here we give only a partial list of guidelines by the NOAA (National Oceanic and Atmospheric Administration) Blue Ribbon Panel (for a complete discussion about the NOAA guidelines see Arrow et al., 1993):

   (a) face to face interviews with pre-test for interviewer effects in order to minimize non-response rates;
   (b) conservative design, when aspects of the survey design and analysis of the responses are ambiguous;
   (c) elicit willingness to pay rather than willingness to accept;
   (d) dichotomous choice referendum format;
   (e) incorporate follow-up questions investigating the specific reasons why the respondent answered 'yes' or 'no' to the payment questions;
   (f) remind the respondent of substitute commodities;
   (g) remind the respondent of budget constraint.

REFERENCES

Arrow, K., R. Solow, R. Radner and H. Schuman (1993), 'Report of the NOAA panel on contingent valuation', *Federal Register*, **58** (10), 4601–15.

Bateman, I.J., M. Cole, P. Cooper, S. Georgiou, D. Hadley and G.L. Poe (2004), 'On visible choice sets and scope sensitivity', *Journal of Environmental Economics and Management*, **47** (1), 71–93.

Baumol, W. (1987), 'Superfairness and applied microtheory', *Atlantic Economic Journal*, **15** (1), 1–9.

Cooper, J. (1993), 'Optimal bid selection for dichotomous choice contingent valuation surveys', *Journal of Environmental Economics and Management*, **24**, 25–40.

Cooper, J., M. Hanemann and G. Signorello (2002), 'One and one-half bound dichotomous choice contingent valuation', *The Review of Economics and Statistics*, **84** (4), 742–50.

Hanemann, M. (1994), 'Valuing the environment through contingent valuation', *Journal of Economic Perspectives*, **8** (4), 1–64.

Hanemann, M., J. Loomis and B. Kanninen (1991), 'Statistical efficiency of double-bounded dichotomous choice contingent valuation', *American Journal of Agricultural Economics*, **73** (4), 1255–63.

Krinsky, I. and A. Robb (1986), 'Approximating the statistical properties of elasticities', *Review of Economics and Statistics*, **68**, 715–19.

Pretty, J.N. (1995), *Regenerating Agriculture*, London: Earthscan.

Renn, O., T. Webler and P. Wiedmann (eds) (1995), *Fairness and Competence in Citizen Participation: Evaluating Models for Environmental Discourse*, Dordrecht: Kluwer Academic Publishers.

St Aquinatis, T. (1897), 'A Secunda Secundae Summae Theologiae', *A Quaestione LVIII ad Quaestionem CXXII*, (Tomus Nonus), Leonis XIII, P.M. (ed.), Rome, Italy: Ex Typographia Polyglotta.

Welsh, M.P. and R.C. Bishop (1993), 'Multiple discrete choice models', in *Benefits and Costs Transfer in Natural Resource Planning*, J. Bergstrom (ed.), Western Regional Research Publication, W-133, Sixth Interim Report, Department of Agricultural and Applied Economics, University of Georgia, pp. 331–52.

Welsh, M.P. and G.L. Poe (1998), 'Elicitation effects in contingent valuation: comparisons to a multiple bounded discrete choice approach', *Journal of Environmental Economics and Management*, **36**, 170–85.

Zajac, E. (1995), *Political Economy of Fairness*, USA: MIT Press.

4. Travel cost estimation conditional on leisure consumption[*]

Joseph C. Cooper, Federico Perali,
Nicola Tommasi and Marcella Veronesi

4.1 INTRODUCTION

This chapter applies the travel cost method (TCM) in order to estimate the recreational demand of a visitor to the West Garda Regional Forest in Italy conditional on her leisure consumption. We consider the number of trips to the natural area as an approximation of the consumed quantity of the environmental good, while the expenditure on the visit as an approximation of the price for the good. No previous studies have applied travel cost method to the West Garda Regional Forest.

We explore two issues in empirical demand analysis: the estimation of a single demand equation, and the estimation of a complete demand system with the incorporation of demographic characteristics. We propose 'translating' as a general method for incorporating demographic variables into complete systems of demand equations (Pollak and Wales, 1978). The estimation of only single demand equations may give us a wrong picture because interactions between demands for commodities are ignored. In addition, some of the properties, or restrictions of a well-behaved utility function, as imposed by economic theory can not be tested if they appear as cross-equation restrictions (such as Slutsky symmetry or adding-up restrictions).

In this case we have to consider that the individual can visit different natural areas in one year. Bockstael et al. (1987) present the problem of choice in two steps: the first one is of macro-allocation and it consists of choosing the number of trips in one year; the second step is of micro-allocation since the choice is about where to go in one specific trip. Provencher and Bishop (1997) apply a dynamic model in which the individual chooses every day if and where to make a trip.

Complete demand systems have two principal advantages over existing valuation models in the literature. First, by incorporating the budget constraint into the analysis, the complete system approach forces recognition of the fact that an increase in expenditure on one consumption category must be balanced by decreases in the expenditure on others. Second, the complete system approach permits the separation of demographic effects from own and cross-price effects as well as income effects. Unless such a separation is made, there is no presumption that demographic effects estimated from one price situation will be relevant in another.

In the first stage of our complete demand system the individual decides, given her income, how much to allocate to food, leisure and other goods. In the second stage the leisure consumption is allocated between trips to the West Garda Regional Forest, trips to other natural areas and expenditure on other leisure activities.

If we focus on the visitor's expenditure, we can identify at least three variables significantly affecting patterns of spending: income, prices and the socio-demographic characteristics of the visitor. A demand system which incorporates demographic variables helps to examine these effects at the same time. This chapter attempts to contribute towards that by using a complete demand system within the framework of the almost ideal demand system (AIDS) of Deaton and Muellbauer (1980) modified according to translating demographic transformation. The difficulty in estimating the recreational demand functions for this second stage is that many visitors are observed to have zero demand for trips for sites different from West Garda Regional Forest. The demand equations for the second stage are estimated taking into account this problem of censoring. Ordinary least square estimates become biased because of the censoring. In order to transform the data into a form that mitigates the problem of censoring, we will use the generalized Heckman procedure (Arias et al., 2003).

We also explore the behavioural implications, estimate the demand model and compute the resulting benefits (consumer surplus) of access to the forest. Income and price elasticities provide the information on the visitor's response to income and price changes.

The chapter is organized as follows. Section 2 outlines the approach with a single demand equation and the almost ideal demand system (AIDS) to estimate a complete demand system conditional on leisure consumption. In Section 3 we describe the empirical application to the West Garda Regional Forest in Italy and we present the study site and the data. In Section 4 we report and discuss the results. Section 5 concludes the study. In the Appendix we present two feasible methods of estimation for recreational demand systems of equations with censored variables: the generalized Heckman procedure and the simulated maximum likelihood method (SML).

4.2 ECONOMETRIC MODELS FOR THE TRAVEL COST METHOD CONDITIONAL ON LEISURE CONSUMPTION

We propose the following estimation procedure in two steps. In a first step, we estimate the single demand equation for the visitor to the West Garda Regional Forest and her willingness to pay for a visit to the natural area by estimating the consumer surplus. In a second step, we estimate the complete demand system conditional on leisure consumptions using the almost ideal demand system (AIDS) of Deaton and Muellbauer (1980) and the Heckman procedure, in order to take into account the problem of censored variables, such as the number of trips to alternative sites.

4.2.1 Single Demand Equation Model and Consumer Surplus Estimation

The basic premise of the travel cost method is that the time and travel cost expenses that people incur to visit a site represent the 'price' of access to the site. Thus, people's willingness to pay to visit the site can be estimated based on the number of trips that they make at different levels of expense on travel. The basic idea of the travel cost method (TCM) is that visitors will choose the annual number of trips to a recreational site based on the cost of travelling to the site. The number of trips will be inversely related to the travel costs. Once information on the travel costs and trips taken during one year to a recreational site is obtained from visitors, a demand curve can be estimated.

The general form for the recreational demand for the natural area is:

$$N_i = \alpha(d_i, q_i) + \sum_{j=1}^{J} \gamma_j \ln p_j + \beta \ln y_i + u_i, \tag{4.1}$$

where:

- N_i is the annual number of visits to the natural area by individual $i = \{1, \ldots, K\}$;
- $\alpha = \alpha_0 + \Sigma_{\delta=1}^{\Delta} \alpha_\delta d_\delta + \Sigma_{\theta=1}^{Q} \alpha_\theta q_\theta$ is a linear function reflecting the 'translating' effects of:
  - a) the socio-demographic variables $d_\delta = \{d_1, d_2, \ldots, d_\Delta\}$ such as education, sex, occupation, number of family members, number of children under 12, logarithm of the annual expenditure on leisure, logarithm of the willingness to pay a fee in order to preserve the natural area for the present and future generations;
  - b) the qualitative variables of the natural area $q_\theta = \{q_1, q_2, \ldots, q_Q\}$ such as the quality of the natural area considering the

characteristics and functions that the respondent could enjoy, level of crowding, place where the survey was conducted;

- $\ln p_1$ is the logarithm of the travel cost per car to visit the area object of study;
- $\ln p_j = \{\ln p_2, \ldots, \ln p_j\}$ is the logarithm of the annual travel cost by car to visit alternative sites j different respect the natural area object of study;
- $\ln y_i$ is the logarithm of the individual i's monthly net income from the previous year;
- u_i is the stochastic term representing both measurement errors and information about the visitor unobservable to the researcher.

This recreational demand model uses count data such as the number of trips to the natural area. Smith (1988) and Shaw (1988) address the sample selection problem with a count variable using the Poisson distribution.

The basic premise of the travel cost method is that the time and travel cost expenses that people incur to visit a site represent the 'price' of access to the site. Thus, people's willingness to pay to visit the site can be estimated based on the number of trips that they make and how much they pay to travel. This is analogous to estimating people's willingness to pay for a marketed good based on the quantity demanded at different prices. The willingness to pay, or consumer surplus, is estimated by calculating the areas below the demand curve and between the actual cost of travelling to the natural area and the maximum cost, above which the number of visits to the natural area is zero.

The consumer surplus (CS) measure of access to good x for consumer i is given by

$$CS_i = \int_{p_0}^{\tilde{p}} x_i(p,y)dp, \tag{4.2}$$

where $x(p, y)$ is the Marshallian demand function for individual i, p_0 is the current price and $x(\tilde{p}) = 0$ (Bockstael et al., 1990). Figure 4.1 shows that the consumer surplus is measured as the area to the left of the Marshallian demand curve and between the two prices p_0 and $\tilde{p}$. The consumer surplus is a monetary measure of the willingness to pay of the visitor for a trip to the natural area.

4.2.2 A Complete Demand System Conditional on Leisure Consumption

The analysis of visitor choices takes into account decisions between consumption and leisure, as well the allocation of expenditure over commodities. The study of the disaggregated categories of expenditures

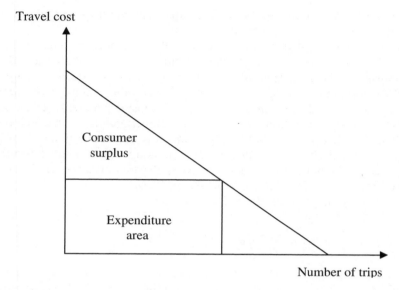

Figure 4.1 Consumer surplus

implies several complementary and substitutability relationships. One solution to this problem is to analyse visitor patterns by the two-stage budgeting procedure (Shenggen et al., 1995).

This procedure assumes that the visitors' utility maximization decision can be decomposed into two separate steps. In the first step, the total income is allocated among broad groups of goods. In the second step, visitors decide how to distribute group expenditure on individual commodities. In this way consumption is partitioned into subsets that include commodities that are closer substitutes or complements among them.

Weak separability is a prerequisite for two-stage budgeting and both a necessary and sufficient condition for estimating the second stage. According to this idea, the marginal rate of substitution among goods belonging to the same group is independent of any other good outside the group. Since it reduces the original problem to a sequence of decisions, the advantage of this approach is that each step requires only information on prices and expenditure at that specific decision level.

Given a weakly separable utility function in a partition of commodities into N groups ($N > 2$), price aggregation is possible if and only if the direct utility function is strongly separable into generalized Gorman polar forms, homothetically separable forms or a combination of the two (Gorman, 1958). We choose a strongly separable utility function, with each group function corresponding to a specific group of commodities and taking the generalized Gorman polar form.

The almost ideal demand system (AIDS) developed by Deaton and Muellbauer is used for the two stages estimation. We estimate the AIDS because it has numerous advantages: it gives an arbitrary first-order approximation to any demand system; it satisfies the axioms of choice; it can be aggregated over consumers without imposing parallel Engel curves (like the linear expenditure system); it has a functional form which is consistent with known household-budget data; it is simple to estimate, largely avoiding the need for non-linear estimation; and it can be used to test the restrictions of homogeneity and symmetry through linear restrictions on fixed parameters (Deaton and Muellbauer, 1980).

The share equation for the AIDS model is:

$$\omega_{i,I} = \alpha_{i,I} + \frac{1}{2}\sum_{j\in I}\gamma_{ij}\log p_{j,I} + \beta_{i,I}\log\frac{E_i}{P_I} + e_{i,I} \tag{4.3}$$

where $\omega_{i,I}$ is the budget share of good i in commodity group I; $e_{i,I}$ is the disturbance term; $p_{j,I}$ is the price of commodity j in group I; E_i is the ith group's total expenditure and P_I is the I-th group price index:

$$\log P_I = \alpha_{0,I} + \sum_{i,I}\alpha_{i,I}\log p_{i,I} + \frac{1}{2}\sum_{i,I}\sum_{j,I}\gamma_{ij,I}\log p_{i,I}\log p_{j,I}, \tag{4.4}$$

with the following restrictions:
homogeneity:

$$\sum_{j,I}\gamma_{ij,I} = 0;$$

adding-up:

$$\sum_{i,I}\alpha_{i,I} = 1; \quad \sum_{i,I}\beta_{i,I} = 0; \quad \sum_{i,I}\gamma_{ij,I} = 0;$$

symmetry:

$$\gamma_{ij,I} = \gamma_{ji,I}$$

The assumption of weak separability between commodities in the different commodity groups implies that the effects of the price change in one commodity group are captured through the group expenditure. Note that in the second stage the I-th group is represented by the leisure expenditure and the i-th commodity is represented by different configurations of leisure expenditure. In this way we define the complete demand system conditional on leisure consumption.

Following Blanciforti et al. (1986) conditional uncompensated price elasticities of commodity i with respect to commodity j's price, in the same group, are

$$\eta_{ij,I} = \delta_{ij,I} + \frac{\gamma_{ij,I}}{\omega_{i,I}} - \frac{\beta_{i,I}\alpha_{i,I}}{\omega_{i,I}} - \frac{\beta_{i,I}}{\omega_{i,I}}\sum_{j\in I}\gamma_{ij,I}\ln p_{i,I},$$

where:

$$\delta_{ij,I} = -1 \;\; if \; i = J, \;\; \delta_{ij,I} = 0 \; \text{otherwise}.$$

We define the conditional expenditure elasticity as:

$$\varepsilon_{i,I} = 1 + \left(\frac{\beta_{i,I}}{\omega_{i,I}}\right)$$

and the compensated elasticity by the Slutsky matrix:

$$\varepsilon^c_{ij,I} = \frac{\gamma_{ij,I}}{\omega_{i,I}} - \delta_{ij,I} + \omega_{i,I}$$

Note that there is a close relation between the effects of changes in demographic variables and the effects of changes in total expenditure. A change in any demographic variables (for example, family size) causes a reallocation of expenditure among the consumption categories.

In this chapter demographic effects are introduced into the system of demand equations by the translating method. The model follows the Barten–Gorman approach in that it translates the budget line through the fixed cost element (translating) but it does not consider the scale effect of the Barten–Gorman model that makes it highly nonlinear.

The AIDS budget share with translating effect becomes:

$$\omega_{i,I} = \alpha_{i,I} + \sum_{k\in I}\delta_{k,I}\log d_{k,I} + \frac{1}{2}\sum_{j\in I}\gamma_{ij,I}\log p_{j,I} + \beta_{i,I}\log\left(\frac{E_i}{P_I * \Delta_I}\right) + e_{i,I},$$

$$(4.5)$$

where $\omega_{i,I}$ is the budget share of good i in commodity group I; $p_{j,I}$ is the price of commodity j in group I; $e_{i,I}$ is the disturbance term; E_i is the ith group's total expenditure and P_I is the Ith group price index defined in equation (4.4); $d_{k,I}$ is the kth socio-demographic variable for group I; and

$\Delta_I = \Sigma_{k \epsilon I} \delta_{ik,I} d_k \log p_{j,I}$ reflects translating effects of the socio-demographic variables $d_{k,I}$.

Note that the complete demand system is characterized by corner solutions. The expenditure for visits to other sites is zero for a part of the sample. If only nonzero visit observations are used in the parameter estimation, ordinary least square procedures would yield inconsistent estimates from selectivity bias. The generalized Heckman procedure described in the Appendix is employed in this study to circumvent the problem.

4.3   STUDY SITE AND DATA GATHERING

The sample is drawn from the survey conducted by the Department of Economics of the University of Verona in Italy, on the west side of Garda Lake, in June–October 1997. This survey was part of an integrated analysis on the multi-functionality of the West Garda Regional Forest in order to define cooperative policies between institutions, local operators and visitors. The survey took the form of on-site[1] interviews of adult visitors (mean age of 39 years).

This area was picked because it was felt that there would be many single-destination, single-purpose trips, which are a necessary assumption of the travel cost method (TCM) (Freeman, 1993). It was also felt that owing to Garda Lake's popularity with tourists from throughout the country and abroad there would be sufficient variation in distance travelled, time and trip cost.

In order to estimate the complete demand system, several questions were included in the survey to analyse the annual expenditure of the family. The first relevant question for this purpose asked the respondent her mean monthly expenditure on food and leisure including the visit to the West Garda Regional Forest. Questions that solicited information for the second stage of the complete demand system asked the respondent to recall the number of annual trips made to West Garda Regional Forest and the number of trips to other natural areas during the year, to allow screening of the sample between those visitors on single-destination and multiple-destination trips.

In order to have a double check on the declared costs, visitors were asked to specify their place of residence, the distance between the natural area and their residence, the journey time and for those who were on vacation, the distance from the forest to the vacation lodging.

Moreover, the following data were collected for each individual: means of transportation used, number of passengers per means of transportation, how many were the family members and how many shared the expense of the trip; if stops were made at other places before going to the natural area; how many days the trip lasted; individual and family transportation expenditure to go to the forest; individual and family expenditure in food, lodging and activities during the trip. This information was used to construct three travel cost variables:[2] cost per payer (*sppag_rt* – mean value 49.37 euros), cost per car, equal to the cost per payer times the number of paying passengers (*spmac_rt* – mean value 60.12 euros per 2.84 paying passengers), cost per family (*spfam_rt* – in mean 5.5 euros per 3.19 members).

In order to estimate the expenditure on alternative sites the visitor was asked about the distance from their residence, number of visits to each site, the quality of the area and the purpose of the trip.[3]

Moreover note that the head of household will spend more if her family members travel with her. The mean travel distance of a visitor travelling alone is about 185 km, while it is about 250 km if at least one member of the family participates in the trip. Thus, we can separate the sharing of expenditure into two categories:

- *Case 1*. The individual pays their own travel cost themselves, independent of the fact that someone else travels with them.
- *Case 2*. The individual travels only if somebody else shares the travel cost.

The data show that the number of payers is equal to the number of passengers for 35 per cent of the sample (case 1); the remaining 65 per cent is composed by visitors who pay for friends or for family members travelling together (case 2).

4.4   RESULTS

In this section we present first the results of the single demand equation approach and then the results of the AIDS model applied to a complete demand system conditional on leisure consumption. They are examined in detail in the following sections.

4.4.1   Single Recreational Demand Equation Model and Consumer Surplus Estimation

The recreational demand equation was estimated using the Poisson distribution. The variables used in the estimation of the recreational demand equation are described in Tables 4.1 and 4.2. The dependent variable is the annual number of visits to the natural area (*nvai*), which has a mean of

Table 4.1   Definition of the variables in the single equation model

Variable	Definition
nvai	Annual number of visits to the natural area
ln_*clsr*	Log (annual interval income) in euros
ln_*sp2*	Log (annual leisure expenditure) in euros
spm	Travel cost per car in euros
ln_*sp1mc*	Log (annual travel cost per car for visits to 1st alternative site) in euros
ln_*sp2mc*	Log (annual travel cost per car for visits to 2nd alternative site) in euros
istrz	Education
eta	Age
*brclv*1	Type of job
nmfl	Number of family members
ln_*vltxi*	Log (willingness to pay a tax to preserve the natural area) in euros
area	Place where the survey was conducted
qtai	Quality of the natural area
affl	Level of crowding

*Table 4.2   Descriptive statistics for selected variables in the single
equation model*

Variable	Mean	Std. Dev.	Min.	Max.
nvai	6.823	11.913	1	90
spm	60.101	109.104	1.033	898.635
qtai	7.378	1.255	4	10
affl	4.630	1.672	1	10
ln_*clsr*	9.904	0.519	9.068	11.034
ln_*sp2*	7.515	0.682	5.225	9.127
istrz	12.687	4.084	5	21
eta	39.355	14.321	14	85
area	2.717	1.494	1	6
*brclv*1	3.119	0.771	1	4
nmfl	3.186	1.317	1	8
ln_*sp1mc*	1.831	2.311	0	6.023
ln_*sp2mc*	0.405	1.936	0	6.166
ln_*vltxi*	1.027	1.908	0	6.142

Note: 361 observations.

Table 4.3   Poisson estimates of the single demand equation model

Variable	Coeff.	Std. Dev.	*t*-stat.
constant	3.140	0.512	6.132
ln_*clsr*	0.230	0.050	4.592
ln_*sp2*	0.309	0.034	9.118
spm	−0.007	0.001	−8.127
ln_*sp1mc*	−0.034	0.011	−3.123
ln_*sp2mc*	−0.023	0.013	−1.784
istrz	−0.023	0.006	−3.873
eta	0.004	0.002	2.566
brclv1	−0.220	0.027	−8.170
nmfl	−0.047	0.018	−2.641
ln_*vltxi*	0.053	0.011	4.895
area	0.089	0.013	6.938
qtai	−0.111	0.017	−6.658
affl	0.019	0.012	1.508

Note: 361 observations.

about six trips per year. The independent variables are the logarithm of the visitor's monthly net income of previous year (ln_*clsr*), the logarithm of the annual leisure expenditure (ln_*sp2*), the annual travel cost per car to visit the West Garda Regional Forest (*spm*), the logarithm of the annual travel cost per car to visit the first alternative site (ln_*sp1mc*) and the second alternative site (ln_*sp2mc*), education (*istrz*), age (*eta*), occupation (*brclv1*), number of family members (*nfml*), logarithm of willingness to pay a tax in order to preserve the natural area for the present and future generations (ln_*vltxi*); quality of the natural area (*qtai*), level of crowding (*affl*) and the place where the survey was conducted (*area*).

The estimated parameters in equation (4.1) are given in Table 4.3. The signs and significance of variable coefficients suggest interesting conclusions.

As expected, the number of visits to the natural area decreases if the travel cost per car (ln_*spm*) and the number of family members (*nfml*) increase (all these variables have a negative sign and are significant at the 5 per cent level); if income (ln_*clsr*), age (*eta*) and the expenditure in leisure (ln_*sp2*) increase then the number of trips increases. These variables have positive and significant coefficient at less than 1 per cent level of significance.

It is interesting to note that the level of crowding of the area (*affl*) is the less significant coefficient (10 per cent level) and has a positive sign. This could mean that visits to the natural area are not significantly affected by

*Table 4.4   Willingness to pay (WTP) for a one day visit by single
           equation demand model (in euros)*

WTP per trip and per car (g)	71.41
Average number of passengers (h)	2.84
WTP per trip and per passenger ($i = g/h$)	25.14
Average number of days of one trip (l)	5.78
WTP per passenger and per one day of visit ($m = i/l$)	4.35

the level of crowding because the forest is located in a tourist area on the
lake where people come for reasons other then visiting the forest (sailing,
swimming, visiting historic centres), so that crowding is not a real problem
for the forest. The positive sign could be due to the fact that if a lot of people
go to the forest this could mean that it is a valuable place to be visited.

The variables involving travel costs to alternative sites have a negative and
significant coefficient. If expenditure on other sites increases then the
number of visits to the West Garda Lake decreases. It is interesting to note
that the travel cost for the second site (ln_$sp2mc$, significant at less than 1 per
cent) affects the number of trips to the West Garda Regional Forest less
than the travel cost for the first site (ln_$sp1mc$, significant at the 10 per cent
level).

Another remarkable result is that the number of trips increases if the environmental concern of visitors increases. The coefficient of the variable willingness to pay a tax to preserve the area for the present and future generation
is positive and significant at every significant level. Instead the negative and
significant coefficients of the variables quality of the area ($qtai$), education
($istrz$) and type of work ($brclv1$) are the opposite of our expectations.

The estimates of consumer surplus experienced by the visitors are listed
in Table 4.4. By equation (4.2) we found a consumer surplus per car and per
trip of 71.41 euros. Dividing this amount by the average number of passengers and the average number of days per trip we found that the average
willingness to pay per one day of visit at the West Garda Regional Forest
is about 4 euros. As an indicator of the willingness to pay, the consumer
surplus is defined as the difference between the amount an individual would
be willing to pay for a good with a constant per-unit price and with a given
income, versus the amount actually paid.

4.4.2 Travel Cost Estimate Conditional on Leisure Consumption

According to the idea of complete demand system conditional on leisure
consumption in two-stage budgeting, visitors of the West Garda Regional

Forest proceed to allocate total income (ln_*redda*) among the broad groups food ($w1$), leisure ($w2$) and other goods ($w3$). In a second step, visitors decide how to distribute the expenditure for leisure (ln_*sp2*) in trips to West Garda Regional Forest ($w4$), trips to other sites ($w5$) and other leisure ($w6$).

The shares of each good are specified as a system of equations according to the almost ideal demand system (AIDS) described in equation (4.6). The descriptive statistics for the selected variables are presented in Tables 4.5 and 4.6. The shares of the first stage are the ratio between the expenditure of each group and the total annual income. The shares of the second stage are the ratio between the commodity expenditure and the total expenditure on leisure. The independent variables included in the AIDS model are the prices of the commodities of each stage,[4] the demographic variables age and education and, respectively for the first and second stage, the logarithm of annual income and the logarithm of annual leisure expenditure.

Maximum likelihood estimates for the AIDS were obtained using the maximum likelihood routine in the computer package Gauss. Table 4.7 shows the estimated means of the expenditures shares for each good in the first and second stage. The estimated share equations were found to be consistent with the underlying theory.[5]

As indicated in previous sections, effects on the intra-household distribution of expenditures can come through three channels: changes in income, price and demographic variables. They are presented by the budget/income elasticities, the compensated elasticities and the elasticities with respect to the demographic variables. Table 4.8 presents the elasticities for the first stage where the demographic variables are age and education.

It is of interest to examine the cross-price effects. From the Slutsky equation of consumer theory, it is known that compensated cross-price effects must be symmetric in order for the demand functions to be consistent with the utility maximization hypothesis. Note that the elasticity with respect to food price is positive (0.01) and so contrary to our expectation. The elasticities with respect to the price of leisure and other goods are negative, at -0.029 for leisure and -0.052 for other goods.

In line with the economic theory, the income elasticities are positive: 0.153 for the food expenditure, 3.967 for leisure expenditure and 0.614 for the expenditure in other goods.

Note that the complete demand system is characterized by corner solutions in the second stage. The expenditure on visits to other sites is zero for part of the sample. If only nonzero visit observations are used in the parameter estimation, ordinary least square procedures would yield inconsistent estimates from selectivity bias. The generalized Heckman procedure described in the Appendix is applied in this study to circumvent the

Table 4.5 Definition of the selected variables in the complete demand system

Variable	Definition
First Stage	
$sp1$	Annual food expenditure in euros
$sp2$	Annual leisure expenditure in euros
$sp3$	Annual expenditure on other goods in euros ($= redda - (sp1 + sp2)$)
$redda$	Annual income in euros
$w1$	Food annual share ($= sp1/redda$)
$w2$	Leisure annual share ($= sp2/redda$)
$w3$	Other goods annual share ($= sp3/redda$)
$\ln p\_w1$	Log food price ($= log\,(sp1)$) in euros
$\ln p\_w2$	Log leisure price ($= log\,(sp2)$) in euros
$\ln p\_w3$	Log other goods price ($= log\,(sp3)$) in euros
$\ln\_redda$	Log (annual income) in euros
eta	Age
$istrz$	Education
Second Stage	
$sp4$	Annual West Garda Regional Forest visits expenditure in euros
$sp5$	Annual expenditure on other site visits in euros
$sp6$	Annual other leisure expenditure in euros ($= sp2 - (sp4 + sp5)$)
$nvai$	Annual number of visits to the natural area
$nvai2$	Annual number of visits to other sites
$w4$	Leisure annual share to West Garda Regional Forest ($= sp4/sp2$)
$w5$	Leisure annual share to visit other sites ($= sp5/sp2$)
$w6$	Other leisure annual share ($= sp6\,/\,sp2$)
$\ln p\_w4$	Log West Garda Regional Forest visits price ($= log\,(sp4/nvai)$) in euros
$\ln p\_w5$	Log other site visits price ($= log\,(sp5)/(nvai + nvai2)$) in euros
$\ln p\_w6$	Log other leisure price ($= log\,(sp6)$) in euros
$\ln\_sp2$	Log (annual leisure expenditure) in euros
eta	Age
$istrz$	Education
dum	Heckman dummy
$brclv1$	Occupation
$fgs12$	Children under 12
$cdzlv1$	Type of job
$distr$	Distance of residence from the natural area

Table 4.6   Descriptive statistics for selected variables in the complete demand system

Variable	Mean	Std. Dev.	Min.	Max.
First Stage				
w1	0.258	0.144	0.010	0.811
w2	0.117	0.085	0.005	0.682
w3	0.625	0.181	0.048	0.980
$\ln p\_w1$	8.382	0.579	5.225	10.710
$\ln p\_w2$	7.515	0.682	5.225	9.820
$\ln p\_w3$	9.3743	0.816	6.419	11.014
ln_redda	16.815	0.534	15.725	18.027
eta	39.355	14.321	14	85
istrz	12.687	4.084	5	21
Second Stage				
w4	0.088	0.143	0.002	0.896
w5	0.032	0.063	0.000	0.691
w6	0.880	0.163	0.091	0.997
$\ln p\_w4$	3.108	1.286	0.032	6.801
$\ln p\_w5$	2.952	1.199	−2.924	6.061
$\ln p\_w6$	7.355	0.813	3.279	9.792
ln_sp2	7.515	0.682	5.225	9.820
eta	39.355	14.321	14	85
istrz	12.687	4.084	5	21
dum	0.568	0.496	0	1
brclv1	3.119	0.771	1	4
fgs12	0.357	0.724	0	4
cdzlv1	2.194	1.664	1	6
distr	0.209	0.316	0.005	2.500

Note: 361 observations.

problem. In order to apply this procedure we create a dummy variable (*dum*) equal to zero when the expenditure for other sites is zero and equal to one otherwise.

Further insights can be gained into the nature of our estimated share equations and their underlying preference ordering by examining the share elasticities. Table 4.9 presents the elasticities for the second stage where we consider the compensated price elasticities, the leisure expenditure elasticities instead of the income elasticity and the elasticities in respect of the socio-demographic variables age and education.

As expected the signs are positive for the compensated elasticities and negative for the elasticites respect to the leisure expenditure. An increase

*Table 4.7   Maximum likelihood (ML) and simulated maximum likelihood
(SML) estimates of first stage and second stage shares*

First Stage		
	Shares (ML)	
	Prediction	Actual
Food	0.242	0.258
Leisure	0.148	0.117
Other goods	0.609	0.625
	Shares (SML)	
	Prediction	Actual
Food	0.286	0.258
Leisure	0.123	0.117
Other goods	0.591	0.625

Second Stage		
	Shares (Heckman)	
	Prediction	Actual
Trips to West Garda Regional Forest	0.095	0.088
Trips to other sites	0.024	0.031
Other leisure activities	0.881	0.880
	Shares (SML)	
	Prediction	Actual
Trips to West Garda Regional Forest	0.126	0.088
Trips to other sites	0.258	0.031
Other leisure activities	0.616	0.880

Note: 361 observations.

of the leisure expenditure of 10 per cent corresponds to an increase of
55.2 per cent in the expenditure for trips to West Garda Regional Forest
and of 52.48 per cent in the expenditure on other leisure activities. The
Slutsky condition is satisfied since the compensated elasticity matrix has all
the elements of the main diagonal negative.

Table 4.8   Elasticities for first stage of the complete demand system

	Compensated elasticities		
	Food	Leisure	Other goods
Food	0.010	−0.029	0.019
Std. Dev.	0.014	0.007	0.010
t-stat.	0.728	−3.972	1.822
Leisure	−0.048	−0.135	0.183
Std. Dev.	0.012	0.009	0.011
t-stat.	−4.076	−15.241	17.095
Other goods	0.008	0.045	−0.052
Std. Dev.	0.004	0.002	0.004
t-stat.	1.805	17.753	−12.212

	Income elasticities		
	Food	Leisure	Other goods
Annual Income	0.153	3.967	0.614
Std. Dev.	0.041	0.046	0.014
t-stat.	3.694	86.601	43.639

	Socio-demographic elasticities		
	Food	Leisure	Other goods
Age	0.004	0.001	−0.002
Std. Dev.	0.005	0.002	0.019
t-stat.	0.885	0.305	−0.110
Education	0.003	−0.017	0.003
Std. Dev.	0.005	0.018	0.007
t-stat.	0.517	−0.927	0.421

Note: 361 observations.

4.5   CONCLUSIONS

In this chapter we explored two issues in empirical recreational demand analysis: first, the estimation of a single recreational demand equation and the consumer surplus of a visitor to the West Garda Regional Forest in Italy; second, the estimation of complete demand systems of demand equations conditional on leisure consumption.

This study on recreational demand has applied the travel cost technique to the West Garda Regional Forest for the first time. The visits to the natural

Table 4.9   Elasticities for second stage of the complete demand system by Heckman procedure

	Compensated elasticities		
	Trips to West Garda Regional Forest	Trips to other sites	Other leisure
Trips to West Garda Regional Forest	−0.342	0.095	0.247
Std. Dev.	0.022	0.037	0.035
t-stat.	−15.401	2.570	7.114
Trips to other sites	0.381	−0.360	−0.012
Std. Dev.	0.096	0.192	0.184
t-stat.	3.987	−1.926	−0.064
Other leisure	0.027	−0.000	−0.026
Std. Dev.	0.004	0.005	0.003
t-stat.	7.094	−0.066	−8.085
	Income elasticities		
	Trips to West Garda Regional Forest	Trips to other sites	Other leisure
Leisure Expenditure	5.520	5.248	0.398
Std. Dev.	0.205	1.537	0.018
t-stat.	26.865	3.415	22.425
	Socio-demographic elasticities		
	Trips to West Garda Regional Forest	Trips to other sites	Other leisure
Age	0.010	0.123	−0.004
Std. Dev.	0.019	0.003	0.351
t-stat.	0.531	47.491	−0.013
Education	0.025	0.232	−0.009
Std. Dev.	0.111	0.070	0.009
t-stat.	0.228	3.312	−1.048

Note: 361 observations.

area produce a high value of consumer surplus to the users, 25 euros per trip per person. The corresponding willingness to pay per day is about 4 euros.

   This chapter has presented a recreational demand model that exploits the notion of separability to derive a two-stage demand system conditional on leisure consumption. Visitors to the West Garda Regional Forest proceed to allocate total income among the broad groups food, leisure and other goods. In a second step, visitors decide how to distribute the expenditure for leisure in trips to the West Garda Regional Forest, trips to other sites and other leisure activities.

The complete demand system has two principal advantages over existing valuation models in the literature. First, by incorporating the budget constraint into the analysis, the complete system approach forces recognition of the fact that an increase in expenditure on one consumption category (such as recreation, for our purposes) must be balanced by decreases in the expenditure on others. Second, the complete system approach permits the separation of demographic effects from own and cross-price effects as well as income effects. Unless such a separation is made, there is no presumption that demographic effects estimated from one price situation will be relevant in another.

The economic results are presented in the context of the almost ideal demand system (AIDS) of Deaton and Muellbauer (1980) modified into a Gorman form by translating the demographic effect of the socio-demographic variables. The resulting demand coefficient estimates suggest the empirical tractability of estimating a complete demand system for a visitor to a natural area combining information about the travel cost and a priori information from consumer theory about the expenditure on leisure by the visitor. The proposed approach may be especially useful in disaggregate demand analysis.

Estimation of demand functions provides us with the means to calculate income and price elasticities. The measurement of income and price elasticities is necessary input to the economically optimal design of many different policies. For example, efficient policy design for indirect taxation and subsidies requires knowledge of these elasticities for taxable commodities and services (Deaton, 1988).

An aspect of the AIDS which has made it attractive is its simplicity. In the empirical estimation of the Engel curves of some commodities, non-linearities appeared to be important. For instance, Banks et al. (1997) show that the Engel curves for clothing and alcohol in the UK are non-linear in the logarithm of expenditures. Since the AIDS demand curves are linear in the logarithm of expenditures, they are not appropriate for the estimation of these Engel curves. We suggest in the future estimating the expenditure share using the quadratic almost ideal demand (Banks et al., 1997).

Note finally that individuals, and not households, have utility. What is relevant is not the preferences of a given household, but rather the preferences of the individuals that compose it (Browning et al., 2003). Estimation of comparisons at the individual level following the earlier literature about the collective approach to household behaviour proposed by Browning et al. (2003) are left for future research.

APPENDIX: ECONOMETRIC METHODS FOR CENSORED VARIABLES

The difficulty in estimating recreational demand functions is that a proportion of the population in a given geographical region are likely to be non-participants in the alternative recreational areas. That is, they are observed to demand zero trips. We are interested in a problem in which many people demand zero trips for alternative sites.

There are many examples in economics of models that can be represented by systems of equations with several censored variables: systems of demand equations where some consumers choose not to buy several of the goods in the system (Wales and Woodland, 1983; Phaneuf, 1999; Perali and Chavas, 2000); systems of input demand and supply equations where firms choose not to produce several outputs or not to use several inputs in the system (Huffman, 1988); systems with censored prices (Arias and Cox, 2001) or models of labour supply (Heckman, 1974).

We present two methods of estimation for systems of equations with censored variables: the generalized Heckman procedure and the simulated maximum likelihood method (SML).

The generalized Heckman procedure is an extension to a system of equations of the two-step Heckman estimator (Heckman, 1974 and 1979), while the simulated maximum likelihood method (Hajivassiliou et al., 1996; Arias and Cox, 2001) uses multiple integrals that are computed with a simulated algorithm to reproduce the statistical process that generated the zero realizations.

Generalized Heckman Procedure

The generalized Heckman procedure consists of transforming the system of censored equations into a system of uncensored equations by using the appropriate correction. Following Arias et al. (2003), we consider the unconditional mean:

$$
\begin{aligned}
E[y_i|x_{it}] &= E[y_i|y_i > 0]\Phi\left(\frac{f_i(x_i,\beta_i)}{\sigma_i}\right)\\
&= f_i(x_i,\beta_i)\Phi\left(\frac{f_i(x_i,\beta_i)}{\sigma_i}\right) + \sigma_i\phi\left(\frac{f_i(x_i,\beta_i)}{\sigma_i}\right),
\end{aligned}
$$

where, ϕ and Φ are respectively the probability density function and the cumulative density function of a standard normal distribution, y_i is the endogenous variable corresponding to the i-th equation in the censored system, x_i is a vector of explanatory variables, β_i is a vector of parameters. Using the expression for the unconditional expected value of each endogenous variable we consider the following system of uncensored equations:

$$y_i = f_i(x_i, \beta_i) \Phi\left(\frac{f_i(x_i, \beta_i)}{\sigma_i}\right) + \sigma_i \phi\left(\frac{f_i(x_i, \beta_i)}{\sigma_i}\right) + \xi_i,$$

where $\xi_{it} = y_{it} - E[y_i | x_{it}]$. This system can be estimated by limited maximum likelihood assuming that:

$$\xi \sim MVN(0, \Omega)$$

where, ξ is a random vector whose i-th element is ξ_i. An important detail stressed by Arias et al. (2003) is that this is a straightforward maximum likelihood estimation since the latter system does not contain any censored equation. We use this approach to generate reasonable starting values for the method of simulated maximum likelihood.

Simulated Maximum Likelihood Method

Following Arias and Cox (2001) the likelihood function for an observation in which the n first endogenous variables out of m are censored is:

$$L_2 = \int_{-\infty}^{c1} \cdots \int_{-\infty}^{cn} df(u_1, \ldots, u_m) du_1 \cdots du_n$$

$$= df_1(u_{n+1}, \ldots, u_m) \int_{-\infty}^{c1} \cdots \int_{-\infty}^{cn} cf(u_1, \ldots, u_n | u_{n+1}, \ldots, u_m) du_1 \cdots du_n$$

where df_i is the marginal probability density function of the uncensored portion and cf is the probability density function of the censored variables conditional on the uncensored ones. This expression represents a portion of the likelihood function with an n-dimensional definite integral. Under the assumption of multivariate normality of the disturbances of the system, this integral does not have a close form solution. Therefore, estimating the system of equations by maximum likelihood requires an efficient method for evaluating the high dimensional definite integrals.

Simulated maximum likelihood consists of simulating rather than calculating these integrals using probability simulation methods, which are based on the fact that the integral of interest represents the probability of an event in a population (Lerman and Manski, 1981; Stern, 1992; Börsh-Saupan and Hajivassiliou, 1993; Hajivassiliou et al., 1996).

Table 4.10   *Elasticities for second stage of the complete demand system*
              by simulated maximum likelihood method (SML)

	Compensated elasticities		
	Trips to West Garda Regional Forest	Trips to other sites	Other leisure
Trips to West Garda Regional Forest	−0.347	0.082	0.265
Std. Dev.	0.023	0.019	0.018
t-stat.	−15.070	4.397	14.524
Trips to other sites	0.237	−0.523	0.285
Std. Dev.	0.052	0.056	0.045
t-stat.	4.561	−9.389	6.402
Other leisure	0.029	0.011	−0.030
Std. Dev.	0.002	0.002	0.002
t-stat.	12.293	4.874	−18.347

	Income elasticities		
	Trips to West Garda Regional Forest	Trips to other sites	Other leisure
Leisure expenditure	5.430	3.019	0.441
St. Dev.	0.180	0.350	0.009
t-stat.	28.622	8.616	45.003

	Socio-demographic elasticities		
	Trips to West Garda Regional Forest	Trips to other sites	Other leisure
Age	0.008	0.059	−0.003
Std. Dev.	0.020	0.002	0.168
t-stat.	0.423	30.846	−0.019
Education	−0.021	0.247	−0.003
Std. Dev.	0.040	0.074	0.007
t-stat.	−0.428	3.333	−1.033

Note: 361 observations.

We present the estimated elasticities for the second stage of the complete demand system conditional on leisure consumption using simulated maximum likelihood method (Hajivassiliou, 2000; Arias and Cox, 2001) in Table 4.10. Table 4.7 presents a comparison of the estimated shares of the first and second stage of the complete demand system applied to the travel cost estimate. We conclude that SML is the preferable approach to the censored variable problem.

NOTES

* The views presented here are those of the authors and do not necessarily represent the views or policies of the Economic Research Service or the United States Department of Agriculture.
1. Visitors were interviewed in the following places: Passo Spino (27.98 per cent of the respondents), Valvestino (17.17 per cent), Tignale (30 per cent), Tremosine (12.47 per cent), Tremalzo (4.16 per cent) and others ones (8 per cent). There were 400 respondents but after skimming the actual sample consists of 361 observations.
2. Every travel cost variable comprehends the opportunity cost of time spent travelling to the natural area. Several studies apply and compare different values to estimate the opportunity cost of time (for example, Cesario, 1976; McConnell and Strand, 1981; Johnson, 1983; Smith et al., 1983; Chavas et al., 1989; Bockstael et al., 1990; McKean et al., 1996). In this study we evaluate travel time at one-third of the wage rate (Cesario, 1976).
3. There may be some concern over how accurately the respondent can recall the information above. Champ and Bishop (1996) found recall bias is less likely to be a problem with questions on total expenditures but it is thought to be a common problem with questions on the number of trips.
4. We use the logarithm of the expenditure as an approximation of the price for each commodity.
5. Estimated parameters of the AIDS in equation (4.5) are available on request.

REFERENCES

Arias, C. and T.L. Cox (2001), 'Estimation of a US dairy sector model by maximum simulated likelihood', *Applied Economics*, **33** (9), 1201–11.
Arias, C., V. Atella, R. Castagnini and F. Perali (2003), 'Estimation of the sharing rule between adults and children and related equivalence scales within a collective consumption framework', in G. Ferrari and C. Dagum (eds), *Household Welfare and Poverty*, Physica Verlag.
Banks, J., R. Blundell and A. Lewbel (1997), 'Quadratic Engel curves and consumer demand', *Review of Economics and Statistics*, **79** (4), 527–39.
Blanciforti, L., R. Green and G. King (1986), 'US consumer behavior over the postwar period. An almost ideal demand system analysis', *Giannini Foundation of Agricultural Economics*, Monograph Series, paper MS40.
Bockstael, N.E., W.M. Hanemann and C.L. Kling (1987), 'Estimating the value of water quality improvements in a recreational demand framework', *Water Resources Research*, **23** (5), 951–60.
Bockstael, N.E., I.E. Strand, K.E. McConnell and F. Arsanjani (1990), 'Sample selection bias in the estimation of recreational demand functions: an application to sportfishing', *Land Economics*, **66** (1), 40–49.
Börsh-Saupan, A. and V.A. Hajivassiliou (1993), 'Smooth unbiased multivariate probability simulators for maximum likelihood estimation of limited dependent variable models', *Journal of Econometrics*, **58**, 347–68.

Browning, M., P.A. Chiappori and A. Lewbel (2003), 'Estimating consumption economies of scale, adult equivalence scales, and household bargaining power', in G. Ferrari and C. Dagum (eds), *Household Welfare and Poverty*, Physica Verlag.

Cesario, F.J. (1976), 'Value of time in recreation benefit studies', *Land Economics*, **52**, 32–41.

Champ, P.A. and R.C. Bishop (1996), 'Evidence on the accuracy of expenditures reported in recreational surveys', *Journal of Agricultural and Resource Economics*, **229**, 150–59.

Chavas, J., J. Stoll and C. Sellar (1989), 'On the commodity value of travel time in recreational activities', *Applied Economics*, **21**, 711–22.

Deaton, A. (1988), 'Quality, quantity, and spatial variation of price', *American Economic Review*, **78**, 418–30.

Deaton, A. and J.J. Muellbauer, (1980), 'The almost ideal demand system', *American Economic Review*, **70** (3), 312–26.

Freeman III, A.M. (1993), *The Measurement of Environmental and Resource Values: Theory and Values*, Washington DC: Resources for the Future.

Gorman, W.G. (1958), 'Separable utility and aggregation', *Econometrica*, **27**, 469–88.

Hajivassiliou, V.A. (2000), 'Some practical issues in maximum simulated likelihood', in Roberto Mariano, Melvyin Weeks and Til Schurmann (eds), *Simulation-Based Inference in Econometrics: Methods and Applications*, Cambridge: Cambridge University Press.

Hajivassiliou, V.A., D. McFadden and P. Ruud (1996), 'Simulation of multivariate normal rectangle probabilities and their derivatives: theoretical and computational results', *Journal of Econometrics*, **72**, 85–134.

Heckman, J.J. (1974), 'Shadow prices, market wages, and labor supply', *Econometrica*, **42**, 679–94.

Heckman, J.J. (1979), 'Sample selection bias as specification error', *Econometrica*, **47** (1), 153–60.

Huffman, W.E. (1988), 'An econometric methodology for multiple-output agricultural technology: an application of endogenous switching models', in S.M. Capalbo and J. Antle (eds), *Agricultural Productivity Measurement and Explanation*, Resources for the Future, Washington, DC: John Hopkins University Press, pp. 229–44.

Johnson, T.G. (1983), 'Measuring the cost of time in recreational demand analysis: comment', *American Journal of Agricultural Economics*, **65**, 169–71.

Lerman, S. and C. Manski (1981), 'On the use of simulated frequencies to approximate choice probabilities', in C.F. Manski and D. McFadden (eds), *Structural Analysis of Discrete Data with Econometric Applications*, Cambridge, MA: MIT Press.

McConnell, K.E. and I. Strand (1981), 'Measuring the cost of time in recreational demand analysis: an application to sportfishing', *American Journal of Agricultural Economics*, **65** (1), 153–6.

McKean, J.R., R.G. Walsh and M.D. Johnson (1996), 'Closely related good prices in the travel cost model', *American Journal of Agricultural Economics*, **78** (3), 640–46.

Perali, F. and J.P. Chavas (2000), 'Estimation of censored demand equations from large cross-section data', *American Journal of Agricultural Economics*, **82** (4), 1022–37.

Phaneuf, D.J. (1999), 'A dual approach to modelling corner solutions in recreation demand', *Journal of Environmental Economics and Management*, **37**, 85–105.

Pollack, R.A. and T.J. Wales (1978): 'Estimation of complete demand systems from household budget data: the linear and quadratic expenditure systems', *The American Economic Review*, **68** (3), 348–59.

Provencher, B. and R.C. Bishop (1997), 'An estimable dynamic model of recreation behaviour with an application to Great Lakes angling', *Journal of Environmental Economics and Management*, **33**, 107–27.

Shaw, D. (1988), 'On-site samples regression', *Journal of Econometrics*, **37**, 211–23.

Shenggen, F., E.J. Wailes and G.L. Cramer (1995), 'Household demand in rural China: a two-stage LES-AIDS model', *American Journal of Agricultural Economics*, **77**, 54–62.

Smith, V.K. (1988), 'Selection and recreation demand', *American Journal of Agricultural Economics*, **70**, 29–36.

Smith, V.K., W.H. Desvouges and M.P. McGivney (1983), 'The opportunity cost of travel time in recreation demand models', *Land Economics*, **59**, 259–78.

Stern, S. (1992), 'A method for smoothing simulated moments of discrete probabilities in multinomial probit models', *Econometrica*, **60**, 943–52.

Wales, T.J. and A.D. Woodland (1983), 'Estimation of consumer demand systems with binding non-negativity constraints', *Journal of Econometrics*, **21** (3), 263–85.

PART II

Management

5. Identifying the best combination of environmental functions using multi-criteria analysis

Paola De Agostini

5.1 INTRODUCTION

Recent research has regarded the implementation of multi-criteria analysis (MCA) as a method able to represent conflicts arising from the use of environmental resources. One of the most common uses of MCA methods is for environmental impact evaluation. These techniques enable decision makers to handle large amounts of information.

MCA techniques can be used to identify the most preferred option, to rank options, to short-list a limited number of options for subsequent detailed appraisal, or simply to distinguish between acceptable and unacceptable possibilities.

Forestry systems have peculiar characteristics. Forestry productive processes produce both market and non-market goods (collective goods). The first, for example timber and fruits, imply the use of soil, while collective goods, for example recreational and entertainment activities and fauna protection, require protection and maintenance of the ecological system. The management of natural resources is often complex because it involves managing a wide variety of contrasting objectives.

Forestry productive processes usually develop over a long period. Therefore, once an area has been allocated for a specific use, it will be constrained by that particular use for several years. And even if management decided it was necessary to change its use, a long time would still pass before obtaining the expected results.

Finally, the demand for public services, as for example landscape preservation, is increasing and more attention is given to forest management also in this prospective. Conflicts between the users of the forest arise because they have different expectations, goals and ways to achieve them and they are interested in different forestry products. In order to solve these conflicts suitable methodologies are necessary to support the decision-making process respecting environmental natural characteristics and users' preferences.

When the decision-making process considers the preferences of both the forest manager and various interest groups and citizens regarding the management and use of the forest area, the process is usually called a *participative process*. Obviously this is not always in place, and sometimes the decision maker might undertake forest planning based only on his own priorities. The advantage of using a participative process approach is that it enables the administrative government to collect new ideas and information from people affected by the planning. It will then be able to consider new managerial alternatives and interpret the results, and the final decision is made after anticipating possible conflict situations arising.

Multi-objectivity is typical in forest planning. Forests should promote fauna and flora conservation and supply appropriate tourist services and timber production.

Multi-criteria analysis has recently reached a high level of technical sophistication and it has been widely used to analyse multi-objective forest management strategies. It uses more flexible mathematical instruments and several types of mathematical methods. There are models suitable for solving each specific managerial problem. The choice of the most appropriate model affects the results. Therefore it is important to focus on the research's main objective and choose the model, depending on both technical and decisional characteristics of that objective.

The aim of this chapter is to describe the methodological aspects of the multi-criteria analysis applied to the forest's management. In doing so we consider two alternative forest management plans: the first describing a non-participative decision process where management planning involves only the administrative government's preferences; the second, called the *participative regional management programme*, where priorities among objectives take into account users' opinions. We compare the optimal combination of managerial interventions in an alternative management plan resulting from the maximization of net benefits measured in quantitative levels obtained from the forest's management with a new approach that integrates bio-ecological information obtained from geographical information systems (GIS) analysis taking into account the forest users' preferences derived from the contingent valuation method (CVM). In doing so, we define the best combination of managerial interventions, which maximizes the administration's revenues by including users' preferences in every alternative management plan. We apply this method to the West Garda Regional Forest.

The chapter is organized as follows. Section 2 outlines the forest planning approach describing the decision process and empirical analysis process. Section 3 describes the multi-criteria analysis (MCA) methodology and

Section 4 describes the multi-objective models typically used in forest planning. Section 5 reports the empirical application of MCA to the West Garda Regional Forest in Italy as traditionally applied in forest planning, and discusses the results. In Section 6 we identify the best combination of forest objectives integrating the MCA model with GIS and contingent valuation data. Section 7 concludes the study. The Appendix presents some basic definitions of the metric used in multi-criteria analysis.

5.2   FOREST PLANNING

5.2.1   The Decision-making Process

The main problem that forest administration faces when designing a forest plan is to search for the best outcome through different scenarios in order to anticipate the future and reduce the likelihood of unexpected events.

A natural area represents a natural habitat for different species of wild fauna and it is often affected by naturalistic and geological emergencies. Multi-criteria analysis has been widely used to analyse forest management strategies. It helps to answer the three main questions that starting a forest planning imposes: what to do? Where and when to do it?

Multi-criteria analysis has recently reached a high level of technical sophistication. It uses more flexible mathematical instruments and several types of mathematical methods. There are models suitable for solving each specific managerial problem. The choice of the most appropriate model affects the results. Therefore it is important to focus on the research's main objective and, depending on both technical and decisional characteristics of that objective, choose the model. Although adopting different techniques, all multi-criteria methods applied to natural resource management problems follow a similar approach. It can be summarized as follows:

1. Explorative phase:
    a. identifying objectives;
    b. identifying options for achieving the objectives;
    c. identifying criteria (indices, alternatives techniques, etc.) to compare the options;
    d. evaluation of the natural area's strength and definition of the main targets.
2. Analysis phase:
    a. definition of Pareto-efficient alternatives management systems;
    b. evaluation of each objective level (using a specific indicator for measuring each objective) for each alternative management system.

The final outcome of this process is a set of management programmes that optimizes the combination of the objectives over the forest territory.

Once the managerial programmes have been identified following a rigorous definition of priorities and preferences, during the decisional phase (see Chapter 7) the decision maker and/or decisional group's preferences for each managerial objective will be evaluated and the option that gains the highest consensus will be identified, evaluating the agreement level achieved in the planning process.

5.2.2   Identifying Planning Strategies

The identification of a planning strategy can be based on two approaches:

1.   multi-attribute analysis: identifying a finite set of alternatives;
2.   multi-objective analysis: identifying alternatives and selecting them by solving a multi-objective mathematical problem.

The first approach is usually used in environmental impact evaluation analysis to generate discrete planning models, while the second approach is typical in forestry planning problems and generates continuous planning models.

The most important characteristic of planning models is their ability to represent all possible acceptable alternatives applicable to a particular territory. However, this mathematical approach suffers from some limitations both from a general point of view and in particular when applied to forest areas.

A first limitation is identifiable in the difficulty or impossibility of building a mathematical model able to predict and represent all the possible implications of forest management.

A second limitation is the decision makers' difficulty in setting their preferences by assigning a weight to each goal of the model. Although many methods exist for identifying preferences and weights, it is always difficult for the decision maker to give exact indications about his preference structure.

Finally, these models often consider only the case with one decision maker, while nowadays, it is common that management choices arise from a combination of different group interests and in particular that group preferences are able to affect public administration plans.

Therefore in order to overcome the issues described above, MCA applies a methodology based on a finite set of possible alternatives known as *multi-attribute analysis*. The aim of this analysis is to identify the alternative that best satisfies the decision maker within the set of alternatives considered.

When there is more than one decision maker this method is called *multi-decisional analysis*.

The application of multi-attribute analysis assumes that planning alternatives have been identified. In forest planning such alternatives may be identified using technical principles.[1] However in some cases this way of proceeding might not be possible, in particular when there are too many goals considered significant from a managerial point of view, or when the area of study is characterized by many soil types needing different agricultural and/or forest treatments. Moreover, it is possible that the set of possible alternatives identified are not efficient. In order to sort this problem out one often uses a mixed approach. In such a case, first we solve a mathematical programming problem and identify a set of efficient solutions. Second, we re-examine the set of solutions using technical principles, and then the final solution derives from solving a multi-attribute or multi-decisional model.

Although it is not always possible to find a model that summarizes all kinds of intervention or to apply multi-decisional techniques, the main advantage in using multi-objective models is that it represents all possible Pareto-efficient alternatives. Therefore, researchers developed techniques that can identify a sufficient number of solutions that represent the Pareto-efficient frontier (these techniques are called discretization techniques). In this case, the solutions obtained represent the finite set of planning alternatives.

5.2.3   Forest Planning Models

In order to overcome the complexity of forest planning and to make the management process efficient, two fundamental theoretical approaches are used: *mix multi-use planning* based on the idea that all forestry systems must supply all environmental services simultaneously, and the *sharing planning strategy*, based on the thesis that each forestry system must supply its prevalent functions depending on its characteristics. However this problem is not always easy to overcome. The best planning strategy identification depends on three main decisional components: (a) the ability of the area to supply natural services and products; (b) the interaction of different objectives; and (c) the socio-economic status of the whole area.

In forest planning models the decisional variables represent areas to be allocated to each managerial alternative. For example X^S, Z^S, W^S represent the total hectares to be allocated to each technical alternative S within the areas X, Z and W. In general forest types are represented by homogeneous forestry area, by geography, families of trees, and vegetation and infrastructure characteristics.

The estimated coefficients produced from this model express temporal benefit (yearly or seasonally) and variations in productivity due to policy variations. One can consider the following cases:

1. yearly benefits (for example food available for fauna) and temporal agricultural productivity varying over time;
2. yearly benefits (for example production of food for fauna) and agricultural services that imply lasting improvement over time (for example high trees to be cut randomly);
3. periodic benefits (for example income deriving from timber production and occupation).

Once technical coefficients have been identified, it is possible to define the form of the objective function. The maximum level that each objective function could reach is limited by physical and technical constraints. In particular in territorial planning it is necessary to take into account the following constraint factors:

1. resources available;
2. institutional constraints as derived from public laws and regulations;
3. contractual constraints (for example with unions);
4. managerial needs.[2]

When explicitly taking time into account we talk about dynamic planning models. The decisional variables X_{te}^S represent the total hectares used by the managerial alternative S in time t in class of age e. The constraints of this model come from having to analyse all possible strategic interventions over the area.

These models work on two temporal scales. The first is the horizontal plan representing the length of time within which the alternatives will be realized. In this case, the period of time depends directly on the age and type of vegetation present within a particular natural area. The horizontal plan consists of short time periods within which each alternative is applied. Usually this time period is longer than one year and corresponds to the expected development period of the natural area.

One advantage of using dynamic models is that they allow for controlling the variation over time of forest services supply. In general, for territorial planning and in particular for forest systems it is often not sufficient to maximize the economic products and services variation. It is also necessary that services supply does not decline over time. For example, if the habitat quality deteriorated suddenly, it would directly affect the fauna population and it would be difficult to compensate by an immediate intervention.

In the same way, variation in occupation affects forestry employment Therefore, it is important to set the constraints in such a way that enable positive variation of objective functions or at least that discourage negative variation over time.

5.3   MULTI-CRITERIA ANALYSIS

One approach to solving forest-planning problems is represented by mathematical programming models (MP). These models are used because:

1.   they formally represent all possible sets of managerial alternatives;
2.   they allow the selection of a set of Pareto efficient alternatives;
3.   they allow selecting the best alternative through interactive processes with decision makers.

Multi-criteria methods use specific indicators to measure physical, ecological, social and economic effects of a particular managerial plan on the territory. Therefore, the efficiency of the planning process depends directly on the ability of these techniques to cope with the challenges that decision makers might face in handling a large amount of complex information in a consistent way.

Several mathematical programming models can be used for practical decision-making regarding the forest. In the past the most used optimization instrument was linear programming. In recent years, interpretative models have become more common. These methods identify the objective function of public administration and help it with interpreting results and making a final decision; they can be also used to simulate future choices.

The multi-criteria approach, because of its stability and using parametric analysis, has allowed researchers to overcome the limitations of linear programming. In particular, it is widely recognized that it is not realistic to assume a unique linear objective function as the optimization criterion because it represents a special case within a general situation where there are multiple objective functions often contrasting with each other. This is one of the main reasons researchers have looked for other methods that are able to identify more than one optimal solution point when more objectives are present.

Multi-criteria analysis techniques are different in how they combine data, in resolution methods used and in model characteristics. However, they present some common aspects, such as multiple-objective functions and conflicts between objectives. MCA can be used to identify a single most preferred option, to rank options, to short-list a limited number of options or to distinguish acceptable from unacceptable possibilities. It establishes preferences between options using relative importance weights and judging the contribution of each option to each performance criterion.

The best way of representing the set of alternative strategies of the decision maker consists of using its utility function. The level of satisfaction of the decision maker depends on multiple factors. The simultaneous optimization of all objectives is often impossible. So researchers usually use two methods and both of them reduce the main problem to a single objective function problem.

1. The first method uses only one objective function, and imposes limitations on all the others. In other words, other goals are treated as constraints and added to the set of constraints of the problem.
2. The second method defines an additive function, usually called global utility function, and optimizes that function. This means optimizing the following function:

$$U = f(O_1, O_2, \ldots, O_k),$$

where U is called global utility function and O_r (with $r = 1, 2, \ldots k$) represents each single objective or goal.

It is important to notice that both these approaches are really subjective. In the first one the researcher decides which objective to keep as objective function and which others to consider as constraints; while in the second case, the researcher has to choose the U function form. It is clear that depending on which kind of analysis has been chosen, the results obtained from these two approaches might be very different. Therefore it is important to keep this in mind when evaluating the final solution.

Among several techniques elaborated for solving MCA problems we can distinguish three mathematical approaches that seem to offer the most powerful capability of territorial planning: multi-objective programming, goal programming and compromise programming.

1. *Multi-objective programming*: optimizes several objectives simultaneously subject to a set of linear constraints. Given this assumption it does not identify one optimal solution, but a set of Pareto-efficient solutions.
2. *Goal programming (GP)*: the model appears very similar to the traditional linear programming model. Here the set of constraints can be divided into two main sets. One contains flexible constraints represented by the goals, which take the mathematical forms indicated below; while the other set of constraints contains non-flexible con-

straints (the usual constraints). While in the case of multi-objective analysis objective function contains decisional variables, in goal programming the objective function contains variables that represent the deviation from the expected value of each goal. The main principal of the GP analysis consists of minimizing those differences: that is, to minimize the possibility of not achieving all the goals. The optimization process might be realized either by adopting a priority list of goals (*lexicographic goal programming*), or by weighting each goal based on its importance for the decision maker (*weighted goal programming*).

3. *Compromise programming*: identifies the set of solutions not dominated by other solutions (also known as Pareto's front of objective vectors) (Marangon, 1990). This model is based on Zeleny's theory (Cochrane and Zeleny, 1973). In particular, the solutions chosen minimize the distance from an ideal point. The distance concept takes a particular meaning here. It is considered as a proxy of preferences, expressing the dissatisfaction in trying to reach a goal. This technique reduces the efficient set into a subset, called a *compromise set*, which covers only a fraction of the Pareto-efficient frontier.

5.4   MULTI-OBJECTIVE MODELS: SOLUTION METHODOLOGY

5.4.1   Using Linear Programming in Multi-objective Problems

The goals in models of MCA are expressed as mathematical functions O_r, with $r = 1, 2 \ldots k$ as:

$$O_r = f_r(x_1, x_2, \ldots, x_n),$$

and their values depend from n decisional variables $(x_1, x_2, \ldots, x_n)$ representing the optimal problem solution.

A specific and realistic level that the general function can assume is its expected value or target, T_r. This is used for measuring at which level the model achieves each particular objective. When one objective is linked with a particular target, it is usually said that a goal has been defined.

The r-th objective may take one of the following mathematical forms:

$$f_r(x_j) \geq T_r,$$
$$f_r(x_j) \leq T_r,$$
$$f_r(x_j) = T_r,$$

where $j = 1, 2 \ldots n$.

Goals have the same mathematical structure as any other constraint in the traditional linear programming problem. However, in multi-criteria analysis, constraints represent a conceptual subgroup of goals. Constraints cannot be thought of as flexible goals because the right-hand side of the above equation must be satisfied by the model solution; otherwise the results are not acceptable. On the other hand, when we move objectives to where constraints define targets, there might be some goal not completely satisfied, and others that exceed their expected value. The difference in respect to usual linear programming models is in the philosophy of this model (MCA). We do not look only for optimal alternatives but for a strategy that best achieves the decision makers' criteria.

5.4.2   Pay-off Matrix

Problems of this type, where the decision variables are infinitely variable, subject to constraints and where there are multiple objectives, are often called *multiple-objective decision-making problems* (MODM). Although constraints and objective functions are often assumed to be linear, this is not always necessary. Where the problem is linear, its representation is just like that of the LP problem above, except that there are now several objective functions, not just one.

Nowadays the utility of using linear programming for solving multi-objective problems arises from its capacity of obtaining useful information on decisional problem characteristics. That information is widely used in more advanced processes.

The first step of this analysis controls for the so-called pay-off matrix. This matrix reports level values of each objective function obtained from optimizing separately each objective function entered in the multi-objective problem. At this stage goals are not yet settled. The solutions to those models are represented by the main diagonal of the matrix. The other elements of the matrix are the levels reached by other objectives in each LP problem (at each optimal point). Elements over the principal diagonal are called ideal values, while the minimum value of each column is called anti-ideal value. Using this matrix, it is possible to analyse the 'degree of conflict' between objective functions considered.

5.4.3   Pareto-efficient Frontier

Solution methods for MODM problems are often strongly problem-specific. However, a common feature of the search process for a solution is a concern to identify *efficient* solutions. The aim, broadly, is to restrict consideration to a (relatively small) set of solutions to the MODM problem that are explicitly not dominated by others.

The concept of Pareto efficiency has a fundamental rule within the multi-objective analysis, because each multi-objective technique works on seeking for solutions that lie on the frontier. This means that the solutions to these multi-objective models are such that none of them might reach a better level without implying for the others a lower level. The set of Pareto-efficient solutions identifies an area called 'Pareto-efficient frontier'. This is characterized by the fact that an objective function can reach a better level value only if that is compensated from a negative variation of some other objective function.

Using linear programming methods one can identify the frontier. This is obtainable by optimizing one objective function, and considering the others as constraints. Therefore solving as many LP problems as the number of objective functions considered and setting the others as constraints, it is possible to identify the frontier, ideal and anti-ideal values.

5.4.3.1 Discretization models

Techniques used for identifying a finite set of efficient alternatives are known as discretization methods. There are two main methods belonging to this class:

1. methods working on the full efficient frontier;
2. methods working only on part of the frontier.

Multi-objective analysis belongs to the first group. Among those, the most used methods are the *constrained method* and the so-called *weighting method*. The constrained method uses linear programming to optimize one objective function, moving the remaining objectives to the constraint set. In this case the Pareto frontier is obtained by evaluating the remaining functions at the optimal solution. On the other hand, weighting methodology maximizes an adding function of all objectives. A weight is attributed to each function depending on the decision maker's preferences. Solutions derive from weight variations.

The main inconvenience with these two methods is the huge number of solutions generated. Consequently recently researchers have been working on the identification of a reduced number of alternatives. In this case they speak about '*filtering techniques*'. The most simple is known as *predetermined convex combinations* (Steuer, 1986). This method works on a convex weight set applied at *compromise programming*.

5.4.4   The Trade-off between Two Objectives

The *trade-off* between objectives represents another basic concept in multi-objective analysis. This indicates the amount one objective function has to lose in order to increase by one unit the level reached by another objective function. So, for example, if we consider two efficient solutions A and B, their trade-off between j and k is given by:

$$T_{j,k} = \frac{f_j(A) - f_j(B)}{f_k(A) - f_k(B)}.$$

Multi-objective analysis can be considered as the first stage of finding the solution to multi-objective problems. MODM techniques therefore start by implementing a search for efficient solutions. Once these have been identified, they then move into a second phase in which different solutions are explicitly compared using the range of objective functions that are defined for the problem in question. In this first step it is not necessary to introduce into the model the preferences structure of the decision maker about the objectives defined.

The second stage involves identification of alternative strategic plans and of one unique solution for the model. This can be done using several methods, but it is first necessary to explicitly derive decision makers' preferences. Often this will involve explicit interaction with the user, who, directly or indirectly, will ultimately have to input views on the trade-offs or other measures of relative importance that he/she holds to be important between the competing objectives. Often the solutions found in this way cannot be *proved* to be optimal; the best that can be hoped for is that they are relatively good.

5.4.5   Using Compromise Programming

Compromise programming can be considered as a natural extension of multi-objective analysis. In fact by using multi-objective analysis we can identify a subset of possible solutions satisfying Pareto-efficiency conditions. The best solution for the decision maker, assuming that he is rational, is within that subset of solutions. In order to identify the optimal combination of objective functions considered, it is necessary to take into account the decision maker's preferences.

The main axiom of compromise programming is that the decision maker tends to achieve the solution closest to the ideal point (choice axiom). It is defined as that non-achievable solution – utopia – that would realize the whole set of objective functions at the same time. The ideal solution represents the reference point of the decision maker. In other words, the decision maker minimizes the distance between the ideal point and a possible efficient solution.

The unique assumption of this technique is that any decision maker tends to look for the closest solution to the ideal one. In order to evaluate the distance of one solution from the ideal one, it is necessary to introduce into the model a distance function. In the case of the West Garda Regional Forest the concept of distance is not used within its geometrical sense, but it represents a behaviour indicator of the decision maker's preferences.

The first step in applying the CP technique consists of defining a metric. (See the appendix to this chapter for the basic 'metric' concept).

Mathematically, the contribution of a single objective to the total variation from the ideal point is obtainable as follows:

$$d_i = y_i^* - f_i(X),$$

where d_i stands for contribution of objective i to the total distance from the ideal point, y_i^* represents the ideal value of objective i and $f_i(X)$ represents objective function while X is the vector of decisional variables. Contribution at the distance from all objective functions differs in general by measurement unit and therefore it needs to be normalized. Normalization can be done computing relative deviation rather than absolute ones as follows:

$$d_i = \frac{y_i^* - f_i(X)}{y_i^* - y_{i*}},$$

where y_{i*} represents the anti-ideal value of objective i. This function varies within the interval [0, 1]. It has value 0 if the function achieves the ideal solution or 1 when function level equals the anti-ideal value. Therefore, the difference to one measures the proportion of objective achievement. A slight variation of L_p – derived from the one reported above – measures the total distance from the ideal point:

$$L_p = \left[\sum_{i=1}^{n} \left| w_i \frac{y_i^* - f_i(X)}{y_i^* - y_{i*}} \right|^p \right]^{\frac{1}{p}},$$

where w_i represents the weight attached to each objective i-th from the decision maker. From a decisional point of view, introducing a weight expresses the contribution of the distance related to decision-maker preferences (the result proportional to the weight). For such a reason weighted distance value represents the 'distance' such as we think it is felt from the decision maker.

Therefore seeking the lowest value of L_p represents the best compromise solution because it results in being closer to the ideal solution respect to the others. Therefore when $p = 1$, the best compromise solution can be obtained solving the following problem:

$$\min_X L_1(X) = \left[\sum_{i=1}^{n} \left| w_i \frac{y_i^* - f_i(X)}{y_i^* - y_{i*}} \right| \right],$$
$$S.T. \Omega \in \mathfrak{R}_+^0$$

using the simplex method and introducing explicitly variables d_i in LP model:

$$\min \sum_{i=1}^{n} d_i$$

s.t.

$$f_i(X) + d_i \frac{y_i^* - y_{i*}}{w_i} \geq y_i^*$$

$$\Omega \in \mathfrak{R}_+^0.$$

Even in the case where $p = \infty$ we can use the simplex method applied to the following problem:

$$\min d$$

s.t.

$$f_i(X) + d \frac{y_i^* - y_{i*}}{w_i} \geq y_i^*$$

$$\Omega \in \mathfrak{R}_+^0.$$

However, non-linear algorithms need to be used when the metric is within the range $[0, \infty]$.

It is very useful for interpreting the results to measure how well the model performs in achieving each goal. To do so we define an index called *degree of goals achievement* as follows:

$$\left[1 - \frac{y_i^* - O_i}{y_i^* - y_{i*}} \right] \cdot 100.$$

Here, we use the actual solution for measuring the level O_i reached from goal i and compare it with the ideal and anti-ideal values.

5.4.5.1 Metric choice

One of the central issues of CP analysis is the metric choice. The best compromise solution, *ceteris paribus*, might change with the metric chosen.

Therefore the kind of metric used might have a precise effect on the decision made. As Yager (1978) pointed out, when $p = 1$, the minimization of $L_p(w)$ reflects the decision maker's interest in respect to the difference between each goal and its ideal point. In other words, the difference between the sum of achieved goal values by the actual solution and the sum of function levels at the ideal point corresponds to the case in which there is an 'absolute compensation' among all goals and a decrement in the objective function might be due to variation within objective functions.

Vice versa, if $p = \infty$ the model minimizes the maximum distance between different deviations: the same importance is attributed to all objectives. This means that goals do not compensate. In this case we consider as significant the objective function with the maximum variation from its ideal point, independently from what other functions do. The final evaluation of the solution can be improved by implementing the value of the function with the lowest value. The multi-objective model is forced to make all weighted distances as equal as possible.

In practice, experiences on natural resources planning and in particular on forest planning (Krawiec et al., 1991) have demonstrated that using metrics with $p > 1$ gives results more coherent and less biased than L_1. In fact, the main issue to be considered while setting managerial territorial plans is that many natural resources are unique and rare and thus difficult to rebuild and recover once damaged. They supply services that are important from many points of view, for example aesthetic, cultural and historical. Therefore, it is not plausible to justify their measure with an implicit compensation from an increment of other benefits arising from them. The compensation principle results are difficult to apply when solving environmental conflicts. This issue derives from the decision process on which the metric L_1 has been based. However experiences in this field demonstrate that the utility function resulting from this model formulation is not always valid for MODM problems characterized by conflicting goals.

5.5   IDENTIFYING THE BEST FOREST PLAN USING MULTI-CRITERIA ANALYSIS

This section applies methodologies described above to the West Garda Regional Forest using GIS data and decision-maker preferences.

The findings from GIS analysis show that the West Garda Regional Forest is characterized by a wide variety of vegetation (forests of black pine, red fir and chestnut trees, shrubby and herbaceous vegetation and rock vegetation), advantaged or disadvantaged by the environmental conditions of the place where it is located. In Chapter 2, land structure and

Table 5.1   Final macro-area centres from cluster analysis (Chapter 2)

	Areas				
	1	2	3	4	5
Naturalistic function	4.92	7.41	2.52	4.15	5.19
Productive function	5.40	0.35	1.30	1.33	5.68
Protective function	1.15	3.02	1.26	3.78	4.26
Tourist function	5.29	3.68	2.08	4.03	3.95

forest vegetation have contributed very much to the specific identification of five homogeneous macro-areas that represent the basic planning unit for the decision process. They result from area characteristics and therefore they are appropriate for the purpose of identifying an efficient policy from economic, managerial and biological points of view.

The goals identified by the administrative manager for this area are the following:

1. optimization of naturalistic capability: this objective includes conservation of the forest ecosystem, vegetation and fauna (naturalistic function);
2. timber production optimization (productive function);
3. hydrologic protection optimization: ensuring protection of the ecosystem from natural catastrophes caused by rain and wind erosion (protective function);
4. maximization of tourist and entertainment capabilities through efficient use of the territory and promotion of recreational purposes (tourist function).

Table 5.1 reports per macro-area (management sub-units) indices representing capability to supply environmental products and services in line with the goals set above. Those coefficients correspond to each cluster's centre resulting from the cluster analysis in Chapter 2. The multi-objective model will be based on these data.

5.5.1 Traditional MCA Application

The first step to be taken is to examine whether conflicts exist between goals and use a so-called *pay-off* (4×4) matrix in order to measure them.

Each element of this matrix derives from solving a maximization linear problem. For example, the first row of the *pay-off matrix* derives from solving the following linear problem:

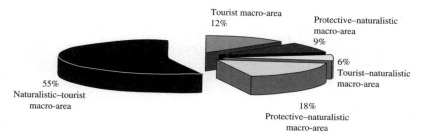

Figure 5.1   *Macro-area proportions*

$$\max_{x} O_r = \sum_{j=1}^{n} c_{jr} x_{rj}.$$
$$s.t.\Omega$$

Where r and j stand respectively for objective r and macro-area j, O_r represents management objective or goal r. Decisional variables x_{rj} represent hectares of area j used for objective r. While c_{jr} are indices representing capability of supplying environmental product and service in line with the goals O_r.

Combining GIS information with cluster analysis results (by macro-areas) we can identify the set of constraints Ω. Five main varieties of vegetation have been identified over the West Garda Regional Forest surface: forests, bushes, grass, rock vegetation and non-vegetation areas. Table 5.2 represents how each vegetation group covers the West Garda landscape in hectares and by macro-area.

Each variety of vegetation may affect the ability of the natural area in supplying naturalistic, productive, protective and/or tourist products and services. In fact it is to be noticed that while the naturalistic function might be improved by any type of vegetation, productive function is applicable only to those macro-areas where trees are present. In the same way, hydrological protection is not supplied in areas of poor vegetation because soil, on its own, cannot resist rain and wind erosion. Therefore in Table 5.3 the hectares in each macro-area are divided into objective functions taking into account constraints imposed by the vegetation distribution (based on information derived in Chapter 1).

We can therefore define five surface constraints: (1) total hectares of each area; (2) maximum number of hectares per function in each area; (3) total hectares per macro-area; (4) maximum number of hectares per macro-area located to each function; (5) minimum number of hectares for each function in the total area in order to ensure that each function is present over the area.[3]

Table 5.2   West Garda Regional Forest main vegetation groups in hectares by macro-area

	Forest [ha]	Bushes [ha]	Grass [ha]	Rock vegetation [ha]	No vegetation [ha]	Other [ha]	Total [ha]
Area 1	1246.50	22.75	10.25	26.00	3.75	25.75	1335
Area 2	171.75	471.25	30.25	49.25	209.50	11.00	943
Area 3	309.50	26.00	32.25	50.00	23.00	180.25	621
Area 4	1234.50	224.00	101.00	266.00	128.00	60.50	2014
Area 5	5796.75	170.75	9.25	71.25	47.00	56.00	6151
Total	8759.00	914.75	183.00	462.50	411.25	333.50	11 064

Table 5.3   Hectares per macro-area per function based on vegetation

	Naturalistic function	Productive function	Protective function	Tourist function	Total
Area 1	1135	1272.25	1331.25	1305.25	1335
Area 2	943	182.75	733.50	684.25	943
Area 3	621	489.75	598.00	548.00	621
Area 4	2014	1295.00	1886.00	1620.00	2014
Area 5	6151	5852.75	6104.00	6032.75	6151
Total	11 064	9092.50	10 652.75	10 190.25	–

The main diagonal of the pay-off matrix, therefore, represents the solution to each of the four problems, while the off-diagonal elements are the values reached by each of the remaining objectives evaluated at the optimal point of each problem.

The pay-off matrix (Table 5.4) highlights that there are some typical contrasts between managerial goals. In particular, there is a deep conflict between the naturalistic function and the use of the landscape for human utility. If the productive function increases, for example, there will be a decrement in naturalistic and hydrologic protective functions.

The ideal alternative is reported in bold characters in the pay-off matrix. This solution would optimize all goals at the same moment. However, because of the conflicts existing and described above, the ideal solution is obviously not achievable. On the other hand, the worst solution, reported in italic in Table 5.4, achieves the minimum value of each goal.

Once we have realized that because of the conflict existing between goals, the ideal solution cannot be achieved, then it is necessary to define a set of

Table 5.4   Pay-off matrix

	Naturalistic function	Productive function	Protective function	Tourist function
Naturalistic function	**5 387 429**	22 247	*27 767*	*60 186*
Productive function	163 598	**4 253 676**	66 552	89 204
Protective function	153 164	74 372	**3 740 676**	91 854
Tourist function	*163 598*	*22 760*	58 017	**4 131 518**

Table 5.5   Weights applied into multi-objective model

Objectives	Scenario A1	Scenario A2	Scenario A3
	Actual forest plan	Non-participative regional management programme	Participative regional management programme
Naturalistic function	30	40	72
Productive function	25	10	17
Protective function	21	20	2
Tourist function	24	30	8

finite management alternatives applicable (scenarios) and chose between them. In doing so, it is important to identify priorities between objectives. A common method used for capturing the preferences of the administrative manager's and interested groups' is to assign a weight to each of the environmental goals considered.

In general in territorial planning studies it is usually possible to identify three types of decision makers: technicians or experts in particular environmental topics, who base their preference on their technical knowledge; policymakers and so called 'participant group' decision makers. However, whoever is the decision maker, the linkage between preferences and weights is the most delicate process of all this analysis.

Thus, in defining the set of possible managerial alternative programmes, we consider here three scenarios (Table 5.5). Each scenario represents different preferences and priorities among naturalistic, protective, productive and tourist function using different weights. The first scenario – A1 – represents the *actual forest planning* of the West Garda Regional Forest. To obtain the actual weights attributed at the four goals, we use a weighted average of total hectares actually allocated per function (Table 5.5 column one). Although leaving little difference in the respective importance attributed to the four environmental functions considered, this policy focuses especially on developing the naturalistic characteristics of the area. In the second scenario – A2 – the managerial policy is defined taking into consideration only managerial and local administrators' preferences and priorities, based on their knowledge of the area. This managerial alternative is therefore called the *non-participative regional management programme*. In this case, weights are derived from direct interviews collected at the Regional Forestry Agency of Lombardy region (ERSAF) and at some local councils of Garda Lake. From Table 5.5, second column, it is possible to see that the manager and administrator of this natural area would prioritize the area for naturalistic and entertainment aims. However, in order to support these two main goals, they need also to maintain good conditions in the area in order to prevent, for example, hydrological catastrophes caused by rain and wind and to conserve the forest itself.

The last scenario – A3 – represents a policy designed taking into account the decision-making process of tourist and resident preferences. Therefore this management alternative is called the *participative regional management programme*. Users' preferences derive from the findings of the contingent valuation method. This group of decision makers is not really participating in the decision-making process, but it is important to take into account views and wishes of users and interested groups in order to ensure that natural resources are useful and available to everybody. In this case users prefer this area to be allocated to naturalistic functions such as fauna habitat and vegetation maintenance.

The alternative scenarios described above represent three possible kinds of intervention that might be named as follows:

A1. multifunctional area with naturalistic tendency (actual forest plan);
A2. naturalistic and tourist area (non-participative regional management programme);
A3. naturalistic area (participative regional management programme).

Compromise programming techniques identify the best combination of goals indicating the proportion of hectares to be allocated to each function within the West Garda Regional Forest and each macro-area.[4] Table 5.6 reports optimal solutions by scenario, while Figures 5.2–5.4 represent graphically the proportion of area allocated to each objective in the whole West Garda Regional Forest and in each macro-area identified in Chapter 2.

It is, at this point, interesting to compare these findings with the vocational function of each macro-area studied in Chapter 2. We expect that the best solution would tend to match with the vocation of each macro-area.

Table 5.6 *Distribution of the functions over the West Garda Regional Forest*

	Area 1	Area 2	Area 3	Area 4	Area 5	Total
Scenario 1: Actual Forest Plan						
Naturalistic function		100	2		31	26
Productive function	3				37	21
Protective function				43	32	26
Tourist function	97		98	57		27
Scenario 2: Non-participative regional management programme						
Naturalistic function	3	100			57	40
Productive function			28			20
Protective function				3	34	19
Tourist function	97		72	97	9	39
Scenario 3: Participative regional management programme						
Naturalistic function	4	100	30	100	85	76
Productive function	96				15	20
Protective function			35			2
Tourist function			35			2

For example, the optimal solution for the first area, called 'tourist area' from the *vocation* analysis, is tourist and entertainment products and service supply in two out of three scenarios. For the second area, called the protective–naturalistic area, the optimal solution obtained from all scenarios is naturalistic use. The third area, previously named tourist–naturalistic area, is mainly associated with tourist activities. Only the non-participative regional management programme would suggest using this area for wood production. The fourth area – the protective–naturalistic area – in the first two scenarios would be mainly used for supply of tourist entertainment and activities and protective services, while in the third scenario it would be much more appropriate to use it for naturalistic aims. Finally the last macro-area, that vocational analysis suggests would be better off when used for naturalistic and tourist purposes, but would also have discrete capabilities for productive and protective functions, has been allocated to a mixture of uses by all scenarios considered above.

Using optimal solutions by scenario, Table 5.7 reports the level to which goals are achieved by each function. Thus, we can reinterpret the optimal solution as distance from the ideal solution computed in a pay-off matrix and evaluate how well each scenario achieves the goals (Table 5.8).

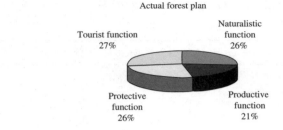

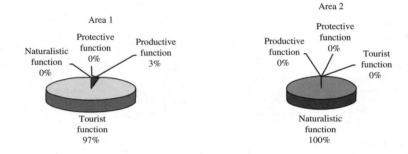

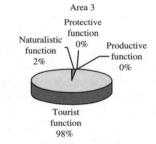

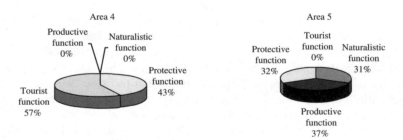

*Figure 5.2   Scenario 1: actual forest plan's optimal combination and
distribution of forest objectives*

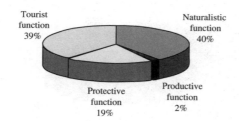

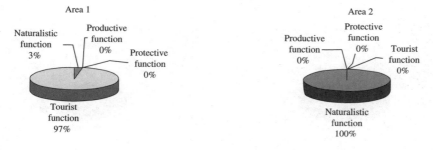

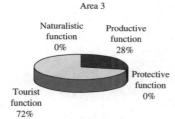

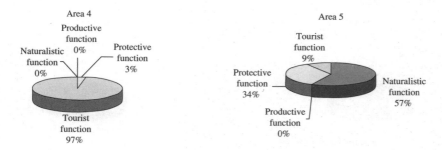

*Figure 5.3   Scenario 2: non-participative regional management
              programme's optimal combination and distribution of forest
              objectives*

Management

Participative regional managerial programme

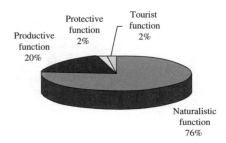

Naturalistic
function
76%

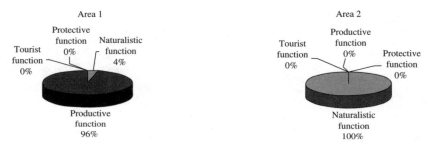

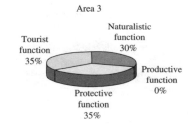

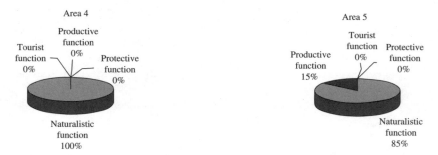

Figure 5.4   Scenario 3: participative regional management programme's
optimal combination and distribution of forest objectives

Table 5.7   *Objective function levels by scenario evaluated at the optimal solution point*

	Naturalistic function	Productive function	Protective function	Tourist function
A1	1 739 967	1 304 808	1 153 162	1 294 221
A2	2 581 081	22 247	896 639	1 784 197
A3	4 336 980	1 198 792	27 767	60 186

Table 5.8   *Achievement of goals by scenario*

	Naturalistic function	Productive function	Protective function	Tourist function
A1	30	30	30	30
A2	46	0	23	42
A3	80	28	0	0

The ideal solution would achieve the optimal value of all functions at the same time. As we noticed above, this is not the case because of conflicts existing between goals. Computing the distance between ideal and anti-ideal solutions, and the level of each objective function we can measure how well each scenario meets the goals using the following index:

$$d_i^k = \frac{y_i^k - y_{i*}}{y_i^* - y_{i*}}.$$

Note that d_i^k tends to 1 when the level of the goal i in scenario k tends to the ideal value. Therefore, we can interpret Table 5.8 as follows:

1. the actual forest plan (A1) realizes all objective functions at a 30 per cent level of the ideal solution.
2. in scenario A2 (non-participative regional management programme) naturalistic and tourist activities are achieved respectively at 46 per cent and 42 per cent level of their ideal values, while the protective function is achieved at 23 per cent of its ideal value.
3. The participative regional management programme achieves 80 per cent level of ideal naturalistic aim and 28 per cent of ideal productive level.

5.6 IDENTIFYING THE BEST FOREST PLAN INTEGRATING GEOGRAPHICAL INFORMATION SYSTEM, CONTINGENT VALUATION AND MULTI-CRITERIA ANALYSIS

The methodology presented so far represents the traditional approach of natural science and urban studies to forest management problems. However, it is important for the decision process to result in integrating completely the physical and biological information noted above with users' and decision makers' preferences, and economic constraints. In doing so, we propose a new multi-objective approach that integrates bio-ecological information obtained from geographical information system (GIS) analysis with users' preferences derived from the contingent valuation method (CVM).

Data collection and data analysis processes can be summarized as follows:

- GIS analysis: quantitative estimation of each objective function.
- Contingent valuation: economic estimation of each objective function.
- Multi-criteria analysis: identification of the optimal combination of functions subject to maximization of managerial revenues and other constraints.

5.6.1   The Data

Quantitative index levels of naturalistic, productive, protective and tourist products supply per macro-area are the same used in the previous analysis and can be obtained from GIS (Table 5.1). The price associated with productive function products derives from the average price of the wood products per hectare on the local market; the prices of naturalistic, protective and tourist activities during the summer derive from contingent valuation findings per hectare assuming that the number of visitors was 11 598 per day. Prices are derived from user preferences on protecting nature, maintenance of entertainment structures and improvement of tourist activities; and the economic value associated with protective function is drawn from the users' willingness to pay for a yearly membership fee for maintaining the conditions of the natural area as they are today and so that future generations would be able to use the park as they do today.

Adding all this new information into our multi-objective model for each scenario and solving it as above it allows the new model to take into account both decision makers' and users' preferences. The decision process becomes fairer for the social groups who are involved in the process of determining which environmental policy should best be applied to each natural area.

5.6.2 Setting a New Multi-objective Function

The integration of biological and economic data allows interpretation of a multi-objective function from an economic point of view. In fact, evaluating each objective function using the prices of its products and services we can rewrite the previous multi-objective model as follows:

Revenue = Sum [price*(function level*hectares)].

While the multi-objective problem solved in section 5.5 represents the maximum net benefits achievable in quantitative levels from the management of the West Garda Regional Forest, the new multi-objective function evaluated at the optimal solution point represents total revenues of public administration obtained by supplying environmental products and services in the area. Formally we can write the new multi-objective problem as follows:

$$\max_{X} R = \phi(p_1 O_1, p_2 O_2, \ldots, p_k O_k)$$
$$S.T.\ \Omega \in \Re_+^0$$

where the policymaker maximizes total revenues as a function of all environmental objectives O_i evaluated at their market price p_i. The set of constraints Ω on forest dimension, macro-area surfaces and minimum supply of each environmental function are the same as before.

In order to be able to compare the results of the new multi-objective problem with the previous ones, we apply a compromise programming model setting the mathematical problem as follows:

$$\min_{X} \Lambda_1(X) = \left[\sum_{i=1}^{n} \left| w_i \frac{p_i y_i^* - p_i f_i(X)}{p_i y_i^* - p_i y_{i*}} \right| \right]$$
$$S.T.\ \Omega \in \Re_+^0$$

The vector of decisional variables X represents again hectares to be allocated at each managerial objective. w_i represents the weight attached to each objective i-th by the regional management programme under examination. $p_i\ y_i^*$ represents the ideal revenue value obtained maximizing expected revenues produced by objective i independently from all the other goals, while y_{i*} represents the anti-ideal revenue value (or minimum revenue) obtainable from objective i.

Table 5.9   *Pay-off matrix with hypothesis of revenue maximization*
                (in euros)

	Naturalistic function	Productive function	Protective function	Tourist function
Naturalistic function	19 802 816.76	62 594.57	95 712.77	279 728.24
Productive function	601 344.34	968 944.93	229 406.75	367 642.84
Protective function	562 991.73	15 994.73	12 894 276.11	426 910.45
Tourist function	601 344.34	340 221.24	199 987.45	19 202 177.38

5.6.3   Multi-criteria Approach

This section recalls the scenario plans reported in Table 5.5 and analyses
them using our new economic hypothesis that administration of the area
should maximize monetary revenues given geographical and morphological constraints (area vocation). In order to distinguish and compare the
new results with previous ones obtained from application of the traditional
approach, we rename the non-participative regional management programme A2 as REV2 and participative regional management programme
A3 as REV3. The analysis process follows the same procedure explained
above. Therefore the first step is to build the pay-off matrix.

The pay-off matrix (Table 5.9) highlights again the existence of conflicts
between managerial goals, in particular that arising from use of the territory
for tourist and entertainment aims and both productive and protective–
naturalistic functions.

Multi-objective model solutions represent hectares allocated to each
function per macro-area in each scenario. Evaluation of the multi-objective
function at an optimal solution point gives the expected total revenue
obtainable by the alternative scenarios. Optimal solutions by scenario are
reported in Table 5.10 and graphically in Figures 5.5 and 5.6 as the proportion of hectares allocated to each goal in the total area and in each
macro-area identified in Chapter 2.

In particular, using the new decisional rule, choosing the natural and
tourist park option (REV2) the optimal allocation of objective functions
would be 65 per cent of the total area to naturalistic purposes, 31 per cent
to tourist entertainment, while protective and productive functions would
be split between the 4 per cent remaining.

On the other hand, if the policymaker decides to follow a participative
regional management programme – naturalistic area (REV3) – the best
combination of environmental functions would designate 94 per cent of the

Table 5.10   *Distribution of the functions over each macro-area by scenario using multi-objective model to maximize administration's total revenues*

	Area 1	Area 2	Area 3	Area 4	Area 5	Total
Scenario A2: Non-participative regional management programme						
Naturalistic function	3	100			100	65
Productive function			28			2
Protective function				11		2
Tourist function	97		72	89		31
Scenario A3: Participative regional management programme						
Naturalistic function	100	100	2	100	100	94
Productive function			28			2
Protective function			35			2
Tourist function			35			2

total park territory to be used for naturalistic purposes, while the remaining environmental services would be left at a minimum level of the usual natural area maintenance. In particular, only the third macro-area (see Chapter 2) is designed as a multi-functional area, while all the others are used for naturalistic aims.

In order to measure how well each scenario achieves managerial goals we compare the optimal value obtained from solving the model and the ideal and anti-ideal values of each goal. Ideal and anti-ideal values of each function are reported respectively in bold and italic type in the pay-off matrix (Table 5.4). Table 5.11 reports expected total revenue obtainable from the application of each scenario, and reinterprets them as a proportion of the total revenue per scenario (by row).

Table 5.12 reports a measure of goal achievement by scenario. Choosing the non-participative regional management programme it would be possible to achieve 73 per cent of the ideal solution of the naturalistic function and 35 per cent of the tourist function. While choosing a participative regional management programme (REV3) the only goal fully achieved would be the naturalistic one.

5.7   CONCLUSIONS

The aim of this chapter is to describe the methodological aspects of the multi-criteria analysis applied to the forest's management. It proposes

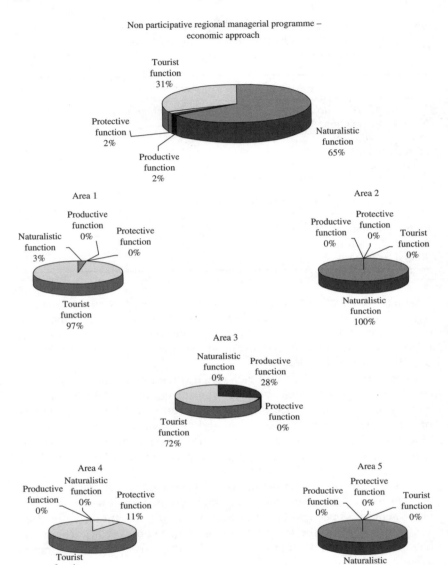

Figure 5.5 *Scenario 2: non-participative regional management programme optimal forest objectives combination and distribution from multi-objective model maximizing administration's total revenues*

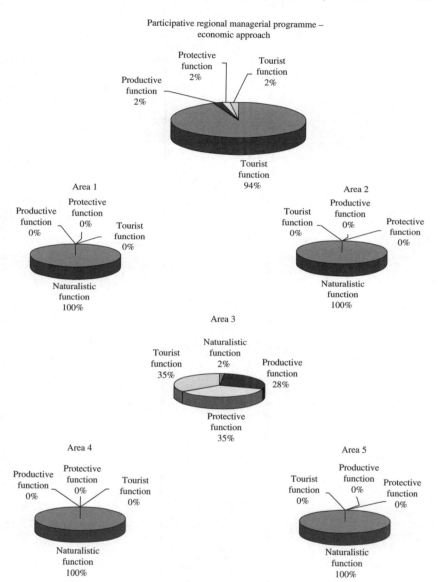

Figure 5.6 Scenario 3: Participative regional management programme optimal forest objectives combination and distribution from multi-objective model maximizing administration's total revenues

Table 5.11 Total revenue by scenario (in euros) and proportion of goal achieved with respect to the ideal solution

	Naturalistic function		Productive function		Protective function		Tourist function		Total euros
	Euros	%	Euros	%	Euros	%	Euros	%	
REV2	14 621 462.92	67	625.95	0	287 138.16	1	6 828 902.99	31	21 738 130.01
REV3	19 802 816.76	98	625.95	6	95 712.89	4	279 728.03	1	20 178 883.63

Table 5.12   Achievement of goals

	REV2	REV4
Naturalistic function	73	100
Productive function	0	0
Protective function	1	0
Tourist function	35	0

a new approach that integrates bio-ecological information obtained from geographical information system (GIS) analysis with the forest users' preferences derived from the contingent valuation method (CVM). In doing so, it defines for each scenario the best combination of managerial interventions, which maximizes expected administrative revenues respecting users' preferences. We apply this methodology to the West Garda Regional Forest.

The first step defines a set of managerial alternative strategies. We simulate three scenarios: (1) a multifunctional park with a naturalistic tendency (the actual forest plan); (2) a naturalist and tourist park (the non-participative regional management programme) where the managerial policy is defined taking into consideration only the management or administrator's preferences, based on their technical knowledge of the area; (3) a naturalistic park (participative regional management programme) which assumes a participatory planning process where decisions are made after finding out the preference structure of users (tourists and residents).

The second step of this chapter compares two different approaches. The first approach maximizes an objective function representing the net benefits in the quantitative levels of functions supplied by the West Garda Regional Forest, while in the second one the objective function acquires an economic meaning: it maximizes the expected revenues of the administrative government. In doing so, the model integrates quantitative function levels supplied by the West Garda Regional Forest with tourists' and residents' (users') willingness to pay a hypothetical entrance ticket and a yearly membership fee for maintenance and improvement of tourist infrastructures and protection of the landscape quality. It is important to notice that the second approach allows decision makers to identify the best location of environmental functions taking into account users' preferences, weighting each function using CVM estimates in all scenarios. In this way the decision process becomes participative in all scenarios. This enables the decision maker to anticipate possible conflicts and to design forest management programmes able to gain maximum satisfaction from all interested groups (such as tourists, citizens, tourist sector unions and so on).

The findings for each alternative management plan can be summarized as follows:

Option 1: Actual Forest Plan

In this case multi-criteria analysis optimizes the objective functions using only the first approach attaching the actual weights assigned to naturalistic, productive, protective and tourist functions derived from GIS analysis (0.30, 0.25, 0.21, 0.24 respectively).

Solutions to these models indicate the proportion of total hectares to be allocated to each function within the West Garda Regional Forest:

Scenario 1	Approach 1 Non-economic approach
Naturalistic function	0.26
Productive function	0.21
Protective function	0.26
Tourist function	0.27

Option 2: Non-participative Regional Management Programme

In this case we consider the West Garda Regional Forest manager's preferences as weights (0.3, 0.1, 0.2, and 0.4). In this case the multi-criteria model optimizes the objective functions using both approaches (approach 1 – non-economic; approach 2 – economic) and the solution by approach in terms of proportion of hectares allocated at each objective would be as follows:

Scenario 2	Approach 1 Non-economic approach	Approach 2 Economic approach
Naturalistic function	0.40	0.65
Productive function	0.02	0.02
Protective function	0.19	0.02
Tourist function	0.39	0.31

Option 3: Participative Regional Management Programme

In the third case, objective functions weight naturalistic, productive, protective and tourist functions based on tourist and resident preference structure. Our findings follow:

Scenario 3	Approach 1 Non-economic approach	Approach 2 Economic approach
Naturalistic function	0.76	0.94
Productive function	0.20	0.02
Protective function	0.02	0.02
Tourist function	0.02	0.02

In general, it is plausible to think that the Regional Forestry Agency of Lombardy region (ERSAF) could extend the methodology suggested in this chapter to other state/regional forest areas and natural reserves. This work integrates GIS territorial analysis, contingent valuation analysis (CVM) and multi-criteria analysis in order to find the optimal multifunctional rule combining naturalistic, productive, protective and tourist functions, taking into account both managers' and users' needs together with geographical and bio-ecological characteristics. The advantage of using multi-criteria analysis is that it helps to combine environmental objectives defining for each managerial plan its optimal combination in the forest territory. However, MCA does not identify the best managerial plan among the set of Pareto-efficient strategies considered. The choice of the best managerial programme for a certain area should derive from comparing the impacts of each managerial alternative on the local economy and anticipating the possible conflicts arising. These issues are left to the following chapters.

APPENDIX: THE CONCEPT OF METRIC

The traditional measure of distance d between two points $x_1 = (x_{11}, x_{12})$ and $x_2 = (x_{21}, x_{22})$ on the plan can be computed using Pythagoras' theorem:

$$d = [(x_{11} - x_{21})^2 + (x_{12} - x_{22})^2]^{\frac{1}{2}}.$$

Such definition can be exported to n-dimensional space as follows:

$$d = \left[\sum_{i=1}^{n} (x_{i1} - x_{i2})^2 \right]^{\frac{1}{2}}.$$

In the nineteenth century the concept of family of distance functions was introduced into mathematics as a generalization of the traditional Euclidean distance, which can be expressed as follows:

$$L_p = \left[\sum_{i=1}^{n} |x_{i1} - x_{i2}|^p \right]^{\frac{1}{p}}.$$

Each value of parameter p is associated with a distance measure definition. Thus the Euclidean measure of distance becomes a special case of the function L_p with $p = 2$. Other special cases from the function L_p are obtained when $p = 1$ (Manhattan distance), $p = 2$ (Euclidean distance) and when $p = \infty$ (Chebychev distance):

$$L_1 = \left[\sum_{i=1}^{n} |x_{i1} - x_{i2}| \right],$$

$$L_2 = \left[\sum_{i=1}^{n} |x_{i1} - x_{i2}|^2 \right]^{\frac{1}{2}},$$

$$L_\infty = \lim_{p \to \infty} \left[\sum_{i=1}^{n} |x_{i1} - x_{i2}|^p \right]^{\frac{1}{p}} = \max_i |x_{i1} - x_{i2}|.$$

It is possible to verify that an increasing p value assumes higher weights for a bigger gap. The extreme case considers $p = \infty$ where the distance measure derives only from the biggest deviation. Such property has no practical application within Euclidean space because distances with $p > 2$ are not possible. It is important to remember that in this study the concept of distance is not its typical geometrical meaning, but it is meant to represent different social behaviour in solving a complex problem involving potential conflict.

NOTES

1. In practice this means to identify management plans: each of those meant to satisfy each goal differently.
2. For example if one section of the park is used as fauna reserve and tourist-naturalistic purposes, it would be necessary to make it easily accessible for tourists. Therefore, it would need new plan metric arrangements and volumetric assessments.
3. With regard to the last, it has been agreed that all the functions must be present in each macro-area at the level of 2 per cent of their total surface.
4. Multi-objective models have been solved using GAMS (general algebraic modelling system).

BIBLIOGRAPHY

Aronoff, S. (1989), *GIS: A Management Perspective*, Ottawa: WDL Publications.
Ausenda, F., R. Rossi and D. Niero (1996), *Studio degli aspetti turistico-ricreativi del Parco Naturale Alto-Garda Bresciano*, ARF – Regione Lombardia, Internal Edition.
Baldani, J., J. Bradfield and R.W. Turner (eds) (2004), *Mathematical Economics*, Mason, OH: Thomson South-Western.
Bazzani, G.M. (1995), 'La teoria della decisione multicriteriale: un'introduzione', *Rivista di Economia Agraria*, **1**, 123–48.
Bendavid-Val, A. (1991), *Regional and Local Economic Analysis for Practitioners*, 4th edn, New York: Praeger Publishers.
Boyle, K.J. and R.C. Bishop (1988), 'Welfare measurements using contingent valuation: a comparison of techniques', *American Journal of Agricultural Economics*, **70**, 20–28.
Buongiorno, J. and J.K. Gilless (1987), *Forest Management and Economics*, New York: Macmillan.
Burrough, P.A. (1986), *Principles of Geographic Information System for Land Resources Assessment*, Oxford University Press: Clarendon.
Castagnoli, E. and L. Peccati (1990), *Matematica per l'Analisi Economica. Ottimizzazione Statica e Dinamica*, vol. 2, Etas Libri, Milan.
Cochrane, J.L. and M. Zeleny, (1973), *Multiple Criteria Decision Making*, Columbia: University of South Carolina Press.
Eastman, J.R., P.A.K. Kyem, J. Toledano and W. Jin (1993), *GIS and Decision Making. Explorations in Geographical Information System Technology*, vol. 4, Geneva: UNITAR.
Folmer, H., H.L. Gabel and H. Landis (1995), *Principles of Environmental and Resource Economics*, Aldershot, UK and Brookfield, USA: Edward Elgar.
Hazell, P.B.H. and R.D. Norton (1986), *Mathematical Programming for Economic Analysis in Agriculture*, New York: Macmillan.
Krawiec, B., I. Bernetti, L. Casini and D. Romano (1991), 'La pianificazione dell'azienda forestale: un'analisi delle moderne tecniche di gestione', *Studi di Economia e Diritto*, **40**, 255–306.
Lebart, L., A. Morineau and M. Piron (1997), *Statistique exploratoire multidimensionnelle*, Paris: Dunod.
Maguire, D.J., M.F. Goodchild and D.W. Rhind (eds) (1991), *Geographical Information Systems*, London: Longman.

Marangon, F. (1990), 'Scelte imprenditoriali e moderne tecniche di gestione dell'azienda agraria', *Bollettino degli Interessi Sardi*, **1**, 51–98.

Nijkamp, P. and P. Rietveldt (1996), 'Multiple objective decision analysis in regional economics', in *Handbook of Regional and Urban Economics*, Amsterdam: North Holland.

Paris, Q. (1991), *Programmazione Lineare. Un'Interpretazione Economica*, Bologna: Il Mulino.

Per-Olov, J. (1993), *Cost–Benefit Analysis of Environmental Change*, Cambridge, UK: Cambridge University Press.

Per-Olov, J. (1987), *The Economic Theory and Measurement of Environmental Benefits*, Cambridge: Cambridge University Press.

Perali, F., A. Zago, N. Gallinaro and M. Carta (1998), 'Studio di Metodologie per la Gestione Multifunzionale dei Complessi Demaniali e delle Riserve Naturali Gestite dall'Azienda Regionale delle Foreste Regione Lombardia – La FDR Gardesana Occidentale', Internal Edition, compiled in Department of Economics, University of Verona.

Rehman, T. and C. Romero (1993), 'The application of the MCDM paradigm to the management of agricultural systems: some basic considerations', *Agricultural Systems*, **41**, 239–55.

Sneath, P.H. and R.R. Sokal (1973), *Numerical Taxonomy*, San Francisco: Freeman.

Steuer, R.E. (1986), *Multiple Criteria Optimization: Theory, Computation, an Application*, New York: John Wiley & Sons, Inc.

Thorndike, R.L. (1953), 'Who Belongs in the Family', *Psychometrika*, **18**, 267–76.

Tomlin, C.D. (1990), *Geographic Information System and Cartographic Modeling*, New Jersey: Prentice-Hall.

Welsh, M.P. and R.C. Bishop (1993), 'Multiple bounded discrete choice models', in John C. Bergstrom (eds), *Benefits and Costs Transfer in Natural Resource Planning: Sixth Interim Report*, compiled in Department of Agricultural and Applied Economics, University of Georgia.

Yager, R.R. (1978), 'Fuzzy decision making including unequal objectives', *Fuzzy Sets and Systems*, **1**, 87–95.

6. Simulating the impact on the local economy of alternative management scenarios for natural areas

Paola De Agostini, Stefania Lovo, Francesco Pecci, Federico Perali and Michele Baggio

6.1 INTRODUCTION

This study estimates the impact on the local economy of alternative management scenarios of the West Garda Regional Forest which is centrally managed by regional authorities located in Milan. Because the forest is part of the High Garda Natural Park[1] (Figure 6.1), which extends over nine municipalities of the Brescia province and is managed locally, the implementation of the best management programme depends critically on the impact on the local economy.

The multi-criteria analysis, described in Chapter 5, identified two alternative optimal combinations of the naturalistic, protective, productive and tourist functions. One is defined as non-participative because it involves only the preferences of central management. The other is the participative strategy which takes into account the users' preferences as revealed by the estimated contingent prices.

We intend to simulate the effects of the participative and non-participative strategies on the entire economy of the park because what is best for the central management, as investigated in the previous chapter, may not be best for the local management that is concerned with maximizing the impact on the local economy and the welfare of the local citizens. The convergence of these objectives is desirable to avoid conflicts between the central and the local management.

The tool used in this study to estimate the impact on the local economy of the different management interests in the West Garda Regional Forest is the SAM multiplier analysis applied at the local level of a territory. The social accounting matrices (SAM) are adequate tools to represent the local

Note: The shaded part of the figure represents the area covered by the West Garda Regional Forest.

Source: ERSAF (Regional Forestry Agency of Lombardy Region).

Figure 6.1 West Garda Regional Forest as a part of the High Garda Natural Park

economy. They define the relationships between local firms and households as well as the physical flows from and to the rest of the economy. They provide a direct and synthetic picture of sector interdependencies, formation of household income, and the dependence of households on local services and productive activities.

To apply the impact analysis at a local level, we need to know with an acceptable level of precision the economic structure of the territory

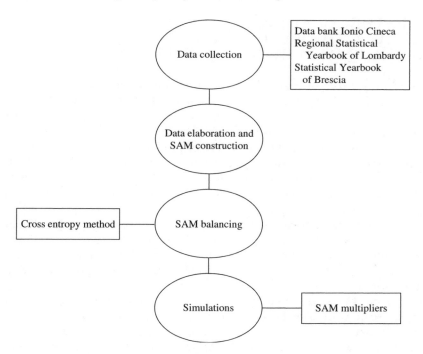

Figure 6.2   Stages of the impact analysis

(Dorward et al., 2003; Bendavid-Val, 1983). The data available from official sources are not organized with the purpose of building tables of sector interdependencies and social accounting matrices at a territorial level. Therefore, the information is often not available at the level of aggregation desirable for the efficient planning of local development activities. This was the most evident constraint faced during the SAM construction.

The SAM analysis shows that the accounting representation of the local economy carries weight and that the participative programme, if chosen by the central regional management, would also be the most desirable programme at the local level.

As described in Figure 6.2, the analysis develops in four phases: data collection and elaboration, construction of the SAM, its balancing, and simulations. This chapter follows the same sequence. Section 2 describes the data required for constructing and balancing the local SAM. Section 3 describes the SAM multiplier analysis. Section 4 presents simulations and results of the impact on the local economic system of the managerial alternatives described above. Section 5 draws some conclusions.

6.2 THE LOCAL SOCIAL ACCOUNTING MATRIX FOR THE WEST GARDA AREA: DESIGN AND DATA REQUIREMENTS

A SAM is a tool of regional analysis providing useful guidelines for the development of a regional economy (Fannin, 2001). It is a system of social accounts which reproduces the economic flows in a particular area. The SAM describes the relevant features of the socio-economic structure and the relationships between the structure of production and the distribution of income and expenditure among households in a particular area. An estimation of the public impact of policies and the examination of the links between social and economic development is useful to support the local policy-making decision process.

A SAM is the natural extension of the input–output model. It includes inter-industry transactions, payments of productive factors, household expenditure, income transfers, government expenditure and transactions with the rest of the economy, defining the circular flows of income within the economic area of interest.

The most evident limitation of this powerful instrument is represented by the scarcity of available information at the regional and local level that is necessary to build a SAM. To describe the High Garda Natural Park's economy we used a simplified SAM which still reflects the structural characteristics of the local economy necessary to estimate the impact of a change of the forest management strategies on the local economy.

Three sectors have been considered: agriculture, tourism and a third aggregate sector including all the other sectors such as industry, construction, commerce and other relatively less important economic activities. Our SAM considers only one social institution, the household, and gives less importance to savings and capital. The structure is reproduced in Figure 6.3 while Box 6.1 describes the SAM contents.

6.2.1 SAM Construction and Balancing

The construction of a local social accounting matrix is a difficult task, mostly because of the scarcity of local statistical information organized at a local level. As a consequence the researcher is forced to use alternative and indirect sources to make hypotheses and get information about local economic entities (Bendavid-Val, 1983).

Within the park, the national statistical office (ISTAT) identifies two local labour systems (LLS) gravitating around the municipalities of Limone and Toscolano Maderno. A local labour system is an area composed by several adjacent municipalities defined on the basis of the

	Agriculture	Tourism	Other sectors	Labour	Capital	Residents	Rest of the economy	Total
Agriculture						Domestic consumption of local agricultural products	Final and intermediate agricultural exported products	Total sales of the agriculture sector
Tourism	Intersector transactions					Expenditure within the park area by resident tourists	Tourist expenditure within the park area by non-resident tourists	Total sales of the tourist sector
Other sectors							'Exported' intermediate and final products and local services	Total sales of other sectors
Labour	Labour employed in agriculture	Labour employed in tourism	Labour employed in other sectors				Income of residents employed in non-local firms, in health and education sectors	Total labour of residents + labour of non-residents employed in local firms
Capital	Capital employed	Capital employed	Capital employed					Total employed capital in local firms
Residents				Labour income			Other income	Resident household incomes
Rest of the economy	'Imported' intermediate goods	'Imported' intermediate goods	'Imported' intermediate goods	Non-resident workers employed in local firms	Capital supply	Domestic consumption of 'imported' goods and services and savings	Balancing account	Balancing account
Total	Total agriculture production	Total tourist production	Total production of other sectors	Labour supply	Capital supply	Total residents' consumption	Balancing account	

Figure 6.3   The local SAM for the High Garda Natural Park

BOX 6.1   DESCRIPTION OF THE SAM CONTENTS

Agriculture: includes cereals, permanent cultivations and livestock. The other productive activities and resident and non-resident consumers' demand for intermediate and final consumption of agricultural goods are included in this row. The value of intermediate goods sold to firms located outside the territory of interest is included in the column 'rest of the economy'. The column includes the consumption of intermediate goods by the agricultural sector and the value of the productive factors, labour and capital, used in the production process. Intermediate goods purchased by firms located outside the territory are listed in the column 'rest of the economy'.

Tourism: includes services offered to the park tourists such as hotels and restaurants, food, drinks, recreational and cultural activities. Hotels and restaurants are included in the tourist sector because their returns are assumed to come entirely from tourism. The other items are partially counted because tourists are only present in some periods of the year and part of the revenue comes from local consumption.

Other sectors: includes all the other sectors in the territory like industry, construction, commercial activities, transport and so on. The main activities are commerce (wholesale and retail), construction and other professional services such as legal consulting, financial consulting, architectural, engineering and other technical activities.

Labour: includes all the professional categories of employees and self-employed. The value of labour employed in agriculture, tourism and other sectors is reported in the row. Resident workers employed in firms outside the territory and in the health and education sectors, which represent 5.4 per cent of the total employed population, are included in the account 'rest of the economy'. This share of value added is distributed among resident and non-resident households (in the columns).

Capital: the total return to capital factor from the three productive activities is indicated in the row. This component of value added is not redistributed because this factor is not relevant for the analysis (in the column). It is then included in the 'rest of the economy' row for the balancing of the SAM.

Residents: includes income and consumption of the inhabitants of the park area. The resident population has been divided into two categories: residents employed in the tourist sector and the remaining resident population. In the SAM, the row indicates the income composition. It consists of labour and other income, including transfers, interest, etc. Considering that other income is not relevant for this analysis, it is indicated in the column 'rest of the economy'. Expenditure on consumption goods is indicated in the column. It is subdivided into consumption of domestic agricultural goods, tourist consumption within the park area and consumption of goods and services provided by other local firms. Savings, taxation and expenditure on consumption goods produced by non-local firms are in the row 'rest of the economy'.

Rest of the economy: includes what is purchased and sold outside the economic area of interest, and those values which are relatively less relevant to the study but necessary for the final balancing of the SAM such as other income, savings and capital supply. The 'rest of the economy' row includes the amount of intermediate 'imported' goods, income of the non-residents employed in local firms, savings, taxes and the consumption of 'imported' goods and services. Intermediate and final goods consumed by non-resident households and demanded by non-local firms are indicated in the column. Non-resident tourists' expenditure, other income and labour income of residents employed in firms outside the territory and in the health and education sectors are also reported.

maximization of commuters' flows within the same area and the minimization of commuters' flows across different areas. The Limone LLS includes also the Tremosine municipality. The Toscolano Maderno LLS includes the municipalities of Gardone Riviera, Gargnano, Magasa, Tignale, Toscolano Maderno and Valvestino. The Salò municipality is at the centre of a third LLS which includes other municipalities all outside the park. For the Limone and Toscolano Maderno LLS, we assume that most inhabitants live and work within the territory. This assumption was not extended to the Salò municipality because there is a relevant movement of workers going in and out. Statistical information on the local labour systems is not fully developed and data cannot be disaggregated either by sectors or by municipality (Faramondi and Paris, 2002). As a consequence, we use the information about local labour systems as a comparison framework in order to evaluate the quality and consistency of the information gathered for constructing the SAM.

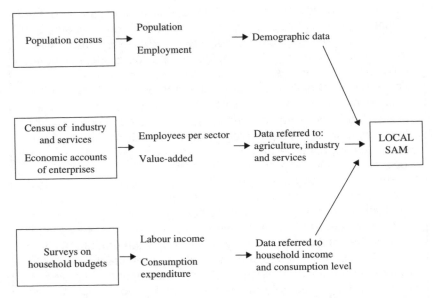

Figure 6.4   Sources and data used for the SAM construction

The productive structure of the area is mainly composed by small firms with fewer than 10 employees (96 per cent of the total firms). The employees mostly work in the tourist and commercial sectors. Their distribution within the territory shows the economic importance of Salò and Toscolano Maderno.

The economy of small municipalities which are near or belong to natural parks is often strongly linked to the tourist presence and their level of expenditure. In Limone for instance, which has about 1000 inhabitants, 70 per cent of the employees work in the tourist sector. Tourism is in fact the most important sector. It is of high quality because hotels with three or more stars are about 65 per cent of the total.

Figure 6.4 describes data and sources used in this chapter for building the local SAM for the High Garda Natural Park.

Table 6.1 reports the aggregate values at the sector level generated following the procedure specified in the Appendix. As expected, tourism plays a relevant role in the local economy within the park boundary.

Considering that the data come from many sources at different points in time, the West Garda SAM is not balanced. Table 6.2 presents the initial unbalanced SAM, computed using the procedure illustrated in the Appendix.

Table 6.1   *Main aggregates of the park productive sectors (in thousands of euros)*

Sectors	Employed	Value-added	Sales	Wages and salaries
Tourism	1837	33 179	81 926	12 185
Other sectors	4203	123 939	398 422	33 245

We use the *cross entropy method* (CE) to correct for this problem as illustrated in detail in the following section.

6.2.2   SAM Balancing using the Cross Entropy Method

The cross entropy method estimates a balanced and consistent matrix starting from an original unbalanced social accounting matrix using information available both at micro- and macroeconomic levels (Robilliard and Robinson, 1999 and Robinson et al., 1998). This approach is based on Shannon's information theory (Shannon, 1948) lately applied to statistical inference by Jaynes (1957). In 1994 Golan, Judge and Robinson used this approach to estimate the coefficients of an input–output table (Golan et al., 1994). The objective is to obtain a new set of coefficients close to those previously available but incorporating updated or additional information about economic aggregates such as value-added or consumption.

Two types of information are considered. The first type of information comes from the observed samples, where weights (coefficients) are computed embodying various demographic information. Weights represent the starting point of the estimating process. The second type of information comes from aggregate sources, such as national accounts. They are provided as aggregate values or weighted averages of the distribution of observed variables among observed households.

The High Garda Natural Park SAM has been balanced fixing the rows and columns totals, except for the tourist account, to their initial average value. The tourist row total has been fixed to the column sum value because of insufficient information on the tourist expenditure reported in the row. The total value-added produced by the industry and services sectors has been fixed to that found in the survey on the local labour systems. We could not use this information for the SAM construction because it refers only to aggregate values (Faramondi and Paris, 2002). However, we adjust the content of the value-added cells using the aggregate data available at the local labour system level.

Table 6.2   The local SAM before balancing (in thousands of euros)

	Agriculture	Tourism	Other sectors	Labour	Capital	Resident population	Rest of the economy	Total
Agriculture	382	281	1135			1545	1255	4597
Tourism	51	1194	744			164	47111	49265
Other sectors	567	3400	25569			159012	209874	398422
Labour	1246	28905	78866				39199	148216
Capital	1350	4274	45074					50698
Resident population				180665	50698		93070	273734
Rest of the economy	1000	43746	247034	4526	50698	113014		460019
Total	4597	81800	398422	185191	50698	273735	390509	

From the initial SAM we obtain the column coefficients $A_{i,j}$:

$$A_{i,j} = \frac{t_{i,j}}{y_j}$$

where $t_{i,j}$ represents the cell in the i-th row and the j-th column and y_j is the total sum of the j-th column.

The estimation process minimizes the cross-entropy distance between the new estimated coefficients and the previous ones:

$$\min I = \left[\sum_i \sum_j A_{i,j} \ln \frac{A_{i,j}}{\overline{A}_{i,j}} \right]$$

subject to the following constraints:

$$\sum_j A_{i,j} y_j^* = \frac{y_j^* + y_i^*}{2}, \quad i = 1, \ldots, n-1$$

$$\sum_j A_{t,j} y_j^* = y_t^*, \quad t = \text{tourist}$$

$$\sum_i \sum_j G_{i,j} T_{i,j} = VA$$

$$0 \leq A_{i,j} \leq 1$$

where $\overline{A}_{i,j}$ and $A_{i,j}$ are respectively the prior and the new estimated SAM coefficients, y^* are rows and columns sums of the n accounts, T is the initial SAM which is multiplied by matrix G which has 1 in the value-added cells (labour and capital) of each sector (agriculture, tourism and other sectors) and 0 elsewhere. VA represents the value-added produced by industry and services sectors found in the survey on the local labour systems. An analytic description of the complete model, where row and column sums involve errors in measurement, is presented in Robilliard and Robinson (1999) and Robinson and El-Said (2000).

The balanced SAM for the High Garda Natural Park is reported in Table 6.3.

The balanced values in Table 6.3 are similar to the original values and the resulting balanced SAM is now ready for the impact analysis.

6.3   THE MULTIPLIER ANALYSIS

We use the SAM multiplier analysis for simulating the impact on the local economic system of changes in relevant exogenous policy variables as

Table 6.3 The local SAM balanced (in thousands of euros)

	Agriculture	Tourism	Other sectors	Labour	Capital	Resident population	Rest of the economy	Total
Agriculture	382	268	905			1 628	1 415	4 597
Tourism	52	1 222	858			227	79 442	81 801
Other sectors	566	3 180	18 888			158 843	216 428	397 905
Labour	1 246	30 829	110 487				42 419	184 981
Capital	1 351	4 610	66 621					72 582
Resident population				180 350	72 582		100 871	281 222
Rest of the economy	1 001	41 691	200 146	4 631		120 524		440 575
Total	4 597	81 801	397 905	184 981	72 582	281 222	440 575	

a result of the interrelations existing among revenue, income and expenditure flows of households and firms. The matrix of multipliers obtained from the SAM captures both the direct and indirect effects on production and income and also the circular effects that are the result of the circular flow of income within the local economy.

The SAM multiplier analysis considers prices as exogenously fixed and implies the following behavioural assumptions:

1. Since prices are given, it is not possible to estimate the impact of price variations and the conclusions must be drawn in terms of quantities.
2. Functional relations use fixed technical coefficients of Leontief technologies and it is therefore not possible to consider changes in the productivity of labour and capital.
3. There are no bounds on goods supply because supply satisfies demand by assumption.

In developing a SAM multiplier model, the first step is to decide which accounts should be exogenous and which are endogenous on the basis of the specific aim of the analysis (De Janvry and Sadoulet, 1995, Pyatt and Round, 1979). Given that in our case the study evaluates the impact of environmental policies on the local economy, the account 'rest of the economy' is considered exogenous.

The matrix of the endogenous transactions, T, can be divided into four sub-matrices. In Figure 6.5, the matrix T_{ij} is the matrix of transactions which is presented also in the input–output model. The matrix T_{ij} represents the composition of the value-added in different sectors of the economy; the matrix T_f represents the distribution of the value added to the endogenous institutions and the matrix T_i corresponds to the expenditures of the endogenous institutions. The column vector X represents the injections from exogenous to endogenous accounts. We can simulate shocks on the endogenous variables by modifying the elements of vector X. L corresponds to the transactions between exogenous accounts and the row vector E shows the leakages from the endogenous to the exogenous accounts. The column vector Y and Y_x represents the total income and the total expenditure of endogenous and exogenous accounts respectively. Considering the matrix of endogenous accounts T, we divide the elements in each column by its column total. We obtain the matrix of coefficients A and inverting the matrix $(I - A)$, where I is the identity matrix, we obtain the SAM multiplier matrix, M. Similarly we divide each element of the row vector E by its column total to obtain the vector of coefficients B.

| | Endogenous accounts | | | | | | | Total | Exogenous accounts | Total |
	(1)	(2)	(3)	(4)	(5)	(6)	(7)		(8)	
(1) Agriculture								N_1	X_1	Y_1
(2) Tourism		T_{ij}					T_i	N_2	X_2	Y_2
(3) Other sectors								N_3	X_3	Y_3
(4) Labour		T_{fj}						N_4	X_4	Y_4
(5) Capital				T_f				N_5	X_5	Y_5
(6) Residents employed in the tourist sector								N_6	X_6	Y_6
(7) Rest of the resident population								N_7	X_7	Y_7
(8) Exogenous accounts	Y_1	Y_2	Y_3	Y_4 E	Y_5	Y_6	Y_7		L	Y_X
Total expenditure									Y_X	

Figure 6.5   Representation of the SAM model

Impacts on total output and income are derived using the following expressions:

- the vector of impacts: $\Delta Y = (I - A)^{-1} \Delta X$;
- the leakages from endogenous to exogenous accounts: $\Delta L = B \Delta Y$;
- the SAM multiplier matrix: $M = (I - A)^{-1}$;
- the vector of exogenous shock. ΔX.

In the High Garda Natural Park case, X is the account 'rest of the economy' and ΔX corresponds to changes in the final demand for agricultural products and the tourists' expenditure of non-residents. The expression describing the impact on leakages ΔL must hold with equality because in a SAM framework total injections from exogenous accounts must be equal to total leakages from the endogenous to the exogenous accounts. In this expression B is the vector of coefficients which represents what the exogenous accounts receive from the endogenous ones.

6.4   SIMULATIONS AND RESULTS

This section estimates the impact of both the participative and non-participative management policies of the West Garda Regional Forest on the local economic system. In line with the analysis developed in the previous chapter, Table 6.4 describes the following three scenarios:

- benchmark – the actual forest plan;
- scenario A – non-participative regional management programme;
- scenario B – participative regional management programme.

Note that in scenario B, the regional manager of the forest based in Milan takes formally into consideration the preferences of the users as revealed by the estimated contingent prices.

In the benchmark scenario, 27 per cent of the forest is devoted to the tourist function while 26 per cent is devoted to the naturalistic function. If the adopted management policy follows scenario A, then the importance of the naturalistic function increases to 65 per cent while the tourist function does not change significantly. On the other hand, if the adopted policy follows scenario B then the importance of the tourist function declines to 2 per cent and the forest mainly offers the naturalistic function in up to 94 per cent of the total area. In both scenarios, protective and productive functions decrease to 2 per cent.

Management

Table 6.4   Combination of functions and their description

Functions	Description	Combinations of functions (%)		
		Benchmark scenario: actual forest plan	Scenario A: non-participative	Scenario B: participative
Naturalistic function	Conserving nature, wildlife and ecosystem	26	65	94
Productive function	Providing market with timber and non-timber products: fodder, mushrooms, resins, etc.	21	2	2
Protective function	Preserving structural features of the canopy and territory	26	2	2
Tourist function	Providing tourist–recreational services: sports, outdoor activities (hunting and fishing, horse riding, biking, etc.)	27	31	2

As it is reasonable to expect, these scenarios attract different flows of tourist and have a differential impact on agriculture as they imply different uses of land. With respect to the participative programme, the non-participative management plan places more importance on the tourist function. Note that more hectares allocated to the tourist function do not necessarily mean higher levels of tourist flows. The tourist function embodies recreational services, sports and natural activities such as fishing, biking and horse riding. These are all anthropic interventions which according to the contingent evaluation analysis seem to be little desired by visitors. Tourists prefer this area to be allocated to naturalistic aims where human interventions are reduced to vegetation and fauna habitat maintenance. For this reason, we simulate that scenario B induces a higher number of visitors than scenario A. In simulating a change in tourist flows, we must also consider that the West Garda Regional Forest is a part of the West Garda Park where most tourists are attracted by cultural and sports events, historical places, monuments and so on. Changes in tourist flows depend also on the efficiency of the future developments in the park's potentialities. Therefore we simulate three possible changes in tourist flows, affecting tourists' expenditure for each scenario.

Table 6.5 The SAM multipliers

	Agriculture	Tourism
Agriculture	1.094	0.007
Tourism	0.014	1.016
Other sectors	0.377	0.316
Labour	0.406	0.473
Capital	0.385	0.112
Resident population	0.396	0.461

Agricultural activities within the park area are partly linked to the productive function of the West Garda Forest. Both scenarios devote only 2 per cent of the territory for productive ends implying a reduction in the land used for agricultural purposes. As a consequence, agricultural activities decline. In the participative scenario (B) the impact is smaller because a larger area is allocated to the naturalistic function. Note that while in tourist areas there is negligible agricultural activity, in naturalistic areas a certain level of agricultural activities is maintained. Therefore we simulate a negative change in the agriculture sector of about 10 per cent in scenario A and of about 5 per cent in scenario B.

Table 6.5 reports the SAM multipliers for the High Garda Natural Park corresponding to changes in the non-resident final demand for agriculture products and tourist services.

The multipliers show the changes in output and income of the local sectors and resident population as a result of exogenous shocks. Inspection of the tourism column reveals that each value can be interpreted as the additional output or income generated in the row account due to a one unit increase in non-resident tourist expenditure. The multipliers show a negligible link between tourism and other local activities (0.007, 0.316) with respect to agriculture (0.014, 0.377). On the other hand, changes in the tourist sector have a larger impact on the resident population income level (0.416).

In the simulation analysis an increase in tourist flows is expected to have a greater direct impact on the tourist sector and smaller indirect effects on other local activities, because of the high share of non-resident tourists' expenditure on the total output of the tourist sector (Table 6.3).

Tables 6.6 and 6.7 respectively show the simulations result expected in terms of changes in production, labour demand and incomes of the resident population.

If there is no change in tourist flows, both strategies have a negative impact on the local economy caused by the shock on the agriculture sector

Table 6.6 Simulation results, variations in production and labour demand (in thousands of euros)

Benchmark scenario: actual forest plan			Scenario A: non-participative			Scenario B: participative		
Change in the agriculture sector (%)			−10	−10	−10	−5	−5	−5
Change in tourists' expenditure (%)			0	+5	+10	0	+10	+20

	Production	Labour	Results					
Agricultural sector	4.597	1.246	−3.36	−2.74	−2.11	−1.67	−0.43	+0.80
Tourist sector	81 800	30 829	−	+4.93	+9.86	−	+9.87	+19.73
Other sectors	402 502	111 732	−1.16	−0.85	−0.55	−1.14	−0.54	+0.54
Total sectors	484 303	142 562	−0.03	+1.05	+2.13	−0.02	+2.16	+4.33

Table 6.7 Simulation results, variations in resident population income level (in thousands of euros)

Benchmark scenario: actual forest plan			Scenario A: non-participative			Scenario B: participative		
Change in the agriculture sector (%)			−10	−10	−10	−5	−5	−5
Change in tourists' expenditure (%)			0	+5	+10	0	+10	+20

		Results					
Income level of residents employed in tourist sector	44 645	−	+3.18	+6.35	−	+6.36	+12.71
Income level of residents employed in agricultural and the other sectors	236 576	−0.02	+0.12	+0.26	−0.01	+0.28	+0.56
Income level of total resident population	281 221	−0.02	+0.60	+1.23	−0.009	+1.24	+2.49

(Table 6.6). However, if the adopted management policy is scenario B, the negative impact is smaller. An increase in tourist expenditure affects positively both the tourist sector and the other activities due to indirect and circular effects. The impact on the local economy generated by the adoption of scenario A is positive given the relevance of the tourist sector to the local economy. On the other hand, the impact is negative for agriculture (2 per cent) and the other sectors. If the management policy is participative, in the case of a 10 per cent increase in tourist expenditure, the results are similar to those of scenario B but the negative effects on agriculture and other sectors are smaller. If the forest is developed incorporating the users' preferences, the increase in tourist expenditure can be even higher. In the case of a 20 per cent increase, the effects on the local economy are markedly positive. The negative impact on agriculture is offset by the positive indirect and circular effects caused by the change in tourist expenditure.

Inspection of Table 6.7 reveals that the impacts on the income level of residents employed in the non-tourist sector are not economically significant. If there is no change in tourist expenditure, residents face a negative but small impact in both scenarios. On the other hand, in the case of a 10 per cent increase, both scenarios have positive effects on the local population. If the participative scenario is adopted, a 20 per cent increase in tourist expenditure causes a positive impact of about 12 per cent on the income level of the resident population employed in the tourist sector.

6.5   CONCLUSIONS

This study analysed the impact of the participative and the non-participative managerial alternatives of the West Garda Regional Forest on the local economy of the High Garda Natural Park, where the forest is located, using a social accounting matrix framework developed at the local level. This approach provides a comprehensive view of the local economic scenario and its basic structural characteristics. The territorial analysis allows us to understand better the social economic and environmental interactions at the local level and to verify the potential sources of conflict between the central management, having jurisdiction over the West Garda Regional Forest, and the peripheral management commanding the High Garda Natural Park.

Although the data available for the area of interest were scattered, the resulting SAM adequately represents the interactions between local economic activities and the resident population. However more and better quality data would permit a more efficient use of the model potentialities.

We simulated the impact of both the participative and non-participative optimal combinations of functions using the SAM multiplier approach that gives an immediate representation of direct, indirect and circular effects. The participative programme is obtained by maximizing the manager's revenues, taking formally into consideration the preferences of users and residents by including the prices that visitors are willing to pay for each function as weights of the objective function. The simulation analysis showed that the participative programme is preferable to the non-participative programme for the impact on both production and income level. It follows that the participative regional management programme matches both the preferences of users and the interests of local institutions because the territory receives a larger benefit from its implementation. However the presence of vested interests among local institutions, associations and actors may be a further source of conflict among the stakeholders. This issue will be analysed in the next chapter.

APPENDIX: DATA SOURCES

In this appendix we describe the data sources used to estimate the values content in the SAM. We collected data mainly from the data bank Ionio Cineca. Local information was provided by the population census (Istat, 1991) and the intermediate census of industry and services (Istat, 1996a). From the regional statistical yearbook of Lombardy region we collected data related to households' incomes and expenditure and employers' professional positions per each observed municipality. Information about value-added and sales of each sector was found in the economic accounts of enterprises yearbook (Istat, 1996b). The value-added produced in agriculture referred to the census of agriculture of 1991 while the agricultural standard gross incomes comes from the INEA yearbook of Italian Agriculture of 1996. Data used to determine value-added, inter-sector transactions, production, income, consumption and labour income are illustrated in sequence.

Value-added

The procedure used for determining the value-added at factor costs produced by local firms includes two phases. First, the number of employees by local economic activity, derived from the intermediate census of industry and services of 1996, is multiplied by the average value-added per employee, assuming that the West Garda's firms produce a value-added similar to the average values of the Lombardy region. The Italian national statistical office (Istat) distinguishes between firms with less than 19 employees and firms with more than 19 employees. We also adopt this classification because within the area considered there are mostly small firms (less than 19 employees). This allows us to be more precise in the estimation. During the SAM balancing process these values have been compared with the data at the Local Labor System level. The obtained value-added is divided into labour and capital remuneration using regional average values. After having determined the amount of labour expenditure, we subtract social contributions, using percentage values calculated at a national level, in order to obtain values as close as possible to the local labour income levels. We verified the congruence between the obtained labour income and the values determined by multiplying the number of employees as derived from the population census of 1991, by the average annual income reported in the statistical yearbook of the Lombardy region. Tables 6.8 and 6.9 report the values obtained. Considering that dependent employees (managers, employees and workers) represent only a part of the total number of employees, we needed to determine the income level of self-employed people. We assumed that the self-employed workers are equally distributed among sectors. Finally, we

Table 6.8   *Value-added, sales and labour costs of the other sectors (in thousands of euros)*

Other sectors	Employed by sector	Value-added	Sales	Wages and salaries
15 Food and drink industries	286	11 074.12	31 461.52	4 147.89
17 Textile industries	66	2 199.77	6 472.96	870.60
18 Clothing industries	56	1 635.86	2 568.24	866.45
20 Wood and wood and cork products	71	1 587.74	3 912.52	429.83
21 Paper and paper products	23	646.19	2 410.15	215.60
22 Publishing and printing	32	988.29	2 631.04	317.87
24 Chemical products, synthetic and artificial fibres	5	222.85	945.89	62.04
25 Gum and plastic products	4	128.29	369.99	39.89
26 Non-metalliferous mineral products	5	135.57	411.87	44.79
28 Metal products	164	5 473.16	10 536.55	1 956.32
29 Machines and mechanical machineries installation, assembly, repair and maintenance	137	6 234.98	12 410.36	2 656.82
31 Machines and NCA electrical set	9	255.18	668.86	86.09
32 Radio, television and communications	3	72.98	198.47	25.05
33 Medical and precision machines, and optical instruments	24	649.50	1 709.27	196.14
35 Motor vehicles	31	765.29	2 364.70	238.32
36 Furniture and other manufacturing industries	26	525.03	1 583.15	172.06
40 Production and distribution of energy, gas and water	1	69.62	363.69	16.28
41 Water collection, purification and distribution	1	39.35	92.50	11.70
45 Construction	731	16 837.84	49 192.16	4 842.52
50 Trade, maintenance and repairing of autos and motor vehicles	175	3 407.32	29 228.88	1 134.03
51 Wholesale of autos and motor vehicles	279	12 481.04	73 601.93	3 048.48

52 Retail, auto and motor vehicles excluded, and repair of personal and household goods	902	15 279.69	81 056.88	3 206.35
60 Land transport services	64	1 976.58	5 113.34	411.63
61 Sea and water transport	6	93.58	201.11	38.70
63 Support and auxiliary transport	46	1 786.53	8 127.28	600.44
64 Post and telecommunications	3	60.27	448.85	28.50
65 Money and financial services	2	40.18	105.87	19.10
67 Auxilairy activity of financial services	81	2 342.65	4 287.88	496.08
70 Estate	171	9 334.80	19 473.27	584.72
71 Hire of machinery and goods for personal use	5	114.65	484.95	23.60
72 Informatic and related activities	47	1 572.92	3 599.76	431.35
73 Research and development	2	94.00	135.62	7.48
74 Other professional activities	571	22 595.31	35 033.75	5 335.92
90 Solid rubbish disposal and drains	5	259.00	791.21	61.98
92 Recreational, cultural and sport activities	26	1 267.59	3 022.62	183.98
93 Other activities	143	1 691.24	3 404.64	436.72
Total	4203	123 938.97	398 421.71	33 245.30

Source: Istat (1996a).

181

*Table 6.9   Value-added, sales and labour costs of the tourist sector
             (in thousands of euros)*

		Employed by sector	Value-added	Sales	Wages and salaries
52.2	Retail of food, drinks and tobacco in specific shops	69	1 169	6 201	245
55	Hotels and restaurants	1 719	30 692	72 710	11 709
92	Recreational, cultural and sporting activities	20	975	2 325	142
93	Other activities	29	343	690	89
	Total	1 837	33 179	81 926	12 185

Source: Istat (1996a).

estimated the value-added produced by the agriculture sector using data
from two sources: the census of agriculture and the Standard Gross Margin
provided by the yearbook of Italian agriculture (INEA, 1996). For the agriculture sector, the value-added is derived from the information available on
gross incomes, which are close to the value-added produced by the agricultural sector (European Commission, 2002). The values obtained are
reported in Table 6.10. The value-added has then been divided into labour
and capital remuneration on the basis of the information on farm budgets
collected by Inea and reported in the 1996 yearbook.

Inter-sector Transactions

Given that local input–output tables are not available, the national
input–output table has been used in order to define the size of inter-sector
transactions under the assumption of constant proportions between the
national, regional and local level. After obtaining the total production of
agriculture, tourism and other sectors we derived the matrix of intermediate transactions using the same fixed proportions between sectors of the
national input–output table. Since firms are rather small and heterogeneous
we assumed that most of the intermediate goods come from firms located
outside the area of interest.

Production

In order to determine the total production of the three sectors considered
in this study (agriculture, tourist and other sectors) we consider that the

Table 6.10   Agriculture sector value-added (in thousands of euros)

	Cereals	Permanent cultivation	Livestock	Total
Gardone Riviera	7.10	47.92	21.81	76.82
Gargnano	36.27	160.28	110.17	306.72
Limone sul Garda	0.63	77.60	0.85	79.07
Magasa	7.94	0.00	62.89	70.83
Salò	334.47	275.72	153.57	763.76
Tignale	88.53	73.25	74.91	236.69
Toscolano-Maderno	76.37	196.23	67.48	340.07
Tremosine	110.79	59.16	475.86	645.80
Valvestino	5.37	0.00	71.37	76.74
Total	667.45	890.15	1038.90	2596.51

Sources: Our elaborations; INEA (1996).

local sales per employee are a reasonable approximation of the average regional values, therefore we multiply average sales per employee by the number of employed, in each sector. The total production of agriculture derives from average regional values. We identified that the value-added produced by the agriculture sector represents the 56 per cent of the total. These values were been compared to those obtained from the input–output table following the procedure described above.

Income

In determining the income and consumption levels of the resident population we need to make further assumptions. Since there is no local information on income and household consumption we assumed that they are similar to the regional and provincial average values. Therefore we derived the average per capita income, labour income and the distribution of consumption expenditure as shown in Table 6.11. The resident population was divided into two categories: residents employed in the tourist sector and the remaining resident population. Table 6.12 shows the income composition of the two categories.

Consumption

Intermediate consumption of local firms' products have been determined assuming that the small and heterogeneous local firms purchase mostly

Table 6.11　Incomes and consumptions of resident population
*　　　　　　　(in thousands of euros)*

Income	
Resident population	27 164
Per capita average annual income (Lombardy region)	10.08
Total income	273 735
Consumption	
% consumption/income (Lombardy region)	94
Total consumption expenditure	257 311
Total savings	16 424
Income composition	
% labour income/total income (Brescia province)	65.87
Total labour income	180 309
Total other income	93 426

Source:　Istat (1996c).

Table 6.12　Composition of the resident population's income

Sources	Resident population employed in the tourist sector	Rest of the resident population
Labour income from domestic sectors		
Agriculture	–	0.52
Tourism	64.45	–
Other sectors	–	45.63
Other incomes (include incomes of residents employed in non-local firms, in education and health sectors)	35.55	53.85
Total	100.00	100.00

from firms located outside the territory of interest. The share of production assigned to final local consumption has been calculated by dividing final consumption by total production derived from the national input–output table (see Table 6.13). By distinguishing among two typologies of visitors, we calculate resident and non-resident tourist expenditure

Table 6.13   Final consumption of goods produced by local firms of the first 8 sectors (in thousands of euros)

Sectors	Employees	Sales	Final consumption/ production	Final consumption
15 Food and drink industries	286	31 462	50.0	15 746
17 Textile industries	66	6 473	21.2	1 370
18 Clothing industries	56	2 568	65.2	1 674
20 Wood and wood and cork products	71	3 913	7.1	276
21 Paper and paper products	23	2 410	6.9	165
22 Publishing and printing	32	2 631	29.7	782
24 Chemical products, synthetic and artificial fibres	5	946	14.1	133
25 Gum and plastic products	4	370	8.7	32
Total	4 203	50 772		20 180

Source: Istat (1996b, 2000).

using information on daily personal expenditure obtained from the travel cost section of the West Garda Regional Forest survey. Moreover, using data on arrivals and the number of nights spent in hotels and supplementary accommodation provided by the Province of Brescia, we determine the average yearly flow of tourists (Table 6.14).

Labour

Estimation of labour income follows the procedure described at the 'value-added' section of this appendix. The number of resident and non-resident workers in firms is calculated by comparing data from the population census and the intermediate census of industry and services. Note that the comparison is difficult because they differ both in terms of heterogeneity of units studied and also for the period they refer to. While the population census refers to households, the intermediate census of industry and services collects information on people employed using local units as a basis.

Management

Table 6.14   Arrivals and nights spent by Italian and foreign tourists in hotels

Period	Italians		Foreign visitors		Total	
	Hotel and supplementary accomodation					
January–December 1998	Arrivals	Nights spent	Arrivals	Nights spent	Arrivals	Nights spent
January	1 492	8 280	423	2 039	1 915	10 319
February	1 904	7 733	725	1 798	2 629	9 531
March	2 942	10 535	6 095	2 238	9 037	32 915
April	10 104	34 513	27 267	129 847	37 371	164 360
May	9 300	47 356	32 964	160 429	42 264	207 785
June	9 684	60 478	28 476	193 178	38 160	253 656
July	11 541	91 189	31 270	234 121	42 811	325 310
August	15 893	139 750	38 223	267 911	54 116	407 661
September	7 842	53 506	31 274	203 132	39 116	256 638
October	3 994	12 662	18 872	101 157	22 866	113 819
November	1 884	6 121	1 219	5 106	3 103	11 227
December	1 805	6 407	713	2 087	2 518	8 494
Total	78 385	478 530	217 521	1 303 043	295 906	1 801 715

Source: Province of Brescia, Ufficio promozione e statistica.

NOTE

1. The High Garda Natural Park extends for about 38 000 hectares, half of which are covered by woods. It embraces the municipalities of Salò, Gardone Riviera, Toscolano Maderno, Valvestino, Magasa, Gargnano, Limone, Tignale and Tremosine. The territory has heterogeneous morphological characteristics. It ranges from a height of 65m to 2000m above the sea level. It presents also very different climatic conditions, typical of a Mediterranean system in the land surrounding the lake shores and the 'alpine systems' on the north-west side of Garda Lake.

REFERENCES

Bendavid-Val, A. (1983), *Regional and Local Economic Analysis for Practitioners*, New York: Praeger Publishers.

De Janvry, A. and E. Sadoulet (1995), *Quantitative Development Policy Analysis*, Baltimore: Johns Hopkins University Press.

Dorward, A., J. Morrison, C. Poulton and T. Hardwick (2003), *Disaggregated Impacts of Agricultural Policy Reform on Rural Households in Malawi*, First Meeting OECD Global Forum Pro-Poor Agricultural Policies, Paris.

ERSAF (Regional Forestry Agency of Lombardy Region) at: http://www.ersaf. lombardia.it/.

European Commission (2002), *Definitions of Variable Used in FADN Standard Results*, RI/CC 8882 Rev. 7.0, Brussels.

Fannin, M. (2001), *Construction of a Social Accounting Matrix for County Fermanagh, Northern Ireland*, Southern Regional Science Association, USA.

Faramondi, A. and M.G. Paris (2002), *Le nuove stime di aggregati socio-economici per i Sistemi Locali del Lavoro*, Sixth Conference of Statistics, Rome.

Golan, A., G. Judge and S. Robinson (1994), 'Recovering information for incomplete or partial multisectoral economic data', *Review of Economics and Statistics*, **76**, 541–9.

INEA (1996), *Agricoltura Italiana Conta*, INEA, Rome.

Istat (1991), 'Censimento della popolazione e delle abitazioni', Istat, Rome; at IONIO Servizio Banche Dati Cineca, n. 13, http://ionio.cineca.it/.

Istat (1996a), 'Censimento intermedio dell'industria e dei servizi', Istat, Rome; at IONIO Servizio Banche Dati Cineca, http://ionio.cineca.it/.

Istat (1996b), *Conti Economici delle Imprese*, Istat, Rome.

Istat (1996c), 'Distribuzione quantitativa del reddito in Italia o nelle indagini sui bilanci delle famiglie', Istat, Rome.

Istat (2000), 'Tavola intersettoriale dell'economia italiana – Anno 1992', Istat, Rome; at INONIO Servizio Banche Dati Cineca, http://ionio.cineca.it/.

Jaynes, E.T. (1957), 'Information theory and statistical mechanics', *Physical Review*, **106** (4), 620–30.

Province of Brescia, Ufficio promozione e statistica at: http://www.provincia. brescia.it/turismo/turismo-uffici.php.

Pyatt, G. and J.I. Round (1979), 'Accounting and fixed price multipliers in a social accounting matrix framework', *The Economic Journal*, **89** (356), 850–73.

Regional Statistical Yearbook of Lombardy region, at http://www.ring. lombardia.it/.

Robilliard, A.S. and S. Robinson (1999), 'Reconciling household survey and national accounts data using a cross entropy estimation method', IFPRI, Discussion Paper no. 50.

Robinson, S., A. Cattaneo and M. El-Said (1998), 'Estimate a social accounting matrix using cross entropy methods', International Food Policy Research Institute, TMD, Discussion Paper no. 33.

Robinson, S. and M. El-Said (2000), 'GAMS code for estimating a Social Accounting Matrix (SAM) using Cross Entropy (CE) methods', International Food Policy Research Institute, TDM, Discussion Paper no. 64.

Shannon, C.E. (1948), 'A mathematical theory of communication', *Bell System Technical Journal*, **27**, 379–423.

7. Resolving conflicts in a natural area

Michele Baggio

7.1 INTRODUCTION

The sustainable development of environmental resources, such as natural areas, represents an opportunity for the economic development of local communities. Managing a natural area efficiently is not an easy task. Its complexity is mainly due to the fact that environmental resources are often subjects of conflicting interests and rights that are not easily assigned and efficiently coordinated. This situation is especially evident in the case of managing a natural area which provides multiple services to local communities and users. The functions provided by the forest can be summarized in four categories: naturalistic, productive, protective and tourist. The lack of convergence of multiple interests may generate conflicts among the interest groups (or stakeholders) and that may seriously hinder the implementation of the best development plan for the natural area. Further, the adoption of different management strategies may cause an unfair distribution of benefits and damages leading to suboptimal management decisions.

This chapter proposes a methodology that intends to help managers of a natural area to implement the best combination of services that a forest may provide by reaching a consensus among the preferences that have been expressed by different interest groups in the forest. Game theory is the tool that is being used to solve the potential conflicts which may arise among the forest's stakeholders in order to allow the forest's authorities to best manage the resource. The methodology is applied in the case of the West Garda Regional Forest where the best plan described in Chapter 5 needs to be implemented after reaching a consensus among the local interest groups. Among the stakeholders interested in the forest's management decisions, we find residents running commercial activities that benefit from the services provided by the natural area. They are naturally interested in management decisions. We gather them under the definition of *providers*. Other stakeholders are *forest management*, *hunters/fishermen* and other *visitors/ tourists*.

Hunting is one of the most traditional activities in the West Garda area. For many years, local hunters held the rights to hunting in the area and they are now reluctant to share it with visitors or tourists. A large part of the society has a negative view of hunters. In Italy in fact, hunting had to face two referenda: on the abolition of hunting (1990) and to forbid the access of hunters to private fields (1997). In both cases the quorum was not achieved to legitimize the ballot, but most of the people who voted (around 90 per cent) favoured banning hunters from entering private fields. The number of hunters has been steadily decreasing in the last 20 years and many more Italians consider hunting as an undesirable activity. In two recent surveys on hunting issues, the majority of those interviewed declared themselves to be against hunting. In the survey about hunting in natural areas, 70 per cent of interviewed in the Lazio region (Taylor Nelson Sofres Abacus, 2002) declared that hunting areas should be reduced, and in a survey on hunting among citizens of the Piemonte region (Albors Research Institute, 2002) more than 84 per cent said that hunting in natural areas should be banned.

Visitors to the forest enjoy many kinds of activities: hiking, biking, bird-watching, picnicking, horseback riding, wildlife, scenery, and many others. Most of these multiple activities can be considered as 'club' goods for those who pay the club fee and to the exclusion of all others. Others, such as wilderness protection or scenery, are considered as pure public goods. The forest's management is interested in getting the highest benefits from the area, but it is also interested in matching the interest of the other stake-holders. Before the project started, it was possible only to guess about the preferences of other stakeholders on the basis of reports and meeting with local interest groups. Because of this lack of information, management decisions were not tailored efficiently. As a consequence of this project, the forest's management decisions can now be made considering all the infor-mation collected, matching most of the interests of stakeholders.

The goal of this work is not to promote any particular interest, but to design a framework able to generate a consensus among those enjoying the park, hunters and visitors, and to resolve the conflicting interests in the forest. Using data and results from the previous chapters, this chapter intends to tie them together by dealing with the implementation phase of the project. As a whole, the project provides the forest's management with a framework that allows them to derive information about intrinsic charac-teristics of the area, the preferences of the stakeholders, and the best alter-native management strategies. It then enables local authorities to implement effectively the chosen management strategy and to resolve the disputes arising from the conflicting interests over the natural area. Specifically, within the project it is possible to obtain:

- *quantities* of services provided by the natural area using GIS techniques;
- *prices* or economic values of those services using preferences elicited through a questionnaire;
- *optimal management strategies* providing the best combination of the services given the natural vocation of the area and the preferences of the park's users;
- *input–output analysis* of the impact on the local economy deriving from the adoption of the optional strategy;
- *best management alternative* that satisfies stakeholders' preferences by using a game theoretic approach.

The information collected with the questionnaire is used in this chapter to set up a game where the players are the stakeholders and the payoffs are the utilities derived from enjoying the services that the natural areas provide for them.

In the following paragraphs, we provide the theoretical background of the analysis with an overview of noncooperative and cooperative games. Finally an application is presented.

7.2   GAME THEORY AND CONFLICT RESOLUTION

Game theory is the study of how rational individuals (agents or players) adopt decisions that determine rewards or penalties (payoffs). Despite its name, games as commonly known are not the subject of the analysis. Game theory aims at finding solutions to disputes arising from the interactions among agents. Firms, corporations, countries, or individuals behave strategically in order to maximize their wealth and their ability to anticipate the actions of the other agent is the necessary endowment to get the highest benefits in a game, a political agreement or economic behaviour. Therefore game theory handles the strategic interaction[1] among agents and it may be applied and modelled to most economic problems.

Following Gibbons (1992), there are four classes of games: static games of complete information, dynamic games of complete information, static games of incomplete information, and dynamic games of incomplete information.[2] Corresponding to these classes, there are four notions of equilibrium that can be summarized in Table 7.1.

Table 7.1   Summary of equilibria under different assumptions

	Complete information	Incomplete information
Static games	Nash equilibrium	Bayesian Nash equilibrium
Dynamic games	Subgame-perfect Nash equilibrium	Perfect Bayesian equilibrium

A game is called static when it is not repeated in time and the players choose simultaneously their strategies just once. In a dynamic game (or supergame), players may choose their strategies in different periods of time (having observed other players' moves–perfect information, or simultaneously–imperfect information). In the noncooperative static games, the players are not able to draw enforceable deals without incurring costs. Each player chooses simultaneously the strategy that represents the best response to the predicted strategies of the other players and reaches a Nash equilibrium. This equilibrium is called self-enforcing because no player has an incentive to deviate from it. In the dynamic games, instead, since players can choose their strategies after observing other players' strategies, they have the incentive to deviate from the Nash equilibrium, and choose the strategy that leads to the highest payoff. In this case, it is necessary to introduce what is called trigger strategy to force players not to deviate. This topic will be discussed later on.

7.2.1   Basic Notions

It is worth introducing some basic notions of game theory. In any game, a strategy represents the plan of action of a player, a feasible action that the player may choose. In a static game a strategy is simply an action. In the case of noncooperative games with complete information,[3] each player chooses the strategy that leads to the highest reward (payoff),[4] given the prediction of other players' chosen strategies. Therefore, each player's strategy[5] is the player's best response to the predicted strategy of the other players. This is the definition of Nash equilibrium (NE). The Nash equilibrium is said to be self-enforcing since no player has the incentive to move from it because any different action would lead to a lower payoff.

As an example, consider the classic prisoners' dilemma (Table 7.2). There are two prisoners, each of which is locked up in a separate cell. Each prisoner can choose between two strategies: to remain silent, RS, or to confess, C. The payoffs are represented by the rewards from confessing or not. Since no communication is possible, the prisoners cannot agree on the strategy to

Table 7.2   Prisoners' dilemma

		Player B	
		Remain silent	Confess
Player A	Remain silent	(5, 5)	(0, 7)
	Confess	(7, 0)	(1, 1)

be taken. They both choose the best strategy given the other player's strategies, which, in this case, is for both to confess (Nash equilibrium). However, the prisoners would both be better off by remaining silent.

Another way to represent the NE consists in representing the best response of players in terms of functions. Let us consider a game with two players. For every feasible strategy that may be chosen by player 2, we can find the player 1's best response, solving

$$\max_{s_1} \pi_1(s_1, s_2^*), \tag{7.1}$$

where π_1 is player 1's payoff function. Player 1 chooses his strategy s_1 given that player 2 has chosen his strategy s_2^*. The first-order conditions for a maximum define player 1's best strategy as a function of player 2's best strategy and vice versa. Thus solving the optimization problem for each player yields the best response functions of the two players

$$\begin{aligned} s_1^* &= R_1(s_2^*) \\ s_2^* &= R_2(s_1^*) \end{aligned} \tag{7.2}$$

In a special case of this problem known as the 'battle of the sexes'[6] (Coffee–Coffee and Sleep–Sleep, Table 7.3), or in another case known as 'matching pennies' (Table 7.4), a Nash equilibrium for pure[7] strategies does not exist, or there are more than one, and it is necessary to look for the NE for mixed strategies. This situation may occur because in these games players are uncertain about what they will do.

A mixed strategy is a probability distribution over the strategies that are feasible for the players. There is Nash equilibrium if each player mixes (or randomizes) his/her strategies to give the best response to the other player's mixed strategy. Each player tries to guess the other player's moves assigning them certain probabilities, and calculate the expected value of the payoffs. The equilibrium is identified for the probabilities that make the player indifferent between strategies. For player 1 the expected playoffs are:

Table 7.3   Battle of the sexes

		Player B	
		Coffee	Sleep
Player A	Coffee	(5, 2)	(0, 0)
	Sleep	(0, 0)	(2, 5)

Table 7.4   Matching pennies

		Player B	
		Heads	Tails
Player A	Heads	(−1, 1)	(1, −1)
	Tails	(1, −1)	(−1, 1)

$$E_1(s_{1j},s_{2k}) = \sum_{k=1}^{K} p_{2k}\pi_1(s_{1j},s_{2k}) \qquad (7.3)$$

where j and k are respectively the jth and the kth pure strategy of players 1 and 2. Contrarily to the NE for pure strategies, a unique NE for mixed strategies always exists. Following the previous example (Table 7.3), we can assign probabilities $(p, 1-p)$ to the player 1's strategies where p is the probability of choosing Coffee, and probabilities $(q, 1-q)$ to the player 2's strategies where q is the probability of choosing Coffee. It is therefore possible to write the expected payoff for player 1 as:

$$E_1\ (Coffee) = q\ (5) + (1-q)\ (0)$$
$$E_1\ (Sleep) = q\ (0) + (1-q)\ (2) \qquad (7.4)$$

Player 1 is indifferent between the two strategies for probability $q^* = 2/7$. Analogously, for player 2:

$$E_2(Coffee) = p(2) + (1-p)(0)$$
$$E_2(Sleep) = p(0) + (1-p)(5). \qquad (7.5)$$

Player 1 is indifferent between the two strategies for probability $p^* = 5/7$. It is possible now to present the players' best responses and the NE for pure and mixed strategies in a simple graphic:

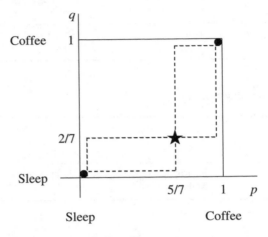

Figure 7.1   Best response correspondences

where the dashed lines are the players' best-response correspondences, while the dots represent the pure-strategies Nash equilibrium (as in the normal form, Table 7.3) and the star signals the mixed-strategies NE.

7.2.2   Noncooperative and Cooperative Games

The two main features that characterize the games are the rules establishing the way actions are taken, affecting the possible attainable outcomes, the number of players and how their actions impact other players. The first main distinction is between noncooperative and cooperative games, and this depends on whether players choose to cooperate or not. If one player decides independently to choose his/her strategy, there is no room for cooperation and the outcomes for the players may not be Pareto-efficient. On the other hand, the players may choose to cooperate to achieve a higher reward by committing themselves to an agreement. This choice is enforced by setting up a credible threat of a lower outcome that applies whenever some of the players decide not to comply with the agreement. While in the noncooperative setting the result is the best for the individual, in the cooperative games the result is the best for the entire group that has been formed. A cooperative outcome may also be obtained in the setting of dynamic games. In this case, players commit themselves to a trigger strategy, and a cooperative outcome may be sustained by a noncooperative equilibrium. Despite that, the crucial distinction between the two settings is due to the presence or absence of binding agreements. If they exist and they are feasible, the game is cooperative, otherwise it is noncooperative. In bargaining games, each player can take no decisive action because the structure of the game decides the outcome. Despite this restriction, cooperative games preserve much of their appeal. A brief introduction on the structure of these games follows.[8]

7.2.2.1 Dynamic games

Threats and expectations about the future can influence players' behaviour in the case of repeated games because repeated interactions between players should have an effect on the predicted outcome of the game. Dynamic games are divided in finitely and infinitely repeated games. This distinction is important because it affects the possibility of achieving cooperative outcomes with an underlying noncooperative equilibrium. A particular feature that makes noncooperative dynamic games particularly fascinating is indeed that the equilibrium set often includes outcomes lying on the payoff possibility frontier representing Pareto-efficient solutions obtainable only through cooperation. In fact, a way to achieve cooperative outcomes in a noncooperative framework is to introduce a trigger strategy, forcing players to act cooperatively. If players deviate from the cooperative strategy, they receive a lower payoff, represented by the payoff obtainable for the noncooperative NE of the static game. This is more likely to happen in the case of infinitely repeated games. To understand why this is possible, it is first necessary to distinguish between games with infinite and finite horizon times.

A game is a finitely repeated game if each game is played T finite number of times, and each stage is played only when the previous one has been observed and the payoffs of the whole game are the sum of each stage's playoffs

$$\pi_i = \sum_{t=1}^{T} \delta^{t-1} \pi_{it}(s_i), \tag{7.6}$$

where π_{it} denotes the payoff to player i in period t, and where $\delta = 1/(1+r)$ is the discount factor of the ith player in the tth period $(0 < \delta < 1)$ and r is interest rate. Recalling the example of the prisoners' dilemma, consider a two-stage game, which satisfies the assumption that for each feasible outcome of the first-stage game, the second-stage game that remains has a unique Nash equilibrium (Gibbons, 1992). The outcome of the remaining game, in the second stage, is the NE (1, 1). Therefore, at the first stage, the payoffs for the second stage are added to each first stage payoff pair, resulting in a unique NE (2, 2).[9] Since there is a unique subgame-perfect NE at each stage, no trigger strategy may be applied (Friedman, 1986) and no cooperation may be achieved. In the case of multiple NE at the first stage of the game, resulting in multiple NE in the whole game, cooperation can be achieved in the first stage of a subgame-perfect outcome of a supergame (Gibbons 1992, pp. 84–8). In some cases, even in the case with no multiple Nash equilibria, it is possible to obtain cooperative payoffs. Radner (1980) and Friedman (1985) state the conditions under which the trigger strategy exists in the context of finite horizon dynamic games. Friedman says that trigger strategies can support games that give each player a payoff that is no lower than the worse they can get with a single-period NE. Radner relies on the concept of *bounded rationality*. Using Friedman's words:

> . . . if players are content to use strategies that are within ε[10] of being best replies, then trigger strategy ε-equilibria are possible in games having sufficiently long, but finite, horizons. . . . The bounded rationality . . . is characterized by compromise between purely instinctive and/or traditional behavior on one hand and full rationality on the other.

His work leads to two solutions using a solution concept expressed earlier. If there is a unique equilibrium point, then a subgame-perfect trigger strategy equilibrium cannot exist, while in the case that there are multiple equilibrium points, then a trigger strategy equilibrium is possible.

When a game has an infinite horizon and is infinitely repeated, the payoffs are represented as follows:

$$\pi_i = (1 - \delta) \sum_{t=1}^{\infty} \delta^{t-1} \pi_{it}(s_i). \tag{7.7}$$

In the infinitely repeated games the players achieve as outcome the discounted sum of the payoffs over an infinite interval of time. Recalling the example of the prisoners' dilemma, the situation represented by the cooperative solution RS–RS may be attained at each stage, even if the equilibrium is still the noncooperative NE. This result is obtainable only if the players have 'cooperated' until the present stage of the game. This result is enforced introducing a plan of actions, called *trigger strategy*, which implies that if a player fails to comply with it, and deviates from the expected pattern, the punishment is to change the strategy to a single period noncooperative outcome forever after. In order to avoid noncredible threats that may distract the player from the optimal point, Selten proposed a refinement of the NE called *subgame-perfect equilibrium*. To be subgame perfect, the Nash equilibrium has to occur for each subgame, where sub-game is defined as a smaller part of the whole game, or repetition of the whole game. If the noncooperative outcome is subgame perfect, and it is worse for every player than those resulting from the agreed strategies, it is self-enforcing because it represents a credible threat. No players intend to deviate from the cooperative strategy and the supergame outcome increases. Aumann (1981) highlighted a common insight cited in the literature that says that if all the discount factors δ are close enough to one where players are concerned about future payoffs, and the individually rational playoff vector is Nash equilibrium (subgame-perfect), the outcome of the infinitely repeated game is the cooperative one. Friedman (1971) states that the definition of threat makes no sense in noncooperative dynamic games because it assumes that players agree on strategies to deal with the threat, and a condition for a noncooperative game setting is that coalitions and bargaining are ruled out and players maximize their payoffs regardless of other players' payoffs. This means that threats are not credible, and there is no incentive for them to exist. He introduces instead a slightly different notion, namely 'temptation'. To explain this notion using Friedman's words: 'If a player can increase his single period profit for a period or so, he may be tempted to do so, but the other players are, in response, likely to revert to a "safe" position.'

That means that players tacitly collude on the choice of strategy. Instead of a clear commitment to the action plan, they assume that every player will have the good sense to choose the strategy leading to the cooperative outcome. In his work, Friedman provides a result in which the noncooperative equilibrium is Pareto-optimal. The convex combination of feasible payoffs from pure strategies in the prisoners' dilemma game in Table 7.2 is represented by the shaded region[11] in Figure 7.2. Denote the trigger strategy for player j in the repeated game $G(T, \delta)$ as follows

$$Player\ j \begin{cases} \text{Play RS if no player has previously deviated} \\ \text{Play C otherwise} \end{cases}, \qquad (7.8)$$

where RS and C correspond respectively to the cooperative strategy and the NE of static game (noncooperative) strategies. The NE outcome C–C is Pareto-dominated by RS–RS, but cooperation is not individually rational. Define $(\pi_1(s_i), \ldots, \pi_n(s_i))$ the n-tuple of feasible payoffs to the n players and $(\pi_1(s^d), \ldots, \pi_n(s^d))$ the payoffs from a Nash equilibrium of a game G. The Folk theorem (Friedman, 1971) states that if $\pi_j(s_i) > \pi_j(s^d)$ for every player j, then there exists a subgame-perfect equilibrium of $G(\infty, \delta)$ that attains $(\pi_1(s_i), \ldots, \pi_n(s_i))$ as the average payoff, provided that δ is sufficiently close

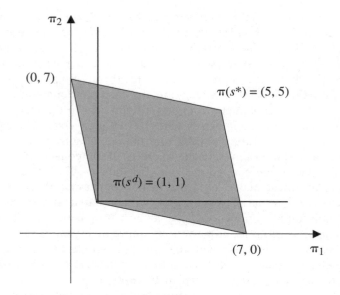

Figure 7.2   Payoffs set and Folk region

to 1. The Folk region of the prisoners' dilemma game described in Table 7.2 is thus defined as:

$$FR = \{(\pi_1, \pi_2) \quad \text{s.t.:} (\pi_1, \pi_2) = \lambda_1(1, 1), \lambda_2(0, 7), \lambda_3(7, 0), \lambda_4(5, 5),$$

with:

$$\sum_1^4 \lambda_i = 1, \quad \lambda_i \geq 0,$$

and

$$\pi_1 > 1, \pi_2 > 1\}.$$

The Folk theorem thus guarantees that in case of an infinitely repeated game, introducing a trigger strategy allows players to obtain even the Pareto-efficient outcome RS–RS with payoffs (5, 5). It is possible to calculate δ such that RS–RS in every period is a trigger strategy equilibrium. The payoff along the equilibrium path is:

$$5 + \delta 5 + \delta^2 5 + \delta^3 5 \ldots = \frac{5}{1 - \delta},$$

and the payoff from deviating is:

$$7 + \delta + \delta^2 + \delta^3 \ldots = 7 + \frac{\delta}{1 - \delta}.$$

Therefore RS–RS is the trigger strategy equilibrium if

$$\frac{5}{1 - \delta} > 7 + \frac{\delta}{1 - \delta}$$

and solving for δ it is found that RS–RS is a subgame-perfect equilibrium if and only if $\delta > \frac{2}{6}$, because the trigger strategy constitutes a Nash equilibrium on every subgame of $G(\infty, \delta)$.

7.2.2.2 Cooperative games

Under the cooperative framework, players commit themselves to binding agreements. There are various kinds of cooperative games, and they mainly depend on the number of players. Part of the literature has concentrated on the two-person cooperative games, while others have extended the analysis to n players. The nature of cooperative games allows thinking in a n players setting. It is natural that in games where agreements are a fundamental component, the formation of *coalitions* among players is a possible realization of this, since a coalition is a subset of those n that make binding agreements. Another distinction is due to the concept of *transferable utility*. It means that each coalition may receive a certain amount of utility and may divide it among its members freely. Another important feature of cooperative games is represented by the concept of *core* which is the set of payoffs attached to strategies that are Pareto-efficient, and therefore, not dominated by any other strategies.

We now introduce an example from Friedman (1986) describing a situation depicted in Figure 7.3 where two persons have a limited supply of two commodities. Each one has an utility function depending on the personal value assigned to those commodities. Suppose that the two players trade the commodities to increase their utility. H represents the compact set[12] of feasible payoffs. The point d represents the status quo, or threat point, representing the payoffs that the players will get in case of disagreement. Its upper bound, line AB, represents the Pareto-optimal set. The line represents the payoffs possibility frontier – the highest feasible payoffs – that is also called the *contract curve*. Each point on it is Pareto-optimal for the players in the game.

The segment CD represents the *core*, defined as the set of Pareto-efficient allocations that are stable in the sense that any other outcome may be blocked by the other player. As appears clearly in Figure 7.3, the core may

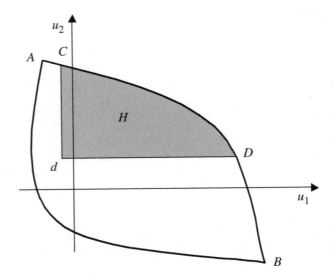

Source: Friedman, 1986.

Figure 7.3   The attainable payoffs in a fixed threat game

consist of many points, or may be empty, but it is unlikely to consist of only one point.

In his seminal works (1950, 1953), John Nash provides a solution that gives a unique outcome (Figure 7.4). The conditions defining the Nash solutions are described by the axioms introduced by Nash (1953):

1.   for each game there is a unique solution, point $N\,(v_1, v_2)$;
2.   if (u_1, u_2) is in N and $u_1 > v_1$ and $u_2 > v_2$ then $(u_1, u_2) = (v_1, v_2)$, the solution is not dominated by any other point in H other than N itself;
3.   the solution is invariant for positive linear transformations of the utilities: $u_1 = a_1\,u_1 + b_1$, $u_2 = a_2 u_2 + b_2$ with $a_1, a_2 > 0$;
4.   symmetry of the solution;
5.   if the set H is restricted to different set, $H' \subset H$, which still contains the solution point of the original game, then this point will be the solution of the new game;
6.   restricting the set of strategies cannot increase the value of the game.

These axioms guarantee the solution to be $(u_1 - d_1)\,(u_2 - d_2)$, individuated by point N in Figure 7.4, a hyperbola asymptotic to the lines starting from the threat point where the product is constant. Assuming an absence of

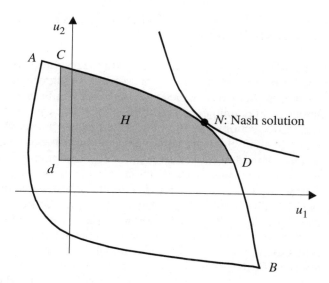

Figure 7.4   The Nash solution

cooperation between subsets of the players, the Nash bargaining solution for the *2-person bargaining problem* can be extended to the *n-person bargaining problem*. Therefore we write the generalized Nash bargaining solution as the point *s* at which

$$\max_{\substack{u \in U \\ u \geq d}} \prod_{j \in P} (u_j - d_j)^{\alpha_j}, \tag{7.9}$$

where U is the bargaining set, u_j is the player's *j*th cooperative payoff and d_j is the player's *j*th disagreement payoff, and $u_j \geq d_j$ for all j, while α_j is player *j*th bargaining power parameter.

It is worth noticing that the disagreement outcomes are not fixed, but depend on the chosen actions. The cooperative game may thus be set as a noncooperative game where the disagreement actions determine disagreement payoffs and the disagreement payoffs determine the cooperative agreement (Friedman, 1986). Nash axioms look for a Nash bargaining equilibrium (a unique one). The solution (equilibrium) of the bargaining process is identified if Nash's axioms hold.

Other approaches to fixed threat bargaining have been presented in the literature. Their review is beyond the purpose of this work.

7.3 CONFLICT RESOLUTION AND SEARCH FOR CONSENSUS

Game theory represents a useful tool to deal with the resolution of conflict. People involved in a conflict may try to solve it by agreeing on some common strategies that are beneficial to both sides. Infinitely repeated dynamic games or bargaining are useful tools for this purpose. As introduced in the above sections, the use of repeated games allows players to achieve cooperative, and therefore Pareto-efficient, outcomes, as well as the bargaining solution used in cooperative games. It is common to find in the literature examples regarding the application of game theory to analysis of conflicts concerning land use, water rights conflicts, fish wars, and other situations where multiple subjects are sharing the same resource for which property rights are not well defined. Conflicts arising over land disputes, which are a problem in many parts of the developing part of the world, can be addressed developing game theoretic models. In fishery economics, game theory is particularly useful in the case of transboundary stocks, i.e. where fish species are highly migratory, and the stocks are shared between countries or fleets. An application to this problem can be found in Munro (2000) where the long-term viability of the UN Fish Stock Agreement is assessed with the aid of both noncooperative and cooperative games. Some authors have suggested cooperative game setting as a framework to study the negotiation process of cooperative agreements (Kaitala and Lindroos (1998), Brasão et al. (2000)). Other authors have proposed management solutions to preserve fish stocks from overexploitation (Arnason et al. (2000), Lindroos and Kaitala (2000), etc.), or further, to analyse the interaction of two parties who harvest the same fish population which is affected by two externalities, the dynamic and the biological interaction between fish species (Fisher and Mirman, 1996).

On the topic of water rights Frisvold and Caswell (2000) make use of game theory to derive a policy dealing with transboundary pollution along the US–Mexican border. They first consider negotiations over the projects as a cooperative game, and secondly they model the issue for border cities seeking other forms of funding for joint water projects as a sequential bargaining game. Another study by Becker and Easter (1999) uses game theory to assess the potential for cooperative management of water resources such as the Great Lakes. They first analyse the noncooperative game setting of the problem which, in their case, does not represent the optimal solution, and then they find that USA and Canada receive higher benefits when cooperating.

7.3.1　Application to the Case of West Garda Regional Forest

The tools of game theory are here applied to a practical case regarding the resolution of conflicts arising among stakeholders of the forest of High Garda Natural Park, located in the north-west part of Garda Lake. The park extends for 38 000 hectares, but only 11 064 belonging to West Garda Regional Forest were actually considered in the project. As discussed in previous chapters, the natural area provides many services and activities, and the forest's stakeholders aim to convince the forest's management (ERSAF) to adopt management strategies giving them the highest benefits. The convergence of multiple interests generates conflicts among these interest groups, preventing ERSAF from implementing optimal management decisions that could lead to higher benefits for themselves and the community. In this situation, ERSAF perpetuates the status quo instead of exploiting the intrinsic characteristics of the natural area as a potential source of economic and environmental benefits.

In the previous chapter developing multi-criteria analysis (MCA), some possible management goals have been maximized subject to the land constraint, deriving a payoff matrix as a result (Table 5.4, Chapter 5). The table is useful in showing the nature of possible conflicts existing between the management's goals, e.g. when it emphasizes productive activities rather than protective ones. These alternatives reflect the interests of the stakeholders because each of the stakeholders has a preference for one management strategy over another. As introduced earlier, the *forest management* pursues the goal of optimizing all the services provided by the area. Alternatively, *hunters* and *fishermen* favour the development of hunting and fishing activities in the forest, asking for more permits for their activities. *Visitors* on the other hand may wish to enjoy a greater presence of wildlife, or to have access to areas of the forest normally devoted to hunting activities.

The analysis develops in two directions. The first follows from the results presented in the previous chapters of the book, making use of the maximum revenues and optimal management alternatives arrived at in Chapter 5. The second approach assumes that the questionnaire was designed to elicit preferences from every group of stakeholders.

Following the first approach, we apply a game setting to a real situation in which all the forest's stakeholders meet around a table to decide on the management of the forest. Recall that the objective of each stakeholder is to maximize the benefits deriving from the forest given the constraint on the amount of land, and the intrinsic characteristics of the area. The information necessary to address this problem is obtained using methods described in the previous chapters. In Chapter 2, GIS techniques are used to work out the levels of services (*quantities*) provided by the natural area. In Chapters 3 and 4, contingent valuation and travel cost methods are used to obtain a valuation of the services (*prices*) by using the preferences elicited through the questionnaire. Finally in Chapter 5, combining the information on prices and quantities, multi-criteria analysis is used to identify the best management strategies according to the hypothesis of maximizing the forest's management revenues.

We set up a static game where the forest's stakeholders are the players. They are instructed in the 'rules' of the game by the 'master of the game', a specialist who provides the information and guides the stakeholders through the steps necessary to the resolution of their disputes. More formally, let the players be providers (P), forest's management (FM), hunters/fishermen (HF), visitors/tourists (VT), $P = \{P, PM, HF, VT\}$, and assume that each player is rational and has complete information about the other players' payoff functions. The strategies of the game are the management alternatives introduced with the MCA, $S = \{A1, A2, A3\}$, and depend on the number of acres devoted to each of the services and activities offered by the natural area. Those are productive (Prod), protective (Prot), naturalistic (Nat), and recreational (Rec) activities as defined earlier. The three management alternatives defined in S are as follows:

1. A1, the actual forest plan, focuses especially on naturalistic characteristics, and expresses the natural vocation of the area;
2. A2, the non-participative regional management programme, focuses on naturalistic-recreational services, and it derives from the preferences expressed by ERSAF management;
3. A3, the participative regional management programme, focuses on improving wildlife, vegetation and landscapes, and it represents visitors' and residents' preferences.

Table 7.5 summarizes the shares of land devoted to each service under each management alternative obtained with MCA according to the hypothesis of maximizing the forest's management revenues (Chapter 5). Payoffs of the game are the maximum revenues/benefits achieved for each player that was interviewed. Recalling from Chapter 5, the maximum revenues for each strategy for the forests' authority (ERSAF), in the case of maximization of its benefits (revenues), are the values in Table 7.6.[13]

Unfortunately, the best combination of services and the maximization of stakeholders' benefit were done only for the forest's management (ERSAF) case. Nevertheless, the framework of the MCA can be applied to the task of maximizing other players' benefits. Using the same approach, we derive the payoffs for the *visitors* according to the hypothesis of maximizing benefits to visitors, Table 7.7[14] (considering an average of 11 598 visitors per year),

Table 7.5   Best combination of services under the different strategies for forest's management

Strategy	Prod	Prot	Nat	Rec
A1	0.02	0.02	0.65	0.31
A2	0.02	0.02	0.65	0.31
A3	0.02	0.02	0.02	0.94

Table 7.6   Maximum revenues-payoffs for forest's management

Strategy	Payoff (euros)
A1	21 738
A2	21 738
A3	20 141

Table 7.7   Payoffs for the visitors

Strategy	Payoff (euros)
A1	50 451
A2	53 030
A3	73 385

and for the two remaining players, *hunters/fishermen* and *providers*. It was not possible to collect enough information on the last two categories of stakeholders and from now on we assume full knowledge of the payoff functions of every player.

The 'master of the game' proceeds as follows. After having provided the players with the necessary information and explained the rules, he lets them play, pursuing their own interests. If rational, the players will choose the feasible strategy that maximizes their personal benefit regardless of which strategy other players choose. In this case the chosen strategies are the Nash equilibrium of the game (NE), and the payoffs attached to those strategies represent the players' rewards. Suppose now that the master allows the players to sign binding agreements before the game starts. So doing, they are able to achieve any payoff in the set X, defined as the convex set formed by the convex combination of the payoffs that can be achieved by the players (feasible payoffs, like the H set in Figure 7.3). The set probably contains payoffs

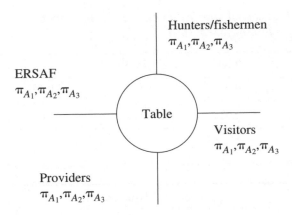

Figure 7.5   Representation of players' interaction

that are higher than the payoffs of NE previously obtained. Indeed, the upper bound of X is the so-called *bargaining set*, that contains all the individually rational, Pareto-efficient payoffs. Now imagine that conditional on this knowledge, the stakeholders decide to sign a binding contract in which they choose to implement the management strategy that gives them the highest payoffs. The 'master of the game' explains to the stakeholders that in case of disagreement no decision will be made other than carrying on the *status quo*. The points in X represent the payoffs obtainable as a consequence of the disagreement. The solution of this new game is now the Nash bargaining solution obtained applying the problem (7.9) to our specific case and it is the only solution that satisfies Nash axioms described in section 7.2.2.2.

7.3.2   Alternative Framework

Suppose enough information was obtained through the questionnaire to estimate a utility function for each category of stakeholders. Suppose the utility function of each stakeholder is a Cobb–Douglas type defined as follows:

$$U_j(s_i) = \prod_{i=1}^{K} A s_i^{\alpha_{ij}}, \qquad (7.10)$$

where s_i is the ith service provided by the forest, α_{ij} is the parameter of the ith service for the jth player, and $\Sigma_{i=1}^{K}\alpha_{ij} = 1$.[15] In this case, the utility function takes the following form:

$$U_j = A \operatorname{Prod}^{\alpha_j} \operatorname{Prot}^{\beta_j} \operatorname{Nat}^{\gamma_j} \operatorname{Rec}^{1-\alpha_j-\beta_j-\gamma_j}, \qquad (7.11)$$

where Prod, Prot, Nat, Rec stand respectively for areas allocated to productive, protective, naturalistic, and recreational activities; α, β and γ are estimated parameters for each stakeholder, and A is a constant. Each stakeholder s maximizes his own utility, given the constraint that the sum of acres allocated for each activity is equal to the total extension of the forest: Prod + Prot + Nat + Rec = Area. Substituting the constraint into the utility function we get the utility function to be maximized

$$U_j = A\,\mathrm{Prod}^{\alpha_j}\mathrm{Prot}^{\beta_j}\mathrm{Nat}^{\gamma_j}(\mathrm{Area} - \mathrm{Prod} - \mathrm{Prot} - \mathrm{Nat})^{1-\alpha_j-\beta_j-\gamma_j} \quad (7.12)$$

Substituting the optimal value for the acres allocated to each activity it is possible to get the maximum value of utility for each group of stakeholders.

We can find the optimal allocation of acres by setting up a game and solving for the Nash equilibrium in both a static and a dynamic framework. This equilibrium will indicate the best management strategy for the forest given the preferences expressed by the stakeholders. More formally, let the players be the same as before $P = \{HK, PM, HF, VT\}$, and the strategies to be now represented by the ratio activities/services. We can then normalize the total forest's area to 1 and the quotas of forest's area allocated to each activity being Prod/Area, Prot/Area, Nat/Area, Rec/Area. The new strategies are $S = \{\mathrm{Prod/Area}, \mathrm{Prot/Area}, \mathrm{Nat/Area}, \mathrm{Rec/Area}\}$, and the payoffs are the maximum values of the utility. In the presence of uncertainty, the players guess what strategy the other players will choose. In the case that players mix their strategies (Section 7.2.1), probabilities are associated with each strategy. These probabilities correspond to the quota of forest area allocated to each activity. More formally, the probability of jth player of playing Prod is $\mathrm{Prob}_j(\mathrm{Prod}) = w1_j$ and it follows that $\mathrm{Prob}_j(\mathrm{Prot}) = w2_j$, $\mathrm{Prob}_j(\mathrm{Nat}) = w3_j$, $\mathrm{Prob}_j(\mathrm{Rec}) = 1 - w1_j - w2_j - w3_j$. Therefore $w1_j$ is the quota of land allocated to production activities, $w2_j$, $w3_j$, and $1 - w1_j - w2_j - w3_j$, to protection, naturalistic, and recreational functions respectively. Suppose that players meet again and behave as explained before, but now they are not allowed to sign any binding agreement. In this case, the NE (pure strategies and/or mixed strategy) gives the optimal combination of acres allocated to each function under the noncooperative setting of the game.

Consider now a dynamic version of the same game, where players repeat it an infinite number of times. It is possible to define a new set of strategies for each group of stakeholders where they play the cooperative strategy if no player has previously deviated, or they play the noncooperative NE[16] otherwise. This time the cooperative strategy corresponds to the collusion behaviour often described in the Cournot model. When players collude and act cooperatively they maximize the total benefit, given by the sum of each player's utility function:

$$W = \max \sum_{j=1}^{4} U_j$$
$$s.t. \ \text{Prod} + \text{Prot} + \text{Nat} + \text{Rec} = \text{Area}$$

(7.13)

Denote as COLL the solution to the above problem, where optimal values for Prod, Prot, Nat, and Rec have been obtained. Denote the trigger strategy for player j in the repeated game $G(T, \delta)$ as follows

$$Player \ j \begin{cases} \text{Play COLL if no player has previously deviated;} \\ \text{Play NE otherwise,} \end{cases}$$

(7.14)

where COLL is the cooperative strategy defined above, and NE is the punishment strategy, which is the Nash equilibrium of static game (noncooperative).[17] Provided that all discount factors δ are close enough to one (players are concerned about future payoffs), and the individually rational playoff vector is a Nash equilibrium (subgame-perfect), the adoption of a trigger strategy guarantees that the outcome of the infinitely repeated game corresponds to the cooperative one, and this guarantees that the forest's stakeholders will act cooperatively in order to reach higher payoffs than those achievable with NE strategies.

7.4   CONCLUSIONS

Designing a questionnaire, instructing interviewers, conducting the interviews, and analysing the collected information are all expensive tasks. It is not possible sometimes, for some small agencies of public administration, for example small provinces or local institutions, to bear the costs of such complex activities. Under this budget constraint, it is possible that public agencies do not have enough information to make a decision on the management of the area, and will therefore decide on a strategy that does not reflect the needs of the stakeholders.

There are other ways to elicit stakeholders' preferences. A Finnish professor, R.P. Hämäläinen and some of his colleagues (Hämäläinen and Lauri, 1995) have made use of different techniques. Instead of quantitative methods, they deduce preferences translating verbal statements into real numbers by comparing alternatives, and assigning weights to them.

The application of the procedure described in this chapter guarantees that a management decision will be taken. Its implementation will lead to higher benefits than those achievable perpetuating the status quo, and the natural area will be finally managed with the consideration and agreement of stakeholders' preferences and the intrinsic characteristics of the area.

This chapter coordinates the qualitative analysis of conflict resolution and the quantitative analysis of preferences in one coherent structure in order to resolve environmental conflicts. The choice of using the techniques of game theory is because of its usefulness in describing the behaviour of social agents facing a strategic decision-making process. The fact that game theory helps to reach management decisions that are Pareto-efficient is of extreme importance, especially when collective choices have to be taken. This allows public administration to adopt measures on the territory that represent the best for the stakeholders of the area.

The management of a natural area does not concern only the forest authority. The ecosystem and the economy of the entire region in which it is located are affected by its activities. It is therefore natural to consider the representatives of all parts of society that are interested. The variety of services provided by natural areas requires the establishment of activities designed to improve the socio-economic and cultural life of local communities, and the opportunities of enjoyment for potential visitors. This highlights the necessity of the considering preferences and interests of all those concerned in the natural area when deciding on a long-term management plan, even if so doing would possibly lead to conflicts among them. This work suggests therefore a way to resolve these conflicts, helping the institution to identify the optimal management decision in consideration of the characteristics of the natural area and the preferences of the stakeholders, guaranteeing that best practices are adopted in the short run and are not left as a burden for future generations.

NOTES

1. Players interact directly, rather than through the market.
2. A game has complete information if each player knows the payoff function of all other players (Gibbons, 1992).
3. Under an assumption of complete information games in which each player has knowledge of other players' payoffs.
4. Payoffs represent the utility attainable by a player using the chosen strategy.
5. The strategies have to be feasible.
6. The version of the game presented here is from Perali (2000) about 'Who makes the coffee?', but the concept is analogous to the classical framework of the 'battle of the sexes'. Here, the game simply represents a dispute about who between wife or husband has to make coffee in the morning.
7. A pure strategy is a strategy that does not have an associated probability distribution.

8. The descripton is restricted to games with complete information. For a more extensive presentation of the theory refer to Gibbons (1992), Friedman (1986), Osborne and Rubinstein (1994), Myerson (1991).
9. This is analogue to backwards-induction outcome. See Gibbons (1992) and Friedman (1986).
10. This can be any positive number.
11. The set has to be compact, that is convex and bounded.
12. The set H is a compact set and the maximum payoff may be attained if the set is convex and both closed and bounded (Friedman, 1986).
13. It is important to point out that these values were obtained considering the natural vocation of the area and preferences of stakeholders. Notice that the forest's authority is indifferent between alternatives A1 and A2, that is $A1 \approx A2 > A3$.
14. Not surprisingly, the visitors prefer alternative A3 to all others; in detail $A3 > A2 > A1$.
15. We are assuming constant elasticity of substitution; the parameters add up to one.
16. In case of more than one NE the one that leads to the lowest payoffs is played.
17. Unless there is another NE (e.g. pure strategy) giving a lower outcome.

REFERENCES

Albors Research Institute (2002), cited in Lega Anti Vivisezione (2003), http://www.infolav.org.

Arnason, R., G. Magnussin and S. Argnarsson (2000), 'The Norwegian spring-spawning herring fishery: a stylized game model', *Marine Resource Economics*, **15** (4), 293–319.

Aumann, R.J. (1981), 'Survey of repeated games', in Aumann et al. (eds), *Essays in Game Theory*, Mannheim: Bibliographisches Institut.

Becker, N. and K.W. Easter (1999), 'Conflict and cooperation in managing international water resources such as the Great Lakes', *Land Economics*, **75** (2), 233–45.

Brasão, A., C.C. Duarte and M.A. Cunha-e-Sá (2000), 'Managing the Northern Atlantic bluefin tuna fisheries: the stability of the UN Fish Stock Agreement Solution', *Marine Resource Economics*, **15** (4), 341–60.

Fischer, R.D. and L.J. Mirman (1996), 'The complete fish wars: biological and dynamic interactions', *Journal of Environmental Economics and Management*, **30**, 34–42.

Friedman, J.W. (1985), 'Cooperative equilibria in finite horizon noncooperative supergames', *Journal of Economic Theory*, **35**, 390–98.

Friedman, J.W. (1986), *Game Theory With Application to Economics*, Oxford: Oxford University Press.

Friedman, J.W. (1971), 'A non-cooperative equilibrium for supergames', *Review of Economic Studies*, **38**, 1–12.

Frisvold, G.B. and M.F. Caswell (2000), 'Transboundary Water Management Game-Theoretic Lessons for Projects on the US–Mexico Border', *Agricultural Economics*, **24**, 101–11.

Gibbons, R. (1992), *A Primer in Game Theory*, Hemel Hempstead: Harvester Wheatsheaf.

Hämäläinen, R.P. and H. Lauri (1995), *Hipre 3+ User's Guide, Systems Analysis Laboratory*, Helsinki: Helsinki University of Technology.

Kaitala, V. and M. Lindros (1998), 'Sharing the benefit of cooperation in high seas fisheries: a characteristic function game approach', *Natural Resource Modeling*, **11**, 275–99.

Lindroos, M. and V. Kaitala (2000), 'Nash Equilibria in a coalition game of the Norwegian spring-spawning herring fishery', *Marine Resource Economics*, **15** (4), 321–39.

Munro, R.G. (2000), 'The United Nations Fish Stocks Agreement of 1995: history and problems of implementation', *Marine Resource Economics*, **15** (4), 265–80.

Myerson, R.B. (1991), *Game Theory. Analysis of Conflict*, Cambridge, MA: Harvard University Press.

Nash, J.F. (1950), 'The Bargaining Problem', *Econometrica*, **18** (2), 155–62.

Nash, J.F. (1953), 'Two-person cooperative games', *Econometrica*, **21** (1), 128–49.

Osborne, M.J. and A. Rubinstein (1994), *A Course in Game Theory*, Cambridge, MA: MIT Press.

Perali, F. (2000), *Microeconomia Applicata. Esercitazioni*, Roma: Carocci editore.

Radner, R. (1980), 'Collusive behaviour in noncooperative epsilon-equilibria of oligopolies with long but finite lives', *Journal of Economic Theory*, **22**, 136–54.

Taylor Nelson Sofres Abacus (2002), cited in Lega Anti Vivisezione (2003), http//www. infolav.org.

Conclusions

Joseph C. Cooper, Federico Perali
and Marcella Veronesi[*]

The research programme developed in this book integrates different survey methodologies using a multidisciplinary approach. The aim was to find the best management strategy for a natural area with multifunctional characteristics. This aim was pursued within the context of the West Garda Regional Forest by combining the evaluation of a natural resource with that of the management of its public resources. To ensure the implementation of the optimal practice, we adopted a participative approach to establish a credible social contract between the area's manager of public resources and its consumers. Balancing the interests of residents, visitors and local businesses, and coupling the development of both the natural potential of the area and the local economy were necessary steps for the best strategy to be adopted.

In order to achieve the objective of best coordinating the natural, productive, protective, and tourist functions based on the manager's and consumers' preferences, the research developed through the following stages:

1. identification and estimation of the level of functions supplied by a natural area;
2. estimation of the economic value of the functions supplied by a natural area;
3. identification of the optimal combination of environmental functions;
4. analysis of the impact of each functional alternative on the local economy;
5. optimal implementation of best actions through credible social contracts.

These phases are summarized below. The first three stages belong to the assessment part of the book, the subsequent two to the management part. Brief policy recommendations follow.

PART I   ASSESSMENT

I   Identification and Estimation of the Level of Functions Supplied by a Natural Area

In this book, we followed two approaches to identifying and estimating the level of functions supplied by a natural area. The first approach, developed in Chapter 1, defined a model of territory evaluation that distinguishes the vegetation components of a natural area and characterizes their specific functionalities. Thanks to the SINGARDO environment information system, the information set (tables, graphics, maps) related to all the system elements can be continuously updated with new information. From the study of the cartographic evidence, the user can estimate each function supply and its territorial distribution.

The subdivision of the West Garda Regional Forest, on the basis of the prevalent functions, showed that 28 per cent of the territory is characterized mainly by naturalistic elements. The tourist function prevails over 10 per cent of the territory and the non-productive function of the West Garda Regional Forest characterizes about 9 per cent of the territory.

Chapter 2 was devoted to the presentation of the second approach, which uses data derived from a detailed GIS mapping system to estimate indices recording the ability of each hectare of territory to offer naturalistic, productive, protective, and tourist products and services. With the aim of aiding decision makers, such as park managers, in defining the most efficient managerial strategy, we identified five macro-areas within the West Garda Regional Forest that are related to each other by either complementary or substitute characteristics. We categorized these macro-areas as tourist; protective–naturalistic; tourist–naturalistic; protective–naturalistic; and naturalistic–tourist. Given this categorization, Chapter 2 applied multi-variate analysis to classify each hectare-cell into homogeneous macro-areas by bio-ecological characteristics and to identify their natural vocation. We used the k-means cluster analysis technique to identify these macro-areas. For each macro-area, we performed factor analysis to identify its natural characteristics. The macro-areas are the territorial units of reference appropriate for the economic evaluation analysis, which cannot be applied on a per-hectare basis for obvious reasons.

II   Estimation of the Economic Value of the Functions Supplied by the Natural Area

We applied two methods to estimate the economic value of the functions supplied by the natural area: (1) the contingent valuation method

(CVM) in Chapter 3; and (2) the travel cost method (TCM) in Chapter 4.

Chapter 3 applied a novel contingent valuation method that we termed fair one-and-one-half-bound (FOOHB) in order to find the values of the functions supplied by the natural area. By allowing the respondent to choose the starting point for the bidding process, FOOHB introduces fairness into discrete choice contingent valuation question format, and should decrease the potential for the respondent to consider the interview to be largely a top-down process that minimizes the input of the respondent to simply a 'yes' or 'no' response. Adding fairness to interactions between policymakers and the household level is a way of encouraging citizen participation in policy decisions as called for by the guidelines for sustainable agriculture and rural development (SARD).

Respondents were asked whether they would be willing to pay for an entrance ticket in order to improve the quality of the management and preservation of the area, and for an annual subscription fee, which would finance projects to improve the quality and quantity of recreational activities. Before asking about their willingness to pay a fee to improve the recreational activities of the area, visitors were asked how they allocated their time during the visit between the functions offered by the forest. Combining this information, we worked out the prices for the different functions that users would be willing to pay. To the best of our knowledge, this is the first study that estimates the price for the functions supplied by a natural area using a single survey.

In order to cross-validate the results obtained with the contingent valuation method, Chapter 4 implemented the travel cost method estimating both a single recreational demand equation and the associated consumer surplus of visitors of the natural area and a complete demand system conditional on leisure consumption. This latter approach presented a recreational demand model that exploited the notion of separability to derive a two-stage demand system conditional on leisure consumption. First, visitors to the natural area proceeded to allocate their total income among the broad groups of food, leisure and other goods. Subsequently, visitors decided how to distribute their expenditure on leisure, between trips to West Garda Regional Forest, trips to other sites and other leisure activities.

The model in Chapter 4 has two principal advantages over the contingent valuation method applied in Chapter 3 and over existing valuation models in the literature. First, by incorporating the budget constraint in the analysis, the complete system approach forces recognition of the fact that an increase in expenditure on one consumption category, such as recreation for example, must be balanced by decreases in expenditure on others. Second, the complete system approach permits the separation of demographic effects from own and cross-price effects as well as income effects. The economic results are presented in the context of the almost ideal demand system (AIDS).

The consumer surplus for the users of the West Garda Regional Forest is about 25 euros per trip. The corresponding per-day willingness to pay is about 4 euros which is very close to the willingness to pay for a ticket estimated by applying the FOOHB contingent valuation method described in Chapter 2. Interestingly, the correct comparison should involve the comparison between the CVM-based willingness to pay and the willingness to pay estimated using a travel cost method that accounts for the travel cost of each member of the family, rather than for the travel cost of the household as a whole. The estimation comparison at the individual level is left for future research.

Combining the knowledge of the quantities of the forest's functions estimated in Chapters 1 and 2 with the knowledge of their values estimated in Chapter 3 and 4, the next step was analysing the optimal management strategies from the point of view of the manager of public resources, the users and the local community.

PART II   MANAGEMENT

III   Identifying the Optimal Combination of Environmental Functions

Chapter 5 described the methodological aspects of the multi-criteria analysis as applied to the management of the forest. We proposed a new approach that integrates bio-ecological information obtained from GIS analysis with the forest users' preferences derived from CVM and multi-criteria analysis. In doing so, we defined the best combination of managerial interventions combining naturalistic, productive, protective and tourist functions, which maximizes administrative revenues including users' preferences and taking into account the geographical and bio-ecological characteristics of the natural area.

The first step defines a set of management alternative strategies. Three scenarios are simulated: (1) a multifunctional park with naturalistic tendency (actual forest plan); (2) a natural and tourist park (non-participative regional management programme) where the managerial policy is defined taking into consideration only the preferences of the management administrator, based on their technical knowledge of the area; and (3) a naturalistic park (participative regional management programme), which assumes participatory planning where decisions are made after finding out the preference structure of users (tourists and residents).

The second step compares the results associated with two different specifications of the objective function. The first approach maximizes an objective function representing the net benefits in quantitative levels of functions supplied by the forest, while in the second approach the objective function maximizes revenues of the administrative government. In doing so, the model integrated the quantitative function levels described in Chapters 1 and 2, with the users' willingness to pay a hypothetical entrance ticket and an annual subscription fee discussed in Chapters 3 and 4. It is important to note that the second approach allows decision makers to identify the best location of environmental functions, taking into account users' preferences by weighting each function using CVM estimates.

In particular, Chapter 5 showed that if decision makers vary the actual forest plan following the non-participative regional management scenario, the optimal allocation of objective functions would be to allocate 65 per cent of the total area surface for naturalistic purposes, 31 per cent for tourist entertainment, while protective and productive functions would be split between the 4 per cent of hectares remaining. On the other hand, if the policymaker decides to follow a participative regional management programme he would designate 94 per cent of the total territory for naturalistic purposes, while the remaining environmental services would be left at a minimum level for natural area maintenance.

IV The Impact of Each Functional Alternative on the Local Economy

Chapter 6 analysed the impact of the participative and the non-participative managerial alternatives of the West Garda Regional Forest on the local economy of the High Garda Natural Park, where the forest is located, using a social accounting matrix (SAM) framework developed at the local level. The SAM is an adequate instrument to represent the local economy and it defines the relationships between local firms and households. The SAM provides a direct and synthetic picture of sector interdependencies, of households' income formation and of the dependence of local households on local services and productive activities.

The simulation analysis showed that the participative programme would be preferable to the non-participative programme for the impact on both production sectors and income levels. It follows that the participative regional management programme matches both the preferences of users and the interests of local institutions because the territory receives more benefit from its implementation.

V Optimal Implementation of Best Actions through Credible Social Contracts

Chapter 7 proposed a methodology that helps managers of a natural area to design the best combination of services provided by a natural area, one which satisfies the preferences of institutions, local economic agents and users. The presence of multiple interests may generate conflicts among interest groups (or stakeholders). Moreover the adoption of different management strategies may cause an unfair distribution of benefits and damages leading to suboptimal management decisions. The optimal management of natural parks does not consider only the institutional authority of the natural area. The ecosystem and the economy of the entire region where it is sited are also affected by the management decisions. The policy-maker should consider the preferences and interests of all the parties concerned with the natural area, even if doing so would lead to conflict.

We used game theory to resolve the conflict arising among the natural area's stakeholders, where the payoffs are the utilities they derive from enjoying the services provided by the natural area. This chapter used the results from previous chapters, and the methodology provides the manager with the possibility of effectively implementing a cooperative management strategy that resolves the disputes arising from sharing the natural area.

We apply game theory techniques to describe the behaviour of social agents facing a strategic decision-making process. The fact that game theory helps identify management decisions that are Pareto-efficient is of extreme importance, especially when collective choices have to be taken. This allows public administration to adopt measures on the territory that represent the best for the stakeholders of the area.

Chapter 7 applied the game to a real situation in which the forest's stakeholders meet around a table to decide on the management strategies of the forest. If rational, the players choose the feasible strategy that maximizes their personal benefit regardless of which strategy other players will choose. In this case the chosen strategies are the Nash equilibrium of the game, and the payoffs attached to those strategies represent the reward of the players. This chapter showed that the forest's stakeholders would act cooperatively in order to reach higher payoffs than those achievable with Nash equilibrium by repeating the game an infinite number of times.

VI Environmental Policy Recommendations for the Development of a Natural Area

This book is intended to be a work that can be used as a reference tool showing how to integrate economic evaluations within the management process related to environmental policy decisions. It combines assessment with public management because assessment helps the manager when making decisions about how best to manage public resources. Such an analysis should be used to define policies that allow for interaction among institutions, local economic agents and the park's users, while accounting for the implications of those policies on the local economy.

It is important that the policymakers have an accurate monetary valuation of the natural resources associated with the park, including valuation of the environmental externalities. Environmental policy has to balance the costs derived from environmental externalities such as pollution with the costs for controlling pollution. Pollution has to be controlled to the point where the marginal cost to reduce pollution is equal to the marginal benefits from the pollution reduction. The optimum reduction of pollution rate is achieved when the social marginal cost for one more unit of pollution reduction is equal to the social marginal benefit for one more unit of pollution's reduction. To achieve this optimum point by means of fiscal policy, for example, requires knowledge of the marginal costs to reduce pollution, which are usually known to the firm but not to the regulator, and the marginal costs of the damages. These are usually not observable but we can deduce them by asking individuals how much they are willing to pay for an improvement to the environment.

The economic instrument has to be chosen considering both the knowledge required and cost of implementation, and its effective acceptance by society. Regulatory requirements, or standards, represent involuntary participation approaches that establish standards that all targeted actors must adhere to. Unlike policy choices in which firm participation is uncertain, regulations require categorically that all firms participate.[1] This feature is particularly important if the consequences of non-compliance are drastic or irreversible. On the other hand, regulatory requirements are a blunt tool and can be the least flexible of all policy instruments, requiring that firms reach a specific environmental goal or adopt specific practices. They are not free to determine their own level of participation, based on their costs. Unless regulators know firm-specific costs (which they are unlikely to) and can use this information to establish firm-specific regulations, environmental effort is not necessarily directed towards firms who can make changes or achieve gains at the lowest cost. Consequently, regulation can be less flexible and less efficient than economic incentives such as taxes and subsidies.

Total tax payments depend on the firm's behaviour; the further from the environmental goal, the higher the payment. The advantages of environmental tax policies are that they are consistent with the 'polluter pays' principle, which argues that the public owns environmental resources and those who pollute these resources must pay compensation to the public. In addition, taxes do not promote expansion of environmentally-damaging activities. On the other hand, taxes have a negative impact on the firm's income.

In general, taxation is an economic instrument that can be applied to reduce the depletion of natural resources, and polluting activities and to finance pollution reduction projects. For example, a tax on polluting emissions can be used to finance investments in structures for pollution control. Taxes paid by the consumer of the public good, such as the entrance ticket to a natural area, should cover both the private opportunity cost of the resource and the social one. The social opportunity cost includes the externalities that derive from using the natural resource, following the travel cost and contingent valuation methods applied in this study. Quantification of the social opportunity cost can be undertaken using the approaches developed in this book on determining the optimal combination of the tourist, productive, protective and naturalistic functions.

It is also important that revenues from taxation policies or entrance tickets to a natural park are allocated as declared. This approach favours the establishment of a credible social contract between the manager and visitors to the park.

NOTES

*   The views presented here are those of the authors, and do not necessarily represent the views or policies of the Economic Research Service or the United States Department of Agriculture.
1.   The term 'firm' here refers to both park visitors and to firms operating in the park, such as mining or timber operators.

Appendix: West Garda Regional Forest survey – a platform for policy analysis

Nicola Tommasi and Marcella Veronesi

OVERVIEW

The West Garda Regional Forest survey was conducted by the Department of Economics of the University of Verona in the north-east of Italy, on the west side of Garda Lake, in June–October 1997. This survey is a primary source of information on the recreational demand, resource use and economic value of the natural, productive, protective and tourist functions of a public forest or park. It provides information about resident and non-resident visitors' preferences and individual consumption. It considers not only the household's total expenditures, but also the distribution and use among members. Such a survey can be used as an example to define policies that allow for interactions among institutions, local economic agents and the park's users, while accounting for implications of those policies on the local economy.

STUDY SITE

The High Garda Natural Park extends over an area of 38 000 hectares (Figure A1) in Brescia province, Lombardy region. Moving from south to north over the west part of the lake, this area covers nine town councils: Salò, Gardone Riviera, Toscolano Maderno, Gargnano, Tignale, Tremosine, Limone sul Garda, Valvestino and Magasa. The Regional Forestry Agency of Lombardy region (ERSAF) is responsible for the management of the park side belonging to the region, called West Garda Regional Forest. This area extends over 11 064 hectares and represents the object of this survey.

Figure A1   West Garda Regional Forest and its location in Italy

DATA COLLECTION

The survey was in the form of on-site[1] interviews of random visitors found in the area of the West Garda Regional Forest. The questionnaire was anonymous and included 97 questions. Respondents spent between 20 and 30 minutes answering all of the questions and, on average, ten people were interviewed per day.

SURVEY ANALYSIS

The survey provides information about:

  I.   the visit to the natural area;
 II.   the quality of the natural area;

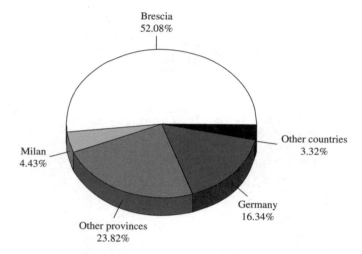

Figure A2   Respondents' nationality

III. an estimation of travelling costs;
IV. an economic valuation:
    a. of the natural area;
    b. of the natural area's functions;
V. visitors' socio-demographic characteristics.

I   Characteristics of the Visit to the Natural Area

On average 52 per cent of visitors come from Brescia province, 28 per cent of the respondents come from other provinces (for example Milan, Verona, Trento) and 20 per cent consist of foreign tourists, of which 16 per cent are German (Figure A2). Twenty per cent of the respondents stay in a house that they own as a vacation home, 20 per cent live in a friend's house, 18 per cent in a hotel and 17 per cent rent a house (Figure A3).

II   Quality of the Natural Area

West Garda Regional Forest is not a crowded area as Figure A4 shows. Only 25 per cent of the sample thinks that the area is crowded, 57 per cent of the respondents think that the level of crowding is low and 18 per cent think that the area is not crowded. The quality of the area is satisfactory for 42 per cent of the sample, but 46 per cent of respondents think that it is good and 5 per cent think it is very good (Figure A5).

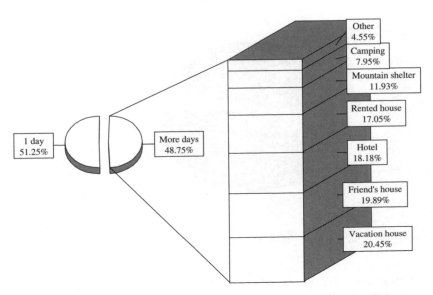

Figure A3   Respondents' accommodation

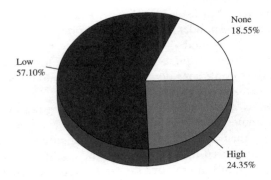

Figure A4   Crowding level

Figures A6, A7 and A8 investigate the quality of the natural area facilities. Regarding the accessibility to the area, 67 per cent of the respondents think that the parking is adequate, though 25 per cent think that an adequate parking facility is lacking. The roads inside the natural area are adequate for 61.5 per cent of the sample, however, 17 per cent think that the area needs more roads and 10 per cent do not want any infrastructure. About half of the respondents think that mountain bike paths and trekking

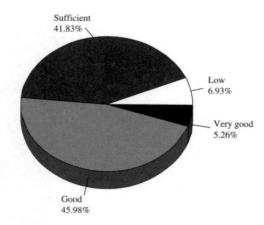

Figure A5   Quality of the area

paths are good, but 11 per cent of respondents do not want any mountain bike paths at all. If we consider picnic areas, we have 52 per cent of respondents who think they are good and 35 per cent who think they have to be improved. Concerning fishing areas, we have contradicting opinions: 42 per cent are not interested in fishing facilities, 27 per cent do not want these areas, 13 per cent of respondents consider them low-quality and only 17 per cent think that they are good.

We can see conflicting opinions about the area for rubbish disposal: 50 per cent of the sample considers them adequate and 40 per cent believe that the natural area needs more of them.

Other questions were asked about the quality of guides or naturalistic teaching programmes: 23 per cent of respondents are not interested, 14 per cent do not want them and if 28 per cent think that they are good, 35 per cent think that they need to be improved. The quality of road signs and information signs in the natural area are considered good by 47 per cent of the sample, but low by 45 per cent. The percentage of respondents not interested in a security service is 22 per cent, while 42 per cent think that this service is good and 28 per cent feel that it should be improved. Another question was about what respondents think about the fauna and flora variety of the area. While 88 per cent of the sample think that the flora is good and only 4 per cent think that the flora quality is low, 65 per cent had a positive opinion about the fauna and 23 per cent had negative views. In general, respondents think that the West Garda Regional Forest's quality is good.

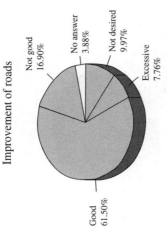

Improvement of roads

Not good
16.90%

No answer
3.88%

Not desired
9.97%

Excessive
7.76%

Good
61.50%

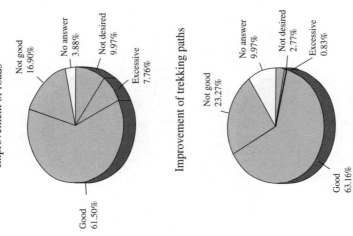

Improvement of trekking paths

No answer
9.97%

Not good
23.27%

Not desired
2.77%

Excessive
0.83%

Good
63.16%

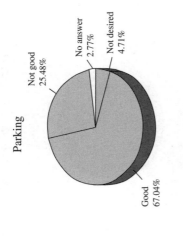

Parking

Not good
25.48%

No answer
2.77%

Not desired
4.71%

Good
67.04%

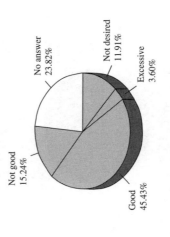

Improvement of mountain bike paths

No answer
23.82%

Not good
15.24%

Not desired
11.91%

Excessive
3.60%

Good
45.43%

Figure A6   Quality of the area's facilities

225

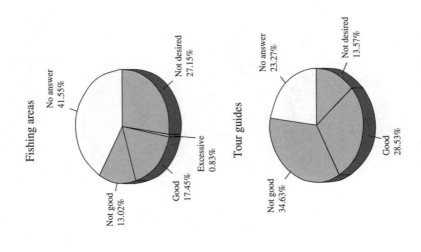

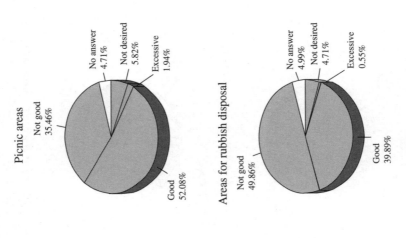

Figure A7 Quality of the area's facilities

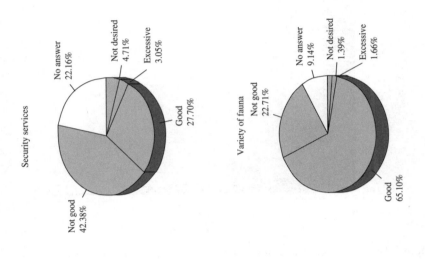

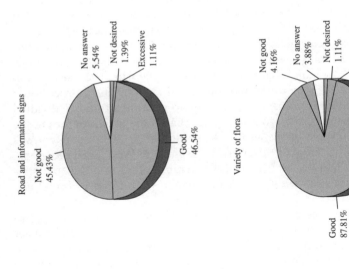

Figure A8   Quality of the area's facilities

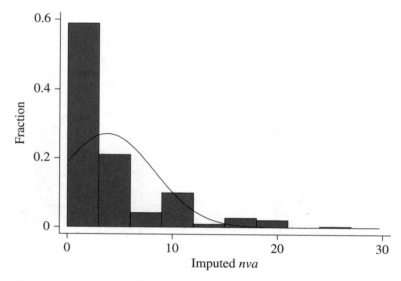

*Figure A9   Respondent's number of trips (*nva*) to the West Garda Regional Forest*

III   Estimation of Travelling Costs

This section provides the researcher with all the information she needs for estimation of travel costs (Figures A9, A10 and A11). It investigates what the respondent's mode of transportation is; how many hours the visitor has travelled to get to the West Garda Regional Forest and to go to alternative sites; how many people travelled with her, how many were family members and how many shared the expense of the trip; if she stopped in other places on the way to the natural area; how long the journey took; individual and family transportation costs to get to the forest; individual and family expenditure on food, lodging, spare-time activities during the trip and the total cost of the visit to the natural area. The respondent was asked to recall the number of annual trips made to West Garda Regional Forest and the number of trips to other natural areas in order to distinguish between visitors with a single destination from those with multiple destinations.

In order to double-check the declared costs, the visitor was asked to specify her place of residence, the distance between the natural area and her residence, journey time and for those that were on vacation, the distance from the forest to the vacation lodging. In order to estimate the expenditure for the alternative sites, the visitor was asked about the distance from her

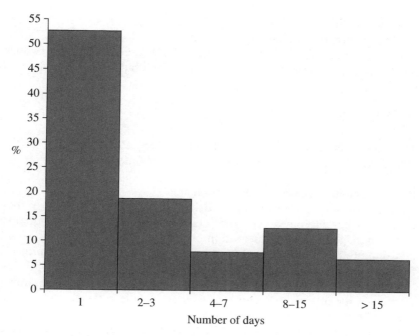

Figure A10   Number of days per visit

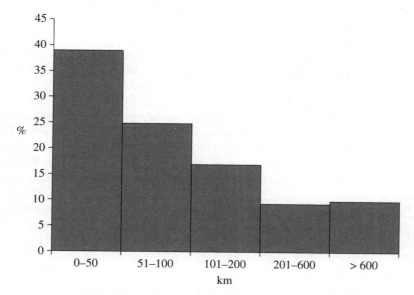

Figure A11   Distance from the place of residence (km)

residence, number of visits to each site, the quality of the area and the purpose of the trip to each alternative site.

The average number of visits per year to the West Garda Regional Forest is 6.79, the average number of days per trip is 5.78, but visitors from Brescia province enjoy more one-day trips.

IV   Economic Valuation

This section is divided into two subsections, one about the value of the natural area and the other about the value of its functions.

IV.1   Economic valuation of the natural area

Access to the forest is currently free. Respondents were asked whether they would be willing to pay an entrance ticket in order to improve the quality of the management and preservation of the area and whether they would be willing to pay an annual subscription fee, which would finance projects to improve the recreational activities. The survey was prepared following the guidelines by the NOAA[2] panel. In order not to incur bias, in the introduction of the survey it was emphasized that the objective is to improve the area and that the prices are hypothetical.

Before asking about their willingness to pay for a ticket, visitors were asked to give an opinion about the area: if it is crowded and if the number of visitors should be regulated. The average respondent thinks that the level of crowding is low and only 11 per cent of respondents think that the number of visitors has to be regulated. Visitors prefer regulating motor vehicles and that parking should be outside the natural area. The average respondent is willing to pay an annual fee of about 20 euros to preserve the natural area.

IV.2   Economic valuation of the natural area's functions

A question about use of time during the visit between functions offered by the area is put to visitors before asking about their willingness to pay a fee to improve the recreational activities of the area. On average, visitors spend about six hours at a time in the natural area. The activities are divided into three categories: recreational, harvest and naturalistic (Figures A12 and A13).

Visitors spend about five hours in recreational activities such as trekking and picnicking. Eighty per cent of respondents carry out these activities respectively for an hour and a half and two and a half hours. Other available activities are horse riding, mountain biking or visiting historic places. Respondents spend only 15 minutes on activities such as hunting and fishing and about 35 minutes harvesting mushrooms and flowers. More time (about 45 minutes) is spent in observing the landscape, flora and fauna.

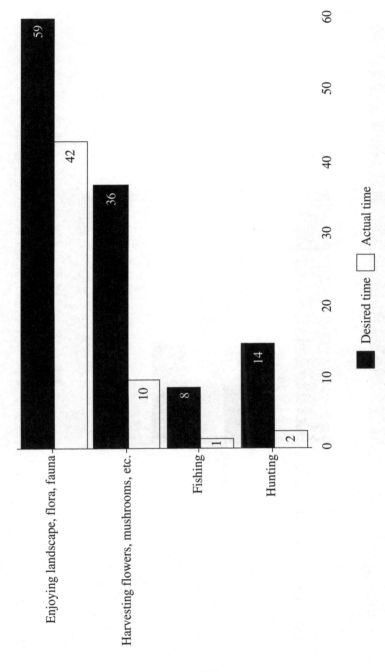

Figure A12   Average time (desired and actual) spent on recreational activities (minutes)

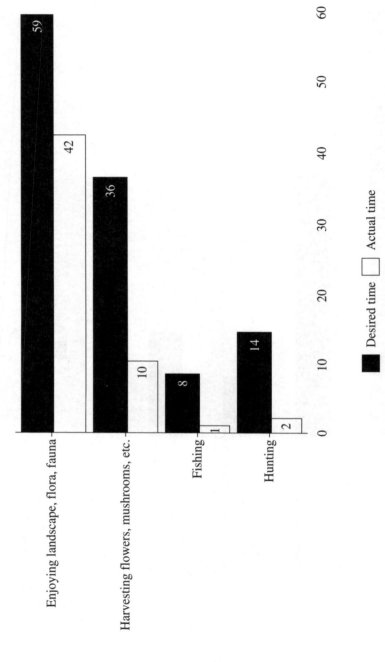

Figure A13 Average time (desired and actual) spent on harvest and naturalistic activities (minutes)

V Socio-economic Characteristics of the West Garda Regional Forest's Visitors

The average visitor is 39 years old, with a secondary education (about 13 years, Figure A14) and middle–high income (around 1807.6 euros, Figure A16). Figure A15 shows the job sector of respondents: 46 per cent work in the service sector, 18 per cent in the secondary sector, 2 per cent in the primary sector and 34 per cent do not work (students, housewives, unemployed, retired). The expenditure on leisure is high since the average visitor spends 10 per cent of her monthly income on leisure (about 185 euros) and 25 per cent on food (426 euros).

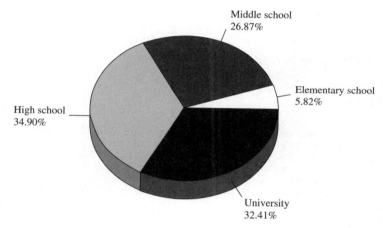

Figure A14   Respondents' education

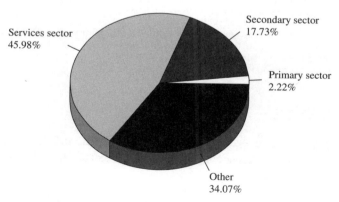

Figure A15   Respondents' job sector

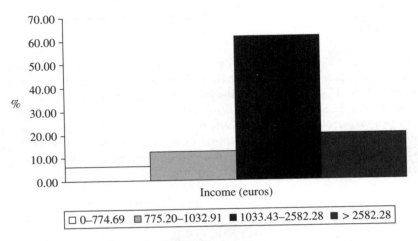

Figure A16   Respondents' monthly income

NOTES

1. Visitors were interviewed in the following places: Passo Spino (27.98 per cent of the respondents), Valvestino (17.17 per cent), Tignale (30 per cent), Tremosine (12.47 per cent), Tremalzo (4.16 per cent) and others locations (8 per cent). There were 400 respondents, but after skimming, the actual sample consists of 361 observations.
2. Here we give a partial list of guidelines by the NOAA (National Oceanic and Atmospheric Administration) Panel (for a complete discussion about the NOAA guidelines see Arrow et al., 1993):
    a) face to face interviews with pre-test for interviewer effects in order to minimize non-response rates;
    b) conservative design, when aspects of the survey design and analysis of the responses are ambiguous;
    c) elicit willingness to pay rather than willingness to accept;
    d) dichotomous choice referendum format;
    e) incorporate follow-up questions investigating the specific reasons why the respondent answered 'yes' or 'no' to the payment questions;
    f) remind the respondent of substitute commodities;
    g) remind the respondent of budget constraint.

REFERENCE

Arrow, K., R. Solow, R. Radner and H. Schuman (1993), 'Report of the NOAA Panel on Contingent Valuation', *Federal Register*, **58** (10), 4601–15.

Index